A thousand miles up the Nile
PART II

A woman's journey among the treasures of
Ancient Egypt

by

Amelia Edwards

TROTAMUNDAS PRESS

Trotamundas Press Ltd.
The Meridian, 4 Copthall House, Station Square, Coventry
CV1 2FL, UK

"A thousand miles up the Nile. Part II" by Amelia Edwards

First published in 1878 by Leipzig Bernhard Tauchnitz

copyright © 2009 of this edition, Trotamundas Press Ltd.

ISBN: 978-1-906393-15-1

Trotamundas Press is an international publisher specializing in travel literature written by women travellers from different countries and cultures.

Our mission is to bring back into print great travel books written by women around the world which have been forgotten. We publish in several languages.

It is our privilege to rescue those travel stories which were widely acclaimed in the past and that are still relevant nowadays to help us understand better the diversity of the countries and the world.

The travel stories also make an enjoyable reading, full of adventure and the excitement of discovery.

We are proud to help preserving the memory of all those amazing women travellers which were unjustly forgotten and hope that you will enjoy reading about their interesting experiences as much as we have enjoyed researching them.

www.trotamundaspress.com

Amelia Edwards (1831-1892)

Amelia Edwards was a prolific novelist, poet, and children's historian. Her earliest travel book was published in 1862 - a children's picture book of Belgium. Soon Amelia went further afield, to northern Italy with a friend, and published a hugely popular book on the Dolomite mountains reprinted under the title *Untrodden Peaks and Unfrequented Valleys - A Midsummer ramble in the Dolomites*. Since there were not yet any proper roads the 'ramble' became a sort of voyage of discovery: she was hooked. A year later she arrived in Egypt - almost by accident, to get out of the European rain on a long holiday - and discovered what was to become her life's passion.

Travelling by dahabiah, a well-appointed sailing craft peculiar to the Nile, and armed with sketch-book and measuring tape, Amelia carefully recorded all she saw of the temples, graves, and monuments - even discovering a buried chapel of her own- and provided in *A Thousand Miles Up The Nile* the first general archaeological survey of Egypt's ruins. The book is full of historical footnotes and careful details.   Amelia Edwards was responsible for founding the first chair in Egyptology (a science she helped create) at University College London, and was behind the appointment of Sir Flinders Petrie. She established herself as one of the authorities on the subject of Ancient Egypt and her book *A Thousand Miles Up the Nile* has remained one of the most inspiring travel books in the subject.

Amelia's book will transport you to a misterious civilization that it still has the power of attraction for adventure and discovery it held over a hundred years ago.

CONTENTS

OF VOLUME II.

A THOUSAND MILES
UP THE NILE.

CHAPTER XIV.

Korosko to Aboo Simbel.

I⊤ so happened that we arrived at Korosko on the eve of the Eed el Kebeer, or the anniversary of the Sacrifice of Abraham; when, according to the Moslem version, Ishmael was the intended victim, and a ram the substituted offering. Now this Eed el Kebeer, being one of the great Feasts of the Mohammedan Kalendar, is a day of gifts and good-wishes. The rich visit their friends and distribute meat to the poor; and every true believer goes to the mosque to say his prayers in the morning. So, instead of starting as usual at sunrise, we treated our sailors to a sheep, and waited till past noon, that they might make holiday.

They began the day by trooping off to the village mosque in all the glory of new blue blouses, spotless turbans, and scarlet leather slippers; then loitered about till dinner-time, when the said sheep, stewed with lentils and garlic, brought the festivities to an end. It was a thin and ancient beast, and must have been horribly tough; but an epicure might have envied the child-like enjoyment with which our honest fellows squatted, cross-legged and happy, round the smoking

cauldron; chattering, laughing, feasting; dipping their
fingers in the common mess; washing the whole down
with long draughts of Nile water; and finishing off
with a hubble-bubble passed from lip to lip, and a
mouthful of müddy coffee. By a little after midday
they had put off their finery, harnessed themselves to
the tow-rope, and set to work to haul us through the
rocky shoals that here impede the current.

From Korosko to Derr, the actual distance is about
eleven miles and a half; but what with obstructions in
the bed of the river, and what with a wind that would
have been favourable but for another great bend which
the Nile takes towards the East, those eleven miles
and a half cost us the best part of two days' hard
tracking.

Landing from time to time when the boat was
close in shore, we found the order of planting everywhere the same, lupins and lentils on the slope against
the water-line; an uninterrupted grove of palms on the
edge of the bank; in the space beyond, fields of cotton
and young corn; and then the desert. The arable soil
was divided off, as usual, by hundreds of water
channels; and seemed to be excellently farmed as well
as abundantly irrigated. Not a weed was to be seen;
not an inch of soil appeared to be wasted. In odd
corners where there was room for nothing else, cu-
cumbers and vegetable-marrows flourished and bore
fruit. Nowhere had we seen castor-berries so large,
cotton-pods so full, or palms so lofty.

Here also, for the first time out of Egypt, we observed among the bushes a few hoopoes and other
small birds; and on a sand-slope down by the river,
a group of wild-ducks. We—that is to say one of the

M. B.s and the Writer—had wandered off that way in search of crocodiles. The two Dahabeeyahs, each with its file of trackers, were slowly labouring up against the current about a mile away. All was intensely hot, and intensely silent. We had walked far, and had seen no crocodile. What we should have done if we had met one, I am not prepared to say. Perhaps we should have run away. At all events, we were just about to turn back when we caught sight of the ducks sunning themselves, half-asleep, on the brink of a tiny pool about an eighth of a mile away.

Creeping cautiously under the bank, we contrived to get within a few yards of them. They were four —a drake, a duck, and two young ones—exquisitely feathered, and as small as teal. The parent-birds could scarcely have measured more than eight inches from head to tail. All alike had chestnut coloured heads with a narrow buff stripe down the middle, like a parting; maroon backs; wing-feathers maroon and grey; and tails tipped with buff. They were so pretty, and the little family party was so complete, that the Writer could not help secretly rejoicing that Alfred and his gun were safe on board the Bagstones.

High above the Libyan bank on the sloping verge of the desert, stands, half-drowned in sand, the little Temple of Amada. Seeing it from the opposite side while duck-hunting in the morning, I had taken it for one of the many stone shelters erected by Mohammed Ali for the accommodation of cattle levied annually in the Soudan. It proved, however, to be a temple, small but massive; built with squared blocks of sand-stone; and dating back to the very old times of the Usur-tasens and Thothmes. It consists of a portico, a

transverse atrium, and three small chambers. The
pillars of the portico are mere square piers. The
rooms are small and low. The roof, constructed of
oblong blocks, is flat from end to end. As an architectural structure it is in fact but a few degrees removed from Stonehenge.

A shed without, this little temple is, however, a
cameo within. Nowhere, save in the tomb of Ti, had
we seen bas-reliefs so delicately modelled, so rich in
colour. Here, as elsewhere, the walls are covered with
groups of Kings and Gods and hieroglyphic texts.
The figures are slender and animated. The head-
dresses, jewellery, and patterned robes are elaborately
drawn and painted. Every head looks like a portrait;
every hieroglyphic form is a study in miniature.

Apart from its exquisite finish, the wall-sculpture
of Amada has, however, nothing in common with the
wall-sculpture of the Ancient Empire. It belongs to
the period of Egyptian Renaissance; and, though inferior in power and naturalness to the work of the
elder school, it marks just that moment of special
development when the art of modelling in low relief
had touched the highest level to which it ever again
attained. That highest level belongs to the reigns of
Thothmes the Second and Thothmes the Third; just
as the perfect era in architecture belongs to the reigns
of Seti the First and Rameses the Second. It is for
this reason that Amada is so precious. It registers an
epoch in the history of the art, and gives us the best
of that epoch in the hour of its zenith. The sculptor
is here seen to be working within bounds already pre-
scribed; yet within those bounds he still enjoys a certain liberty. His art, though largely conventionalised,

is not yet stereotyped. His sense of beauty still finds expression. There is, in short, a grace and sweetness about the bas-relief designs of Amada for which one looks in vain to the storied walls of Karnak.

The chambers are half-choked with sand; and we had to crawl into the sanctuary upon our hands and knees. A long inscription at the upper end records how Amenhotep the Second, returning from his first campaign against the Ruten, slew seven kings with his own hand; six of whom were gibbeted upon the ramparts of Thebes, while the body of the seventh was sent to Ethiopia by water and suspended on the outer wall of the city of Napata, * "in order that the negroes might behold the victories of the Pharaoh in all the lands of the world."

In the darkest corner of the atrium we observed a curious tableau representing the King embraced by a Goddess. He holds a short straight sword in his right hand, and the crux ansata in his left. On his head he wears a blue mitre studded with gold stars and ornamented with the royal asp. The Goddess clasps him lovingly about the neck, and bends her lips to his. The artist has given her the yellow complexion conventionally ascribed to women; but her saucy mouth and nez retroussé are distinctly European. Dressed in the fashion of the nineteenth century, she might have served Leech as a model for his Girl of the Period.

* A city of Ethiopia, now identified with the ruins at Gebel Barkal. The worship of Ammon was established at Napata towards the end of the XXth Dynasty, and it was from the priests of Thebes who settled at that time in Napata, that the Ethiopian conquerors of Egypt (XXIIId Dynasty) were descended.

The sand has drifted so high at the back of the Temple, that one steps upon the roof as upon a terrace only just raised above the level of the desert. Soon that level will be equal; and if nothing is done to rescue it within the next generation or two, the whole building will become engulfed, and its very site be forgotten.

The view from the roof, looking back towards Korosko and forward towards Derr, is one of the finest—perhaps quite the finest—in Nubia. The Nile curves grandly through the foreground. The palm-woods of Derr are green in the distance. The mountain region which we have just traversed ranges, a vast crescent of multitudinous peaks, round two-thirds of the horizon. Ridge beyond ridge, chain beyond chain, flushing crimson in light and deepening through every tint of amethyst and purple in shadow, those innumerable summits fade into tenderest blue upon the horizon. As the sun sets, they seem to glow; to become incandescent; to be touched with flame—as in the old time when every crater was a fount of fire.

Struggling next morning through a maze of sandbanks, we reached Derr soon after breakfast. This town—the Nubian capital—lies a little lower than the level of the bank, so that only a few mud walls are visible from the river. Having learned by this time that a capital town is but a bigger village, containing perhaps a mosque and a market-place, we were not disappointed by the unimposing aspect of the Nubian metropolis.

Great, however, was our surprise when, instead of the usual clamorous crowd screaming, pushing, scrambling, and bothering for backsheesh, we found the

landing-place deserted. Two or three native boats lay
up under the bank, empty. There was literally not a
soul in sight. L. and the Little Lady, eager to buy
some of the basket-work for which the place is famous,
looked blank. Talhamy, anxious to lay in a store of
fresh eggs and vegetables, looked blanker.

We landed. Before us lay an open space, at the
farther end of which, facing the river, stood the Governor's palace; the said palace being a magnified mud
hut, with a frieze of baked bricks round the top, and
an imposing stone doorway. In this doorway, according to immemorial usage, the great man gives audience.
We saw him—a mere youth, apparently—puffing away
at a long chibouque, in the midst of a little group of
greybeard elders. They looked at us gravely, immov-
ably; like smoking automata. One longed to go up
and ask them if they were all transformed to black
granite from the waists to the feet, and if the inhabitants of Derr had been changed into blue stones.

Still bent on buying baskets, if baskets were to be
bought,—bent also on finding out the whereabouts of
a certain rock-cut temple which our books told us to
look for at the back of the town, we turned aside into
a straggling street leading towards the desert. The
houses looked better built than usual; some pains having evidently been bestowed in smoothing the surface
of the mud, and ornamenting the doorways with fragments of coloured pottery. A cracked willow-pattern
dinner-plate set like a fanlight over one, and a white
soup-plate over another, came doubtless from the canteen of some English Dahabeeyah, and were the pride
of their possessors. Looking from end to end of this
street —and it was a tolerably long one, with the Nile

at one end, and the desert at the other—we saw no
sign or shadow of moving creature. Only one young
woman, hearing strange voices talking a strange tongue,
peeped out suddenly from a half-opened door as we
went by; then, seeing me look at the baby in her
arms (which was hideous and had sore eyes) drew her
veil across its face, and darted back again. She
thought I coveted her treasure, and she dreaded the
Evil Eye.

All at once we heard a sound like the far-off qui-
vering cry of many owls. It shrilled—swelled—wavered
—dropped—then died away, like the moaning of the
wind at sea. We held our breath and listened. We
had never heard anything so wild and plaintive. Then
suddenly, through an opening in the houses, we saw a
great crowd on a space of rising ground about a quarter
of a mile away. This. crowd consisted of men only—
a close, turbaned mass some three or four hundred in
number; all standing quite still and silent; all looking
in the same direction.

Hurrying on to the desert, we saw the strange sight
at which they were looking.

The scene was a barren sandslope hemmed in between the town and the cliffs, and dotted over with
graves. The actors were all women. Huddled together
under a long wall some few hundred yards away, bare-
headed, and exposed to the blaze of the morning sun,
they outnumbered the men by a full third. Some were
sitting, some standing; while in their midst, pressing
round a young woman who seemed to act as leader,
there swayed and circled and shuffled a compact phalanx of dancers. Upon this young woman the eyes of
all were turned. A black Cassandra, she rocked her

body from side to side, clapped her hands above her head, and poured forth a wild declamatory chant, which the rest echoed. This chant seemed to be divided into strophes, at the end of each of which she paused, beat her breast, and broke into that terrible wail that we had heard just now from a distance.

Her brother, it seemed, had died last night; and we were witnessing his funeral.

The actual interment was over by the time we reached the spot; but four men were still busy filling the grave with sand, which they scraped up, a bowlful at a time, and stamped down with their naked feet.

The deceased being unmarried, his sister led the choir of mourners. She was a tall, gaunt young woman of the plainest Nubian type, with high cheekbones, eyes slanting upwards at the corners, and an enormous mouth full of glittering teeth. On her head she wore a white cloth smeared with dust. Her companions were distinguished by a narrow white fillet, bound about the brow, and tied with two long ends behind. They had hidden their necklaces and bracelets, and wore trailing robes and shawls, and loose trousers of black or blue calico.

We stood for a long time watching their uncouth dance. None of the women seemed to notice us; but the men made way civilly and gravely, letting us pass to the front, that we might get a better view of the ceremony.

By and by an old woman rose slowly from the midst of those who were sitting, and moved with tottering uncertain steps towards a higher point of ground, a little apart from the crowd. There was a movement

of compassion among the men; one of whom turned
to the Writer and said gently:—"His mother."

She was a small, feeble old woman, very poorly
clad. Her hands and arms were like the hands and
arms of a mummy, and her withered black face looked
ghastly under its mask of dust. For a few moments,
swaying her body slowly to and fro, she watched the
grave-diggers stamping down the sand; then stretched
out her arms, and broke into a torrent of lamentations.
The dialect of Derr * is strange and barbarous; but we
felt as if we understood every word she uttered. Presently the tears began to make channels down her
cheeks—her voice became choked with sobs—and falling down in a sort of helpless heap, like a broken-
hearted dog, she lay with her face to the ground, and
there stayed.

Meanwhile, the sand being now filled in and
mounded up, the men betook themselves to a place
where the rock had given way, and selected a couple
of big stones from the débris. These they placed at
the head and foot of the grave; and all was done.

Instantly—perhaps at an appointed signal, though
we saw none given—the wailing ceased; the women
rose; every tongue was loosened; and the whole became a moving, animated, noisy throng dispersing in a
dozen different directions.

We turned away with the rest; the Writer and the
Painter rambling off in search of the temple, while the
other three devoted themselves to the pursuit of baskets
and native jewellery. When we looked back presently,

---

* The men hereabout can nearly all speak Arabic; but the women of
Nubia know only the Kensee and Berberee tongues, the first of which is spoken
as far as Korosko.

the crowd was gone; but the desolate mother still lay
motionless in the dust.

It chanced that we witnessed many funerals in Nubia; so many that one sometimes felt inclined to doubt
whether the Governor of Assouan had not reported
over-favourably of the health of the province. The
ceremonial, with its dancing and chanting, was always
much the same; always barbaric, and in the highest
degree artificial. One would like to know how much
of it is derived from purely African sources, and how
much from ancient Egyptian tradition. The dance is
most probably Ethiopian. Lepsius, travelling through
the Soudan in A.D. 1844,* saw something of the kind
at a funeral in Wed Medineh, about half-way between
Sennaar and Khartoom. The white fillet worn by the
choir of mourners is, on the other hand, distinctly
Egyptian. We afterwards saw it represented in paintings of funeral processions on the walls of several
tombs at Thebes,** where the wailing women are seen
to be gathering up the dust in their hands and casting
it upon their heads, just as they do now. As for the
wail—beginning high, and descending through a scale
divided, not by semi-tones, but thirds of tones, to a
final note about an octave and a half lower than that
from which it started—it probably echoes to this day
the very pitch and rhythm of the wail that followed
the Pharaohs to their sepulchres in the Valley of the
Tombs of the Kings. Like the zaghareet, or joy-cry,
which every mother teaches to her little girls, and

* Lepsius's *Letters from Egypt, Ethiopia*, etc., Letter XVIII. p. 184.
Bohn's ed. A.D. 1853.
** See an interesting account of funereal rites and ceremonies in Sir
G. Wilkinson's *Ancient Egyptians*, vol. II. chap. X., Lond. 1871. Also wood-
cuts Nos. 493 and 494 in the same chapter of the same work.

which, it is said, can only be acquired in very early
youth, it has been handed down from generation to
generation through an untold succession of ages. The
song to which the Fellah works his shadoof, and the
monotonous chant of the sakkieh-driver, have perhaps
as remote an origin. But of all old, mournful, human
sounds, the death-wail that we heard at Derr is perhaps one of the very oldest—certainly the most
mournful.

The temple here, though dating from the reign of
Rameses II., is of rude design and indifferent execution. Partly constructed, partly excavated, it is approached by a forecourt, the roof of which, now gone,
was supported by eight square columns. Of these
columns only the bases remain. Four massive piers
against which once stood four colossi, upheld the roof
of the portico and gave admission by three entrances
to the rock-cut chambers beyond. That portico is now
roofless. Nothing is left of the colossi but their feet.
All is ruin; and ruin without beauty.

Seen from within, however, the place is not without
a kind of gloomy grandeur. Two rows of square
columns, three at each side, divide the large hall into
three aisles. This hall is about forty feet square, and
the pillars have been left standing in the living rock,
like those in the early tombs at Siout. The daylight,
half blocked out by the fallen portico, is pleasantly subdued, and finds its way dimly to the sanctuary at the
farther end. The sculptures of the interior, though
much damaged, are less defaced than those of the
outer court. Walls, pillars, doorways, are covered with
bas-reliefs. The King and Phtah, the King and Ra,
the King and Ammon Ra, stand face to face, hand in

hand, on each of the four sides of every column. Scenes of worship, of slaughter, of anointing, cover the walls; and the blank spaces are filled in as usual with hieroglyphic inscriptions. Among these Champollion discovered an imperfect list of the sons and daughters of Rameses the Second. Four gods once sat enthroned at the upper end of the sanctuary; but they have shared the fate of the colossi outside, and only their feet remain. The wall sculptures of this dark little chamber are, however, better preserved, and better worth preservation, than those of the hall. A procession of priests, bearing on their shoulders the bari, or sacred boat, is quite unharmed; and even the colour is yet fresh upon a full-length figure of Hathor close by.

But more interesting than all those—more interesting because more rare—is a sculptured palm-tree against which the king leans while making an offering to Ammon Ra. The trunk is given with elaborate truthfulness; and the branches, though formalised, are correct and graceful in curvature. The tree is but an accessory. It may have been introduced with reference to the date-harvests which are the wealth of the district; but it has no kind of sacred significance, and is noticeable only for the naturalness of the treatment. Such naturalness is unusual in the art of this period, when the conventional persea and the equally conventional lotus are almost the only vegetable forms that appear on the walls of the Temples. I can recall, indeed, but one similar instance in the bas-relief sculpture of the New Empire — namely, the bent, broken, and waving bulrushes in the great lion-hunting scene at Medinet Haboo, which are admirably free, and studied apparently from nature.

2*

Coming out, we looked in vain along the courtyard
walls for the battle-scene in which Champollion was
yet able to trace the famous fighting lion of Rameses
the Second, with the legend describing him as "the
Servant of His Majesty rending his foes in pieces." But
that was forty-five years ago. Now it is with difficulty
that one detects a few vague outlines of chariot-wheels
and horses.

There are some rock-cut tombs in the face of the
cliffs close by. The Painter explored them while the
Writer sketched the interior of the Temple; but he
reported of them as mere sepulchres, unpainted and
unsculptured.

The rocks, the sands, the sky, were at a white
heat when we again turned our faces towards the
river. Where there had so lately been a great multitude there was now not a soul. The palms nodded;
the pigeons dozed; the mud town slept in the sun.
Even the mother had gone from her place of weeping, and left her dead to the silence of the desert.

We went and looked at his grave. The fresh-turned
sand was only a little darker than the rest, and but for
the trampled foot-marks round about, we should scarcely
have been able to distinguish the new mound from the
old ones. All were alike nameless. Some, more cared
for than the rest, were bordered with large stones and
filled in with variegated pebbles. One or two were
fenced about with a mud wall. All had a bowl of baked
clay at the head. Wherever we saw a burial-ground in
Nubia, we saw these bowls upon the graves. The
mourners, they told us, mourn here for forty days;
during which time they come every Friday and fill the
bowls with fresh water, that the birds may drink from

it. The bowls on the other graves were dry and full of sand; but the new bowl was brimming full, and the water in it was hot to the touch.

We found L. and the Happy Couple standing at bay with their backs against a big lebbich tree, surrounded by an immense crowd and far from comfortable. Bent on "bazaaring," they had probably shown themselves too ready to buy; so bringing the whole population, with all the mats, baskets, nose-rings, finger-rings, necklaces and bracelets in the place, about their ears. Seeing the straits they were in, we ran to the Dahabeeyah and despatched three or four sailors to the rescue, who brought them off in triumph.

Even in Egypt, it does not answer, as a rule, to go about on shore without an escort. The people are apt to be importunate, and can with difficulty be kept at a pleasant distance. But in Nubia, where the traveller's life was scarcely safe fifty years ago, unprotected Ingleezeh are pretty certain to be disagreeably mobbed. The natives, in truth, are still mere savages *au fond*— the old war-paint being but half disguised under a thin veneer of Mohammedanism.

Some of the women who followed our friends to the boat, though in complexion as black as the rest, had light blue eyes and frizzy red hair, the effect of which was indescribably frightful. Both here and at Ibrim there are many of these "fair" families, who claim to be descended from Bosnian fathers stationed in Nubia at the time of the conquest of Sultan Selim in A.D. 1517. They are immensely proud of their alien blood, and think themselves quite beautiful.

All hands being safe on board, we pushed off at

once, leaving about a couple of hundred disconsolate
dealers on the bank. A long-drawn howl of disappointment followed in our wake. Those who had sold, and
those who had not sold, were alike wronged, ruined,
and betrayed. One woman tore wildly along the bank,
shrieking and beating her breast. Foremost among
the sellers, she had parted from her gold brow-pendant
for a good price; but was inconsolable now for the loss
of it.

It often happened that those who had been most
eager to trade, were readiest to repent of their bar-
gains. Even so, however, their cupidity outweighed
their love of finery. Moved once or twice by the
lamentations of some dark damsel who had sold her
necklace at a handsome profit, we offered to annul
the purchase. But it invariably proved that, despite
her tears, she preferred to keep the money.

The palms of Derr and of the rich district beyond,
were the finest we saw throughout the journey. Straight
and strong and magnificently plumed, they rose to an
average height of seventy or eighty feet. These superb
plantations supply all Egypt with saplings, and con-
tribute a heavy tax to the revenue. The fruit, sun-
dried and shrivelled, is also sent northwards in large
quantities.

The trees are cultivated with strenuous industry by
the natives, and owe as much of their perfection to
laborious irrigation as to climate. The foot of each
separate palm is surrounded by a circular trench into
which the water is conducted by a small channel about
fourteen inches in width. Every palm-grove stands in
a network of these artificial runlets. The reservoir from
which they are supplied is filled by means of a Sakkieh,

or water-wheel—a primitive and picturesque machine
consisting of two wheels, the one set vertically to the
river and slung with a chain of pots; the other a horizontal cog turned sometimes by a camel, but more frequently in Nubia by a buffalo.   The pots (which go
down empty, dip under the water, and come up full)
feed a sloping trough which in some places supplies
a reservoir, and in others communicates at once with
the irrigating channels.   These sakkiehs are kept perpetually going; and are set so close just above Derr,
that the Writer counted a line of fifteen within the
space of a single mile.   There were probably quite as
many on the opposite bank.

The sakkiehs creak atrociously; and their creaking
ranges over an unlimited gamut.   From morn till dewy
eve, from dewy eve till morn, they squeak, they squeal,
they grind, they groan, they croak.   Heard after dark,
sakkieh answering to sakkieh, their melancholy chorus
makes night hideous.   To sleep through it is impossible.   Being obliged to moor a few miles beyond
Derr, and having lain awake half the night, we offered
a sakkieh-driver a couple of dollars if he would let his
wheel rest till morning.   But time and water are more
precious than even dollars at this season; and the
man refused.   All we could do, therefore, was to
punt into the middle of the river, and lie off at a point
as nearly as possible equidistant from our two nearest
enemies.

The native dearly loves the tree that costs him so
much labour, and thinks it the chef d'œuvre of crea-
tion.   When Allah made the first man, says an Arab
legend, he found he had a little clay to spare; so with
that he made the palm.   And to the poor Nubian, at

all events, the gifts of the palm are almost divine;
supplying food for his children, thatch for his hovel,
timber for his water-wheel, ropes, matting, cups, bowls,
and even the strong drink forbidden by the Prophet.
The date-wine is yellowish-white, like whiskey. It is
not a wine, however, but a spirit; coarse, fiery, and un-
palatable.

Certain trees—as for instance the perky little pine
of the German wald—are apt to become monotonous;
but one never wearies of the palm. Whether taken
singly or in masses, it is always graceful, always suggestive. To the sketcher on the Nile, it is simply
invaluable. It breaks the long parallels of river and
bank, and composes with the stern lines of Egyptian
architecture as no other tree in the world could do.

"Subjects indeed!" said once upon a time an
eminent artist to the present Writer; "fiddlesticks about
subjects! Your true painter can make a picture out
of a post and a puddle."

Substitute a palm, however, for a post; combine
with it anything that comes first—a camel, a shadoof,
a woman with a water-jar upon her head—and your
picture stands before you ready made.

Nothing more surprised me at first than the colour
of the palm-frond, which painters of Eastern landscape
are wont to depict of a hard, blueish tint, like the
colour of a yucca leaf. Its true shade is a tender,
bloomy, sea-green grey; difficult enough to match, but
in most exquisite harmony with the glow of the sky
and the gold of the desert.

The palm-groves kept us company for many a mile,
backed on the Arabian side by long level ranges of
sandstone cliffs horizontally stratified, like those of the

Thebaid. We now scarcely ever saw a village—only palms, and sakkiehs, and sandbanks in the river. The villages were there, but invisible; being built on the verge of the desert. Arable land is too valuable in Nubia for either the living to dwell upon or the dead to be buried in.

At Ibrim—a sort of ruined Ehrenbreitstein on the top of a grand precipice overhanging the river—we touched for only a few minutes, in order to buy a very small shaggy sheep that had been brought down to the landing-place for sale. But for the breeze that happened just then to be blowing, we should have liked to climb the rock, and see the view and the ruins—which are part modern, part Turkish, part Roman, and little, if at all, Egyptian.

There are also some sculptured and painted grottoes to be seen in the southern face of the mountain. They are, however, too difficult of access to be attempted by ladies. Alfred, who went ashore after quail, was drawn up to them by ropes; but found them so much defaced as to be scarcely worth the trouble.

We were now only thirty-four miles from Aboo Simbel; but making slow progress, and impatiently counting every foot of the way. The heat at times was great; frequent and fitful spells of Khamseen * wind alternating with a hot calm that tried the trackers sorely. Still we pushed forward, a few miles at a time; till by and by the flat-topped cliffs dropped out of sight and were again succeeded by volcanic peaks, some of which looked loftier than any of those about Dakkeh or Korosko.

* A hot South wind, like our Sirocco,

Then the palms ceased, and the belt of cultivated
land narrowed to a thread of green; and at last there
came an evening when we only wanted breeze enough
to double two or three more bends in the river.

"Is it to be Aboo Simbel to-night?" we asked, for
the twentieth time before going down to dinner.

To which Reïs Hassan replied, "Aiwah" (certainly).

But the pilot shook his head, and added, "Bookra"
(to-morrow).

When we came up again, the moon had risen, but
the breeze had dropped. Still we moved, impelled by
a breath so faint that one could scarcely feel it. Presently even this failed. The sail collapsed; the pilot
steered for the bank; the captain gave the word to go
aloft—when a sudden puff from the north changed our
fortunes, and sent us out again with a well-filled sail
into the middle of the river.

None of us, I think, will be likely to forget the
sustained excitement of the next three hours. As the
moon climbed higher, a light more unreal than the
light of day filled and overflowed the wide expanse of
river and desert. We could see the mountains of
Aboo Simbel standing as it seemed across our path, in
the far distance—a lower one first; then a larger; then
a series of receding heights, all close together, yet all
distinctly separate.

That large one—the mountain of the Great Temple
—held us like a spell. For a long time it looked a
mere mountain like the rest. By and by, however, we
fancied we detected a something—a shadow—such a
shadow as might be cast by a gigantic buttress. Next
appeared a black speck no bigger than a porthole.

We knew that this black speck must be the doorway.
We knew that the great statues were there, though not
yet visible; and that we must soon see them.

For our sailors, meanwhile, there was the excitement of a chase. The Bagstones and three other
Dahabeeyahs were coming up behind us in the path of
the moonlight. Their galley fires glowed like beacons
on the water; the nearest about a mile away, the last,
a spark in the distance. We were not in the mood
to care much for racing to-night; but we were anxious
to keep our lead and be first at the mooring-place.

To run upon a sandbank at such a moment was
like being plunged suddenly into cold water. Our sail
flapped furiously. The men rushed to the punting
poles. Four jumped overboard, and shoved with all
the might of their shoulders. By the time we got off,
however, the other boats had crept up half-a-mile
nearer; and we had hard work to keep them from
pressing closer on our heels.

At length the last corner was rounded, and the
Great Temple stood straight before us. The façade,
sunk in the mountain-side like a huge picture in a
mighty frame, was now quite plain to see. The black
speck was no longer a porthole, but a lofty doorway.

Last of all, though it was night and they were still
not much less than a mile away, the four colossi came
out, ghostlike, vague, and shadowy, in the enchanted
moonlight. Even as we watched them, they seemed
to grow—to dilate—to be moving towards us out of
the silvery distance.

It was drawing on towards midnight when the
Philæ at length ran in close under the Great Temple.
Content with what they had seen from the river, the

rest of the party then went soberly to bed; but the
Painter and the Writer had no patience to wait till
morning.   Almost before the mooring-rope could be
made fast, they had jumped ashore and begun climbing the bank.

They went and stood at the feet of the colossi,
and on the threshold of that vast portal beyond which
was darkness.   The great statues towered above their
heads.   The river glittered like steel in the distance.
There was a keen silence in the air; and towards the
east the Southern Cross was rising.   To the strangers
who stood talking there with bated breath, the time,
the place, even the sound of their own voices seemed
unreal.   They felt as if the whole scene must fade
with the moonlight, and vanish before morning.

CHAPTER XV.

Rameses the Great.

THE central figure of Egyptian history has always been, probably always will be, Rameses the Second. He holds this place partly by right, partly by accident. He was born to greatness; he achieved greatness; and he had borrowed greatness thrust upon him. It was his singular destiny not only to be made a posthumous usurper of glory, but to be forgotten by his own name and remembered in a variety of aliases. As Sesoosis, as Osymandias, as Sesostris, he became credited, in course of time, with all the deeds of all the heroes of the new Empire, beginning with Thothmes III., who preceded him by 300 years, and ending with Sheshonk, the captor of Jerusalem, who lived four centuries after him. Modern science, however, has repaired this injustice; and, while disclosing the long-lost names of a brilliant succession of sovereigns, has enabled us to ascribe to each the honours which are his due. We know now that some of these were greater conquerors than Rameses II. We suspect that some were better rulers. Yet the popular hero keeps his ground. What he has lost by interpretation on the one hand, he has gained by interpretation on the other; and the *beau sabreur* of the Third Sallier Papyrus remains to this day the representative Pharaoh of a line of monarchs whose history covers a space of fifty centuries, and

whose frontiers reached at one time from Mesopotamia
to the ends of the Soudan.

The interest that one takes in Rameses II. begins
at Memphis, and goes on increasing all the way up
the river. It is a purely living, a purely personal, interest; such as one feels in Athens for Pericles, or in
Florence for Lorenzo the Magnificent. Other Pharaohs
but languidly affect the imagination. Thothmes and
Amenhotep are to us as Darius or Artaxerxes—shadows that come and go in the distance. But with the
second Rameses we are on terms of respectful intimacy.
We seem to know the man—to feel his presence—to
hear his name in the air. His features are as familiar
to us as those of Henry the Eighth or Louis the Four-
teenth. His cartouches meet us at every turn; and
even to such as do not read the hieroglyphic character,
those oft-recurring signs soon convey, by sheer force of
association, the pompous style and title of Sun power
of Truth, Approved of the Sun, Son of the Sun, Beloved of Ammon.

This being so, the traveller is ill equipped who
goes through Egypt without something more than a
mere guide-book knowledge of Rameses II. He is, as
it were, content to read the Argument and miss the
Poem. In the desolation of Memphis, in the shattered
splendour of Thebes, he sees only the ordinary pathos
of ordinary ruins. As for Aboo Simbel, the most
stupendous historical record ever transmitted from the
past to the present, it tells him a but half-intelligible
story. Holding to the merest thread of explanation,
he wanders from hall to hall, lacking altogether that
potent charm of foregone association which no Murray
can furnish. Your average Frenchman straying help-

lessly through Westminster Abbey under the conduct
of the verger has about as vague a conception of the
historical import of the things he sees.

What is true of the traveller is equally true of those
who take their Nile vicariously "in connection with
Mudie." If they are to understand any description of
Aboo Simbel, they must first know something about
Rameses II. Let us then, while the Philæ lies moored
in the shadow of the rock of Abshek,* review, as sum-
marily as may be, the leading facts of this important
reign; such facts, that is to say, as are recorded in inscriptions, papyri, and other contemporary monuments.

Rameses the Second** was the son of Seti I., the
second Pharaoh of the XIXth Dynasty, and of a cer-

---

* *Abshek:*—The hieroglyphic name of Aboo Simbel. *Gr.* Aboccis.

** In the present state of Egyptian chronology, it is hazardous to assign
even an approximate date to events that happened before the conquest of
Cambyses. The Egyptians, in fact, had no chronology in the strict sense of
the word. Being without any fixed point of departure, such as the birth of
Christ, they counted the events of each reign from the accession of the sovereign. Under such a system error and confusion were inevitable. To say when
Rameses II. was born and when he died is impossible. The very century in
which he flourished is uncertain. M. Mariette, taking the historical lists of
Manetho for his basis, supposes the XIXth Dynasty to have occupied the
interval comprised within B.C. 1462 and 1288; according to which computation
(allowing 57 years for the reigns of Rameses I. and Seti I.) the reign of
Rameses II. would date from B.C. 1405. Brugsch gives him from B.C. 1407 to
B.C. 1341; and Lepsius places his reign in the sixty-six years lying between
B.C. 1388 and B.C. 1322; these calculations being both made before the discovery
of the stela of Abydos. Bunsen dates his accession from B.C. 1352; while the
method adopted by Mr. Stuart Poole and others would bring the beginning of
his reign fifty-nine years nearer still to our own epoch. Between the highest
and the lowest of these calculations there is, as shown by the following table, a
difference of 800 years:—

Rameses II. began to reign   B.C.

							B.C.
According to	Brugsch	.	.	.	.	.	1407
	Mariette	.	.	.	.	.	1405
	Lepsius	.	.	.	.	.	1388
	Bunsen	.	.	.	.	.	1352
	Poole	.	.	.	.	.	1283

tain Princess Tuaa, described on the monuments as
"royal wife, royal mother, and heiress and sharer of
the throne." She is supposed to have been of the
ancient royal line of the preceding dynasty, and so to
have had, perhaps, a better right than her husband to
the double crown of Egypt. Through her, at all events,
Rameses II. seems to have been in some sense born a
king,* equal in rank, if not in power, with his father.
He is believed to have succeeded to the throne while
yet very young, and to have learned his first war-lesson
in the lands south of the Cataract. The stela of Dakkeh,** which dates from the third year of his reign
speaks of him as already terrible in battle; as "the
bull powerful against Ethiopia, the griffin furious
against the negroes, whose grip has put the moun-
taineers to flight." The events of his second campaign
(undertaken two years later in order to reduce to
obedience the revolted tribes of Syria and Mesopotamia) are immortalised in the poem of Pentaour.***
It was on this occasion that he fought his famous
single-handed fight, against overwhelming odds, in the
sight of both armies under the walls of Kades. Two
years later, he carried fire and sword into the land of
Canaan, and according to inscriptions yet extant upon
the ruined pylons of the Ramesseum at Thebes, took,
among other strong places on sea and shore, the fortresses of Ascalon and Jerusalem†.

The next important record transports us to the

---

* See Chap. VIII. footnote, p. 182, vol. I.
** See Chap. VIII. p. 182, vol. I.
*** *Ibid.* pp. 181, 182.
† L'an 8 de son règne, le roi prit la forteresse de Salem. C'est Salem,
l'ancien nom de Jerusalem, qui designait cette ville avant que les Juifs l'eus-
sent prise."—*Hist. d'Egypte,* BRUGSCH: 1st edition; Leipzig, 1859.

twenty-first year of his reign. Thirteen years have now
gone by since the fall of Jerusalem, during which time
a fluctuating frontier warfare has probably been carried
on, to the exhaustion of both armies. Khetasira, Prince
of Kheta, sues for peace. An elaborate treaty is there-
upon framed, whereby the said Prince and "Rameses,
Chief of Rulers, who fixes his frontiers where he
pleases," pledge themselves to a strict offensive and
defensive alliance, and to the maintenance of goodwill
and brotherhood for ever. This treaty, we are told,
was engraved for the Khetan prince "upon a tablet of
silver adorned with the likeness of the figure of Sutech,
the Great Ruler of Heaven;" while for Rameses Mer-
Ammon it was sculptured on a wall adjoining the Great
Hall at Karnak,* where it remains to this day.

According to the last clause of this curious document, the contracting parties enter also into an agree-
ment to deliver up to each other the political fugitives
of both countries; providing at the same time for the
personal safety of the offenders. "Whosoever shall be
so delivered up," says the treaty, "himself, his wives,
his children, let him not be smitten to death, moreover,
let him not suffer in his eyes, in his mouth, in his feet,
moreover, let not any crime be set up against him."**

* This invaluable record is sculptured on a piece of wall which Mariette-
Bey's latest plan of Karnak (see *Monuments of Upper Egypt,* translated by
Alphons Mariette, Trübner & Co., London, 1877) shows to have formed part of
the boundary-wall of a large hall now destroyed, but formerly standing at right
angles to the south wall of the Hypostyle Hall at Karnak. The treaty faces
to the west, and is situate about half-way between the famous bas-relief of
Sheshonk and his captives, and the Karnak version of the poem of Pentaour.
The former lies to the west of the southern portal; the latter to the east. The
wall of the treaty juts out about sixty feet to the east of the portal. This south
wall and its adjunct, a length of about 200 feet in all, is perhaps the most precious and interesting piece of sculptured surface in the world.
** See *Treaty of Peace between Rameses II. and the Hittites,* translated
by C. W. Goodwin, M.A.—RECORDS OF THE PAST, vol. IV. p. 25.

This is the earliest instance of an extradition treaty
upon record; and it is chiefly remarkable as an illustration of the clemency with which international law was
at that time administered.

Finally, the convention between the sovereigns is
placed under the joint protection of the gods of both
countries:—"Sutech of Kheta, Ammon of Egypt, and
all the thousand gods, the gods male and female, the
gods of the hills, of the rivers, of the great sea, of the
winds and the clouds, of the land of Kheta and of the
land of Egypt."

The peace now concluded would seem to have remained unbroken throughout the rest of the long reign
of Rameses the Second. We hear, at all events, of no
more wars; and we find the king married by and by
to a Khetan princess, who in deference to the gods of
her adopted country takes the official name of Ra-maa-
ur-nofre, or Sun-truth, Beautiful-exceedingly. The
names of two other queens—Nofre-ari and Isi-nofre—
are also found upon the monuments; to say nothing of
a certain Princess-Queen, called Ba-ta-anta, of whom
M. Pierret suggests, unpleasantly enough, that she was
a daughter of Rameses wedded to her own father.

These three were probably the only legitimate wives
of Rameses II., though he must also have been the
lord of an extensive hareem. His family, at all events,
as recorded upon the walls of the Temple at Wady
Sabooah, amounted to no less than 170 children, of
whom 111 were princes. This may have been but a
small family for a great king three thousand years ago.
It was but the other day, comparatively speaking, that
Lepsius saw and talked with old Hasan, Kashef of
Derr—the same petty ruler who gave so much trouble

to Belzoni, Burckhardt, and other early travellers—and he, like a patriarch of old, had in his day been the husband of sixty-four wives, and the father of something like 200 children.

For forty-six years after the making of the Khetan treaty, Rameses the Great lived at peace with his neighbours and tributaries. The evening of his life was long and splendid. It became his passion and his pride to found new cities, to raise dykes, to dig canals, to build fortresses, to multiply statues, obelisks, and inscriptions, and to erect the most gorgeous and costly temples in which man ever worshipped. To the monuments founded by his predecessors he made additions so magnificent that they dwarfed the designs they were intended to complete. He caused artesian wells to be pierced in the stony bed of the desert. He carried on the canal begun by his father, and opened a waterway between the Mediterranean and the Red Sea. No enterprise was too difficult, no project too vast, for his ambition. "As a child," says the stela of Dakkeh,* "he superintended the public works, and his hands laid their foundations." As a man, he became the supreme Builder. Of his gigantic structures only certain colossal fragments have survived the ravages of time; yet those fragments are the wonder of the world.

To estimate the cost at which these things were done is now impossible. Every temple, every palace, represented a hecatomb of human lives. Slaves from Ethiopia, captives taken in war, Syrian immigrants settled in the Delta, were alike pressed into the service of the State. We know how the Hebrews suffered, and to what an extremity of despair they were reduced

* See Chap. VIII. p. 182. vol. 1.

by the tasks imposed upon them. Yet even the Hebrews were less cruelly used than some who were kidnapped beyond the frontiers. Torn from their homes without hope of return, driven in herds to the mines, the quarries, and the brick-fields, these hapless victims were so dealt with that not even the chances of desertion were open to them. The negroes from the South were systematically drafted to the North; the Asiatic captives were transported to Ethiopia. Those who laboured underground were goaded on without rest or respite, till they fell down in the mines and died.

That Rameses II. was the Pharaoh of the captivity,* and that Menephthah, his son and successor, was the Pharaoh ** of the Exodus, are now among the estab-

---

* "Les circonstances de l'histoire hébraïque s'appliquent ici d'une manière on ne peut plus satisfaisante. Les Hébreux opprimés batissaient une ville du nom de Ramsès. Ce récit ne peut donc s'appliquer qu'à l'époque où la famille de Ramsès était sur le trône. Moïse, contraint de fuir la colère du roi après le meurtre d'un Égyptien, subit un long exil, parceque le roi ne mourut *qu'après un temps fort long;* Ramsès II. regna en effet plus de 67 ans. Aussitôt après le retour de Moïse commença la lutte qui se termina par le célèbre passage de la Mer Rouge. Cet événement eut donc lieu sous le fils de Ramsès II., ou tout au plus tard pendant l'époque de troubles qui suivit son règne. Ajoutons que la rapidité des derniers événements ne permet pas de supposer que le roi eût sa résidence à Thèbes dans cet instant. Or, Merenptah a précisement laissé dans la Basse-Égypte, et spécialement à Tanis, des preuves importantes de son séjour."—De Rougé, *Notice des Monuments Égyptiennes du Rez de Chaussée du Musée du Louvre,* Paris, 1875, p. 22.

"Il est impossible d'attribuer ni à Meneptah I., ni à Seti II., ni à Siptah, ni à Amonmesès, un règne même de vingt années; à plus forte raison de cinquante ou soixante. Seul, le règne de Ramsès II. remplit les conditions indispensables. Lors même que nous ne saurions pas que ce souverain a occupé les Hébreux à la construction de la ville de Ramsès, nous serions dans l'impossibilité de placer Moïse à une autre époque, à moins de faire table rase des renseignements bibliques."—*Recherches pour servir à l'Histoire de la XIX Dynastie:* F. Chabas; Paris 1873; p. 148.

** The Bible narrative, it has often been observed, invariably designates the King by this title, than which none, unfortunately, can be more vague for purposes of identification. "Plus généralement," says Brugsch, writing of the royal titles, "sa personne se cache sous une série d'expressions qui toutes ont le sens de la '*grande maison*' ou du '*grand* palais,' quelquefois au duel , des '*deux grandes maisons*,' par rapport à la division de l'Égypte en deux parties. C'est du titre très fréquent ⌐⌐ Per-āo, 'la grande maison,' 'la haute

lished facts of Egyptological science. The Bible and
the monuments confirm each other upon these points,
while both are again corroborated by the results of
recent geographical and philological research. The
"treasure-cities Pithom and Raamses" which the Israelites built for Pharaoh with bricks of their own making,
are the Pa-Tum * and Pa-Rameses ** of the inscriptions. It was from this last that Rameses II. set out
with his army to attack the confederate princes then
lying in ambush near Kades;*** and it was hither that
he returned in triumph after the great victory. A con-

porte,' qu'on a heureusement dérivé le nom biblique *Pharao* donné aux rois
d'Égypte."—*Histoire d'Égypte*, BRUGSCH: 2d edition, part I., p. 35; Leipzig,
1875.
  This probably is the only title under which it was permissible for the
plebeian class to speak or write of the sovereign.
  * Pa-Tum, or the city of Tum, is identified by Brugsch with Heracleopolis
Parva, the chief town of the nome called by the Greeks Sethroites. Tum, or
Atoum, was a solar god, and represented the unrisen sun. He preceded Ra
in the order of the universe.
  ** Pa-Rameses. Authorities differ widely upon the site of this famous city.
M. Chabas supposes it to be Pelusium, while Herr Brugsch identifies it with
Tanis, the modern San, the Zoan of the Scriptures. The French engineers,
however, finding at Tel-el-Mashoota a granite monolith inscribed with the cartouche of Rameses II., long since gave to that place the name of Rameses; a
conclusion which seems likely to be borne out by the recent discoveries of M.
Paponnet, the engineer at present engaged in the construction of the new
fresh-water canal between Cairo and Suez. Some fine sphinxes are reported
of as already exhumed from beneath a deep bed of alluvial deposit, and the
temple to which they led will probably have been discovered by the time these
pages are made public. The site of Tel-el-Mashoota is in many respects a
likely one, being situate on the border of the ancient canal, and in the immediate neighbourhood of a considerable lake, which used formerly to be filled
by the annual inundation. Pa-Rameses was a port, and close to a famous
piece of water called Shet-Hor, or the Pool of Horus. Granted that Tel-el-
Mashouta and Pa-Rameses are one, another possible identification suggests itself.
The site of the nome called by the Greeks *Sethroïtes* has not yet been determined. Here Brugsch conjectures that the original Egyptian name may have
been Set-ro-hata (the Land of the Mouths: *i. e.* the Tanitic, Pelusiac, and
Mendesian Mouths of the Nile). The present writer ventures, with the utmost
diffidence, to submit that *Sethroïtes* may have been a Greek rendering of
Shet-Hor. Pithom and Rameses being brought down some thirty miles farther
inland than Tanis, it follows also that *Set-ro-hata* would cease to be an ap-
plicable derivation.
  *** Kades, otherwise Katesh, Kadesh, or Atesch, a town on the Orontes,
identified by Brugsch with Cadytis,—See *Geog. Inschriften*, Taf. XIX. 105, I.

temporary letter written by one Panbesa, a clerk, describes in glowing terms the beauty and abundance of
the royal city, and tells how the damsels stood at their
doors in holiday apparel, with nosegays in their hands
and sweet oil upon their locks, "on the day of the
arrival of the War-God of the world." This letter is
in the British Museum. *

Other letters written during the reign of Rameses II.
are supposed to make direct mention of the Israelites.

"I have obeyed the orders of my master," writes
the scribe Kauiser to his superior Bak-en-Pthah, "being
bidden to serve out the rations to the soldiers, and
also to the Hebrews who quarry stone for the palace
of King Rameses Mer-Ammon." A similar document
written by a scribe named Keniamon, and couched in
almost the same words, shows them on another occasion
to have been quarrying for a building on the southern
side of Memphis; in which case Toora** would be the
scene of their labours.

These invaluable letters, written on papyrus in the
hieratic character, are in good preservation. They
were found in the ruins of Memphis, and now form
part of the treasures of the Museum of Leyden. ***

---

* Anastasi Papyri, No. III., Brit. Mus.
** See Chap. III., p. 61. vol. I.
*** See *Mélanges Égyptologiques*, by F. Chabas, 1 Série, 1862. There has
been much discussion among Egyptologists on the subject of M. Chabas's
identification of the Hebrews. The name by which they are mentioned in the
papyri here quoted, as well as in an inscription in the quarries of Hamamat, is
Aperi-u. A learned critic in the *Revue Archéologique* (vol. v. 2d série, 1862)
writes as follows:—"La découverte du nom des Hébreux dans les hiéroglyphes
serait un fait de la dernière importance; mais comme, aucun autre point historique n'offre peut-être une pareille séduction, il faut aussi se méfier des illu-
sions avec un soin méticuleux. La confusion des sous R et L dans la langue
égyptienne, et le voisinage des articulations B et P nuisent un peu, dans le cas
particulier, à la rigueur des conclusions qu'on peut tirer de la transcription.
Néanmoins, il y a lieu de prendre en considération ce fait que les Aperiu, dàns
les trois documents qui nous parlent d'eux, sont montrés employés à des

They bring home to us with startling nearness the
events and actors of the Bible narrative. We see the
Israelites at their toil, and the overseers reporting them
to the directors of public works. They extract from
the quarry those huge blocks which are our wonder
to this day. Harnessed to rude sledges, they drag
them to the river-side and embark them for transport
to the opposite bank.* Some are so large and so
heavy that it takes a month to get them down from
the mountain to the landing-place.** Other Israelites
are elsewhere making bricks, digging canals, helping to
build the great wall that reached from Pelusium to
Heliopolis, and strengthening the defences not only of
Pithom and Rameses, but of all the cities and forts
between the Red Sea and the Mediterranean. Their
lot is hard; but not harder than the lot of other workmen. They are well fed. They intermarry. They
increase and multiply. The season of their great oppression is not yet come. They make bricks, it is
true, and those who are so employed must supply a

travaux de même espèce que ceux auxquels, selon l'Écriture, les Hébreux
furent assujettis par les Égyptiens. La circonstance que les papyrus mention-
nant ce nom ont été trouvés à Memphis, plaide encore en faveur de l'assimilation proposée—découverte importante qu'il est à désirer de voir confirmée par
d'autres monuments." It should be added that the Aperiu also appear in the
Inscription of Thothmes III. at Karnak, and are supposed by M. Mariette to be
the people of Ephron. Dr. Birch is of opinion that there were two tribes of
Aperiu, a greater and a lesser, or an upper and a lower tribe. This, however,
would be consistent with the establishment of Hebrew settlers in the Delta,
and others in the neighbourhood of Memphis.

* See the famous wall-painting of the Colossus on the sledge engraved in
Sir G. Wilkinson's *Ancient Egyptians;* frontispiece to vol. II., ed. 1871.

** In a letter written by a priest who lived during this reign (Rameses II.),
we find an interesting account of the disadvantages and hardships attending
various trades and pursuits, as opposed to the ease and dignity of the sacerdotal office. Of the mason he says—"It is the climax of his misery to have to
remove a block of ten cubits by six, a block which it takes a month to drag by
the private ways among the houses."—Sallier Pap., No. II., Brit. Musæ.

certain number daily; * but the straw is not yet with-
held, and the task, though perhaps excessive, is not
impossible.

For we are here in the reign of Rameses II., and
the time when Menepthah shall succeed him is yet far
distant. It is not till the King dies that the children
of Israel sigh, "by reason of the bondage."

There are in the British Museum, the Louvre, and
the Bibliothèque Nationale, some much older papyri
than these two letters of the Leyden collection—some
as old, indeed, as the time of Joseph—but none of
such overwhelming historical interest. In these, the
scribes Kauiser and Keniamon seem still to live and
speak. What would we not give for a few more of
their letters! These men knew Memphis in its glory,
and had looked upon the face of Rameses the Great.
They might even have seen Moses in his youth, while

* "Ye shall no more give the people straw to make brick, as heretofore:
let them go and gather straw for themselves.

"And the tale of the bricks, which they did make heretofore, ye shall lay
upon them: ye shall not diminish ought thereof."—Exodus, chap. v. 7. 8.

M. Chabas says:—"Ces détails sont complètement conformes aux habi-
tudes Égyptiennes. Le mélange de paille et d'argile dans les briques antiques
a été parfaitement reconnu. D'un autre côté, le travail à la tâche est men-
tionné dans un texte écrit au revers d'un papyrus célébrant la splendeur de la
ville de Ramsès, et datant, selon toute vraisemblance, du règne de Meneptah I.
En voici la transcription:—'Compte des maçons, 12; en outre des hommes à
mouler la brique dans leurs villes, amenés aux travaux de la maison. Eux à
faire leur nombre de briques journellement; non ils sont à se relâcher des
travaux dans la maison neuve; c'est ainsi que j'ai obéi au mandat donné par
mon maître.'" See Recherches pour servir à l'Histoire de la XIX. Dynastie,
par F. Chabas. Paris; 1873, p. 149.

The curious text thus translated into French by M. Chabas is written on
the back of the papyrus already quoted (i.e. Letter of Panbesa, Anastasi
Papyri, No. III.), and is preserved in the British Museum. The wall-painting
in a tomb of the XVIIIth Dynasty at Thebes, which represents foreign captives mixing clay, moulding, drying, and placing bricks, is well known from the
illustration in Sir G. Wilkinson's Ancient Egyptians, ed. of 1871, vol. II. p. 196.
Cases 61 and 62 in the First Egyptian Room, British Museum, contain bricks
of mixed clay and straw stamped with the names of Rameses II.

yet he lived under the protection of his adopted mother, a prince among princes.

Kauiser and Keniamon lived, and died, and were mummied between three and four thousand years ago; yet these frail fragments of papyrus have survived the wreck of ages, and the quaint writing with which they are covered is as intelligible to ourselves as to the functionaries to whom it was addressed. That this writing should have reference to a subject race of whose keep and labour an accurate entry was necessarily kept by government scribes appointed for that purpose, is after all the least surprising part of the story. The Egyptians were eminently business-like. From the earliest epoch of which the monuments furnish record, we find an elaborate bureaucratic system in full operation throughout the country. Even in the time of the pyramid-builders, there are ministers of public works; inspectors of lands, lakes, and quarries; secretaries, clerks, and overseers innumerable.* From all these, we may be sure, were required strict accounts of their expenditure, as well as reports of the work done under their supervision. Specimens of their book-keeping are by no means rare. The Louvre is rich in memoranda of the kind; some relating to the date-tax; others to the transport and taxation of corn, the payment of wages, the sale and purchase of land for burial, and the like. If more news of the Hebrews should ever reach us from Egyptian sources, it will almost certainly be through the medium of documents such as these.

* "Les affaires de la cour et de l'administration du pays sont expédiées pas les 'chefs' ou les 'intendants,' par les 'secrétaires' et par la nombreuse classe des scribes. . . . Le trésor rempli d'or et d'argent, et le divan des

An unusually long reign, the last forty-six years of
which would seem to have been spent in peace and
outward prosperity, enabled Rameses II. to indulge his
ruling passion without interruption. To draw up anything like an exhaustive catalogue of his known architectural works would be equivalent to writing an
itinerary of Egypt and Ethiopia under the XIXth
Dynasty. His designs were as vast as his means appear to have been unlimited. From the Delta to
Gebel Barkal, he filled the land with monuments dedicated to his own glory and the worship of the Gods.
Upon Thebes, Abydos, and Tanis, he lavishes structures of surpassing magnificence. In Nubia, at the
places now known as Gerf Hossayn, Wady Sabooah,
Derr, and Aboo Simbel, he was the author of temples
and the founder of cities. These cities, which would
probably be better described as provincial towns, have
disappeared; and but for the mention of them in various inscriptions we should not even know that they
had existed. Who shall say how many more have
vanished, leaving neither trace nor record? A dozen
cities of Rameses* may yet lie buried under some of
those nameless mounds that follow each other in such
quick succession along the banks of the Nile in Middle
and Lower Egypt. Only yesterday, as it were, the re-

dépenses et des recettes avaient leurs intendants à eux. La chambre des
comptes ne manque pas. Les domaines, les propriétés, les palais, et même
les lacs du roi sont mis sous la garde d'inspecteurs. Les architectes du pharaon
s'occupent de bâtisses d'après l'ordre du pharaon. Les carrières, à partir de
celles du Mokattam (le Toora de nos jours) jusqu'à celles d'Assouan, se trouvent
exploitées par des chefs qui surveillent le transport des pierres taillées à la
place de leur destination. Finalement la corvée est dirigée par les chefs des
travaux publics." *Histoire d'Égypte,* Brugsch; second edition, 1875; chap. v.
pp. 34 and 35.
    * The Pa-Rameses of the Bible narrative was not the only Egyptian city of
that name. There was a Pa-Rameses near Memphis, and another Pa-Rameses
at Aboo Simbel, and there may probably have been many more.

mains of what would seem to have been a magnificent
palace were accidentally discovered under the mounds
of Tel-el-Yahoodeh,* about twelve miles to the N.E. of
Cairo. There are probably fifty such mounds, none of
which have been opened, in the Delta alone; and it is
no exaggeration to say that there must be some hundreds between the Mediterranean and the First Cataract.

An inscription found of late years at Abydos shows
that Rameses II. reigned over his great kingdom for
the space of sixty-seven years. "It is thou," says Rameses IV., addressing himself to Osiris, "it is thou
who wilt rejoice me with such length of reign as Rameses II., the great God, in his sixty-seven years. It
is thou who wilt give me the long duration of this great
reign." **

If only we knew at what age Rameses II. succeeded to the throne, we should, by help of this inscription, know also the age at which he died. No

* "Nothing of any interest had been found at Tel-el-Yahoodeh (the
'Mound of the Jews') till 1870, when the fellaheen of the neighbourhood, while
engaged in carrying away the brick-dust, which from the quantity of nitre it
contains forms a valuable top-dressing to the soil, came across the remains of
what had evidently been a magnificent palace. . . . The remains were
apparently those of a large hall paved with white alabaster slabs. The walls
were covered with a variety of bricks and encaustic tiles; many of the bricks
were of most beautiful workmanship, the hieroglyphs in some being inlaid in
glass. The capitals of the columns were inlaid with brilliant coloured mosaics,
and a pattern in mosaics ran round the cornice. Some of the bricks are inlaid
with the oval of Rameses II." See *Murray's Handbook for Egypt*, Route 7,
p. 217.
Case D, in the Second Egyptian Room at the British Museum contains
several of these tiles and terra-cottas, some of which are painted with figures
of Asiatic and Negro captives, birds, serpents, etc.; and are extremely beautiful both as regards design and execution. Murray is wrong, however, in attributing the building to Rameses II. The cartouches are those of Rameses III.
** This tablet is votive, and contains in fact a long Pharisaic prayer offered
to Osiris by Rameses IV. in the fourth year of his reign. The king enumerates
his own virtues and deeds of piety, and implores the God to grant him length
of days. See *Sur une Stèle inédite d'Abydos*, par P. Pierret. Revue Archéologique, vol. XIX. p. 273.

such record has, however, transpired. Brugsch, taking
for his point of departure the vague preamble of the
stela of Dakkeh,* assumes that he became king when
about nine or ten years of age, according to which calculation he must have been about seventy-seven at the
time of his death.

"Thou madest designs while yet in the age of infancy," says this inscription. "Thou wert a boy wearing the side-lock, and no monument was erected, and
no order was given without thee. Thou wert a youth
aged ten years, and all the public works were in thy
hands, laying their foundations." These lines, translated literally, cannot, however, be said to prove much.
They certainly contain nothing to show that this youth
of ten was, at the time alluded to, sole king and ruler
of Egypt. That he was titular king, in some heredi-
tary sense, from his birth** and during the lifetime of
his father, seems tolerably certain. That he should, as

---

* See *Histoire d'Égypte:* BRUGSCH. First edition, 1859, chap. VIII.
p. 130.
** M. Mariette, in his great work on Abydos, has argued that Rameses II.
was designated during the lifetime of his father by a cartouche signifying only
Ra-User-Ma; and that he did not take the additional *Setp-en-Ra* till after the
death of Seti I. The Louvre, however, contains a fragment of bas-relief representing the infant Rameses with the full title of his later years. This important fragment is thus described by M. Paul Pierret:—"Ramsés II. enfant,
représenté assis sur le signe des montagnes *du:* c'est une assimilation au soleil
levant lorsqu'il émerge a l'horizon céleste. Il porte la main gauche à sa bouche,
en signe d'enfance. La main droite pend sur les genoux. Il est vêtu d'une
longue robe. La tresse de l'enfance pend sur son épaule. Un diadème relie
ses cheveux, et un uræus se dresse sur son front. Voici a traduction de la
courte légende qui accompagne cette représentation. 'Le roi de la Haute et
de Basse Égypte, maître des deux pays, *Ra-User-Ma Setp-en-Ra,* vivificateur,
éternel comme le soleil.'" *Catalogue de la Salle Historique.* P. PIERRET.
Paris, 1873, p. 8.
　　M. Maspero is of opinion that this one fragment establishes the disputed
fact of his actual sovereignty from early childhood, and so disposes of the entire
question. See *L'Inscription dédicatoire du Temple d'Abydos, suivi d'un
Essai sur la jeunesse de Sesostris.* G. MASPERO. 4° Paris, 1867. See also
Chap. VIII. (footnote), p. 182, vol. I.

a boy, have designed public buildings and superintended their construction is extremely probable. The
office was one that might well have been discharged
by a crown-prince who delighted in architecture, and
made it his peculiar study. It was, in fact, a very
noble office—an office which from the earliest days of
the ancient Empire had constantly been confided to
princes of the royal blood;* but it carried with it no
evidence of sovereignty. The presumption, therefore,
would be that the inscription (dating as it does from
the third year of the reign of Rameses II.) alludes to
a time long since past, when the king as a boy held
office under his father.

The same inscription, as we have already seen,
makes reference to the victorious campaign in the
South. Rameses is addressed as "the bull powerful
against Ethiopia; the griffin furious against the negroes;" and that the events hereby alluded to must
have taken place during the first three years of his
reign is proved by the date of the tablet. Brugsch expressly says:—"Le jeune roi *débuta* par des guerres
contre les habitants de l'Ethiopie revoltée." ** According, then, to the method of calculation hitherto followed the king, if he came to the throne at nine or
ten years of age, must have brought his first campaign
to a close before he reached the age of thirteen.

Now the famous sculptures of the commemorative
chapel at Bayt el Welly relate expressly to the events
of this expedition; and as they are executed in that

---

* "Le métier d'architecte se trouvait confié aux plus hauts dignitaires de
la cour pharaonique. Les architectes du roi, les *Myrket*, se recrutaient assez
souvent parmi le nombre des princes." *Histoire d'Égypte:* BRUGSCH. Second
edition, 1875, chap, v. p. 34.
** *Histoire d'Égypte:* BRUGSCH. First edition, chap. VIII. 137.

refined and delicate style which especially characterises
the bas-relief work of Goornah, of Abydos, of all those
buildings which were either erected by Seti the First,
or begun by Seti and finished during the early years
of Rameses II., I venture to think we may regard them
as contemporary, or very nearly contemporary with the
scenes they represent. In any case, it is reasonable to
conclude that the artists employed on the work would
know something about the events and persons de-
lineated, and that they would be guilty of no glaring
inaccuracies.

What shall we say, however, when on referring to
these same sculptures* we find this boyish conqueror,
this lad of less than thirteen years of age, accompanied
by his son, Prince Amenhisemif, who is of an age not
only to bear his part in the field, but afterwards to
conduct an important ceremony of state on the occasion of the submission and tribute-offering of the Ethiopian commander? Such, nevertheless, is the fact; as
those who cannot go to Bayt el Welly may see and
judge for themselves by means of the admirable casts
of these great tableaux which line the walls of the
Second Egyptian Room at the British Museum. To
explain away Prince Amenhisemif would be difficult.
We are accustomed to a certain amount of courtly exaggeration on the part of those who record with pen
or pencil the great deeds of the Pharaohs. We expect
to see the king always young, always beautiful, always
victorious. It seems only right and natural that he
should be never less than twenty, and sometimes more
than sixty, feet in height. But that any flatterer
should go so far as to credit a lad of thirteen with a

* See Rosellini, *Monumenti Storici*, pl. LXXI.

son at least as old as himself is surely quite incredible.

Lastly, there is the evidence of the Bible.

Joseph being dead and the Israelites established in
Egypt, there comes to the throne a Pharaoh who takes
alarm at the increase of this alien race, and who seeks
to check their too rapid multiplication. He not only
oppresses the foreigners, but ordains that every male
infant born to them in their bondage shall be cast
into the river. This Pharaoh is now universally believed to be Rameses II. Then comes the old, sweet,
familiar Bible story that we know so well. Moses is
born, cast adrift in the ark of bulrushes, and rescued
by the King's daughter. He becomes to her "as a
son." Although no dates are given, it is clear that the
new Pharaoh has not been long upon the throne when
these events happen. It is equally clear that he is no
mere youth. He is old in the uses of state-craft; and
he is the father of a princess of whom it is difficult to
suppose that she was herself an infant.

On the whole, then, it seems reasonable to conclude that Rameses II., though in some way born a
King, was not merely grown to manhood, but wedded,
and the father of children already past the period of
infancy, before he succeeded to the sole exercise of
sovereign power.

Brugsch places the birth of Moses in the sixth year
of the reign of Rameses II.* This may very well be.

* "Comme Ramsès II. regna 66 ans, le règne de son successeur sous
lequel la sortie des Juifs eut lieu, embrassa la durée de 20 ans; et comme
Moïse avait l'age de 80 ans au temps de la sortie, il en résulte évidemment
que les enfants d'Israël quittèrent l'Égypte une des ces dernières six années
du règne de Menephthah; c'est à dire entre 1327 et 1321 avant l'ère chré-
tienne. Si nous admettons que ce pharaon périt dans la mer, selon le rapport

The fourscore years that elapsed between that time
and the time of the Exodus correspond with sufficient
exactness to the chronological data furnished by the
monuments. Moses would thus see out the sixty-one
remaining years of the King's long life, and release the
Israelites from bondage towards the close of the reign
of Menephthah,* who sat for about twenty years on
the throne of his fathers. The correspondence of dates
this time leaves nothing to be desired.

The Sesostris of Diodorus Siculus went blind, and
died by his own hand; which act, says the historian,
as it conformed to the glory of his life, was greatly admired by his people. We are here evidently in the
region of pure fable. Suicide was by no means an
Egyptian, but a classical virtue. Just as the Greeks
hated age, the Egyptians reverenced it; and it may be
doubted whether a people who seem always to have
passionately desired length of days, would have seen
anything to admire in a wilful shortening of that most
precious gift of the gods. With the one exception of
Cleopatra — the death of Nitocris the rosy-cheeked

---

biblique, Moïse sera né 80 ans avant 1321, ou 1401 avant J, Chr., la *sixième*
année du règne de Ramsès II."—*Hist. d'Égypte:* BRUGSCH. Chap. VIII.
p. 157. First edition, Leipzig, 1859.

* If the Exodus took place, however, during the opening years of the
reign of Menephthah, it becomes necessary either to remove the birth of
Moses to a correspondingly earlier date, or to accept the amendment of
Bunsen, who says "we can hardly take literally the statement as to the age
of Moses at the Exodus *twice over* forty years." Forty years is the mode of
expressing a generation, from thirty to thirty-three years. *Egypt's Place in
Universal History;* BUNSEN, Lond. 1859. Vol. III. p. 184. That Menephthah
did not himself perish with his host, seems certain. The final oppression of the
Hebrews and the miracles of Moses, as narrated in the Bible, give one the impression of having all happened within a comparatively short space of time;
and cannot have extended over a period of twenty years. Neither is it stated
that Pharaoh perished. The tomb of Menephthah, in fact, is found in the
Valley of the Tombs of the Kings (No. 8).

being also of Greek,* and therefore questionable, origin
—no Egyptian sovereign is known to have committed
suicide; and even Cleopatra who was half Greek by
birth, must have been influenced to the act by Greek
and Roman example. Dismissing then altogether this
legend of his blindness and self-slaughter, it must be
admitted that of the death of Rameses II., and of the
place of his burial, we know nothing certain.

His tomb was excavated, or at least begun, in the
Valley of the Tombs of the Kings. It has every appearance of being unfinished, and is choked with rubbish. The rubbish, in fact, looks like the débris of the
excavation; as if the workmen had refilled the place
when the work was abandoned. The Osymandias of
Hecatæus was, however, interred in a magnificent building, the description of which corresponds in all essen-
tial points to the Ramesseum at Thebes. It seems
possible, therefore, that Rameses II. may have begun
the first tomb during the early years of his reign, and
have afterwards abandoned it in favour of the most
gorgeous mortuary temple the world has ever seen.
Future excavations in the area of the Ramesseum, or
the contents of some yet undiscovered papyrus, may
hereafter solve this question.

Such are, very briefly, the leading facts of the history of this famous Pharaoh. Exhaustively treated, they
would expand into a volume. Even then, however, one
would ask, and ask in vain, what manner of man he
was. Every attempt to evolve his personal character
from these scanty data, is in fact a mere exercise of
fancy.** That he was personally valiant may be gathered,

* HERODOTUS, Bk. II.
** Rosellini, for instance, carries hero-worship to its extreme limit when

with due reservation, from the poem of Pentaour; and
that he was not unmerciful is shown in the extradition
clause of the Khetan treaty. His pride was evidently
boundless. Every Temple that he erected was a monument to his own glory; every colossus was a trophy;
every inscription a pæan of self-praise. At Aboo Simbel,
at Derr, at Gerf Hossayn, he seated his own image in
the sanctuary among the images of the gods.* There
are even instances in which he is depicted under the
twofold aspect of royalty and divinity—Rameses the
Pharaoh burning incense before Rameses the Deity.

For the rest, it is safe to conclude that he was
neither better nor worse than the general run of Oriental despots—that he was ruthless in war, prodigal in
peace, rapacious of booty, and unsparing in the exercise
of almost boundless power. Such pride and such des-
potism were, however, in strict accordance with immemorial precedent, and with the temper of the age
in which he lived. The Egyptians would seem, beyond
all doubt, to have believed that their King was always,

he not only states that Rameses the Great had, by his conquests, filled
Egypt with luxuries that contributed alike to the graces of every-day life
and the security of the state, but (accepting as sober fact the complimentary
language of a triumphal tablet) adds that "universal peace even secured to
him the love of the vanquished" (l'universal pace assicurata dall' amore dei
vinti stessi pel Faraone) —*Mon. Storici*, vol. III. part II. p. 294. Bunsen,
equally prejudiced in the opposite direction, can see no trait of magnanimity
or goodness in one whom he loves to depict as "an unbridled despot, who
took advantage of a reign of almost unparalleled length, and of the acquisi-
tions of his father and ancestors, in order to torment his own subjects and
strangers to the utmost of his power, and to employ them as instruments
of his passion for war and building." *Egypt's Place in Universal History*;
BUNSEN. Vol. III. bk. IV. part II, p. 184.

* "Souvent il s'introduit lui-même dans les triades divines auxquelles il
dédie les temples. *Le soleil de Ramsès Meïamoun* qu'on aperçoit sur leur
murailles, n'est autre chose que le roi lui-même déifié de son vivant." *Notice
des Monuments Egyptiennes au Musée du Louvre*. DE ROUGÉ; Paris, 1875,
p. 20.

in some sense, divine. They wrote hymns* and offered up prayers to him, and regarded him as the living representative of Deity. His princes and ministers habitually addressed him in the language of worship. Even his wives, who ought to have known better, are represented in the performance of acts of religious adoration before him. What wonder, then, if the man so deified believed himself a god?

* See *Hymn to Pharaoh* (Menephthah) translated by C. W. Goodwin, M.A. RECORDS OF THE PAST, vol. VI. p. 101.

CHAPTER XVI.

Aboo Simbel.

WE came to Aboo Simbel on the night of the 31st
of January, and we left at sunset on the 18th of February. Of these eighteen clear days, we spent fourteen
at the foot of the rock of the Great Temple, called in
the old Egyptian tongue the Rock of Abshek. The remaining four (taken at the end of the first week and
the beginning of the second) were passed in the excursion to Wady Halfeh and back. By thus dividing
the time, our long sojourn was made less monotonous
for those who had no especial work to do.

Meanwhile, it was wonderful to wake every morning close under the steep bank, and, without lifting
one's head from the pillow, to see that row of giant
faces so close against the sky. They showed unearthly
enough by moonlight; but not half so unearthly as in
the grey of dawn. At that hour, the most solemn of
the twenty-four, they wore a fixed and fatal look that
was little less than appalling. As the sky warmed, this
awful look was succeeded by a flush that mounted and
deepened like the rising flush of life. For a moment
they seemed to glow—to smile—to be transfigured.
Then came a flash, as of thought itself. It was the first
instantaneous flash of the risen sun. It lasted less than
a second. It was gone almost before one could say
that it was there. The next moment, mountain, river,
and sky were distinct in the steady light of day; and

the colossi—mere colossi now—sat serene and stony
in the open sunshine.

Every morning I waked in time to witness that daily
miracle.   Every morning I saw those awful brethren
pass from death to life, from life to sculptured stone.
I brought myself almost to believe at last that there
must sooner or later come some one sunrise when the
ancient charm would snap asunder, and the giants arise
and speak.

Stupendous as they are, nothing is more difficult
than to see the colossi properly. Standing between the
rock and the river, one is too near; stationed on the
island opposite, one is too far off; while from the sandslope only a side-view is obtainable.   Hence, for want
of a fitting standpoint, many travellers have seen nothing
but deformity in the most perfect face handed down to
us by Egyptian art.   One recognises in it the negro,
and one the Mongolian type;* while another admires
the fidelity with which "the Nubian characteristics"
have been seized.

---

* The late Vicomte E. de Rougé, in a letter to M. Guigniaut on the discoveries at Tanis, believes that he detects the Semitic type in the portraits of
Rameses II. and Seti I.;   and even conjectures that the Pharaohs of the
XIXth dynasty may have descended from Hyksos ancestors:—"L'origine de
la famille des Ramsés nous est jusqu' ici complétement inconnue : sa prédilec-
tion pour le dieu *Set* ou *Sutech*, qui éclate dès l'abord par le nom de Séti 1ᵉʳᵉ
(*Sethos*), ainsi que d'autres indices, pouvaient déjà engager à la reporter vers
la Basse Egypte. Nous savions même que Ramsés II. avait épousé une fille du
prince de Khet, quand le traité de l'an 22 eut ramené la paix entre les deux
pays. Le profil très-décidément sémitique de Séti et de Ramses se distinguait
nettement des figures ordinaires de nos Pharaons Thébains." (See *Revue
Archéologique*, vol. IX. A.D. 1864.)   In the course of the same letter, M. de
Rougé adverts to the magnificent restoration of the Temple of Sutech at Tanis
(San) by Rameses II., and to the curious fact that the God is there represented
with the peculiar head-dress worn elsewhere by the Prince of Kheta.

It is to be remembered, however, that the patron deity of Rameses II.
was Ammon Ra.   His homage of Sutech (which might possibly have been
a concession to his Khetan wife) seems to have been confined almost ex-
clusively to Tanis, where Ra-ma-ur-nofre may be supposed to have resided.

Yet, in truth, the head of the young Augustus is
not cast in a loftier mould. These statues are portraits—portraits of the same man four times repeated;
and that man is Rameses the Great.

Now, Rameses the Great, if he was as much like
his portraits as his portraits are like each other, must
have been one of the handsomest men, not only of
his own day, but of all history. Wheresoever we meet
with him, whether in the fallen colossus at Memphis,
or in the syenite torso of the British Museum, or
among the innumerable bas-reliefs of Thebes, Abydos,
Goornah, and Bayt-el-Welly, his features (though bearing in some instances the impress of youth, and in
others of maturity) are always the same. The face is
oval; the eyes are long, prominent, and heavy-lidded;
the nose is slightly aquiline and characteristically depressed at the tip; the nostrils are open and sensitive; the under lip projects; the chin is short and
square.

At Bayt-el-Welly, in a bas-relief commemorative of
his first campaign, we see Rameses II. represented as
a beardless youth with a delicate and Dantesque face,
clutching a captive by the hair with one hand, while
with the other he lifts his mace in act to slay. At
Abydos he appears with a boyish beard, and apparently some three or four years older. But it is at
Aboo Simbel, in the features of the Southernmost and
most perfect of the seated colossi of the great Temple,
that we learn to know him best. This last, whether
regarded as a marvel of size or of portraiture, is the
chef-d'œuvre of Egyptian sculpture. We here see the
great king in his prime. His features are identical
with those of the head at Bayt-el-Welly; but the con-

tours are more amply filled in, and the expression is altogether changed. The man is full fifteen or twenty years older. He has outlived that rage of early youth. He is no longer impulsive, but implacable. A godlike serenity, an almost superhuman pride, an immutable will, breathe from the sculptured stone. He has learned to believe his prowess irresistible, and himself almost divine. If he now raised his arm to slay, it would be with the stern placidity of a destroying angel.

The profile of the southernmost colossus can be correctly seen from but one point of view; and that point is where the sandslope meets the northern buttress of the façade, at a level just parallel with the beards of the statues. The sandslope is steep, and loose, and hot to the feet. More disagreeable climbing it would be hard to find, even in Nubia; but no traveller who refuses to encounter this small hardship need believe that he has seen the faces of the colossi.

Viewed from below, the face is fore-shortened out of all proportion. It looks unduly wide from ear to ear, while the lips and the lower part of the nose show relatively larger than the rest of the features. The same may be said of the great cast in the British Museum. Cooped up at the end of a narrow corridor and lifted not more than fifteen feet above the ground, it is carefully placed so as to be wrong from every point of view and shown to the greatest possible disadvantage.

The artists who wrought the original statues were, however, embarrassed by no difficulties of focus, daunted by no difficulties of scale. Giants themselves,

they summoned these giants from out the solid rock,
and endowed them with superhuman strength and
beauty. They sought no quarried blocks of syenite or
granite for their work. They fashioned no models of
clay. They took a mountain, and fell upon it like
Titans, and hollowed and carved it as though it were
a cherry-stone, and left it for the feebler men of after-
ages to marvel at for ever. One great hall and fifteen
spacious chambers they hewed out from the heart of
it; then smoothed the rugged precipice towards the
river, and cut four huge statues with their faces to the
sunrise, two to the right and two to the left of the
doorway, there to keep watch to the end of time.

These tremendous warders sit sixty-six feet high,
without the platform under their feet. They measure
across the chest 25 feet and 4 inches, from the
shoulder to the elbow, 15 feet and 6 inches; from the
inner side of the elbow joint to the tip of the middle
finger, 15 feet; and so on, in relative proportion.* If
they stood up, they would tower to a height of at
least 83 feet, from the soles of their feet to the tops
of their enormous double-crowns.

Nothing in Egyptian sculpture is perhaps quite so
wonderful as the way in which these Aboo Simbel

---

* Not, however, in strict proportion, according to the canon discovered
some years since by M. Charles Blanc, who found that the middle finger,
taken as the unit of measurement, corresponded to one nineteenth of the
total height of the body. The length of the middle finger of the Aboo Simbel
colossi is exactly three feet, according to which standard the figures would
measure only 57 feet in height without the head-dress. Counting, however,
from the sole of the foot to the rise of the crown of the head inside the pschent,
their actual height, if standing erect, would be full 66 feet, or 83 feet including
the height of the pschent.

A close comparison, however, of certain figures drawn to scale in squares,
some of which are found in tombs at Thebes, one at Memphis, and some in the
portico at Kom Ombo, has satisfactorily proved that the canon of proportion
varied from time to time. It was shorter in the Ptolemaic period than during
the XVIIIth and XIXth dynasties.

artists dealt with the thousands of tons of material to which they here gave human form. Consummate masters of effect, they knew precisely what to do, and what to leave undone. These were portrait statues; therefore they finished the heads up to the highest point consistent with their size. But the trunk and the lower limbs they regarded from a decorative rather than a statuesque point of view. As decoration, it was necessary that they should give size and dignity to the façade. Everything, consequently, was here subordinated to the general effect of breadth, of massiveness, of repose. Considered thus, the colossi are a triumph of treatment. Side by side they sit, placid and majestic, their feet a little apart, their hands resting on their knees. Shapely though they are, those huge legs look scarcely inferior in girth to the great columns of Karnak. The articulations of the knee-joint, the swell of the calf, the outline of the *peroneus longus* are indicated rather than developed. The toe-nails and toe-joints are given in the same bold and general way; but the fingers, because only the tips of them could be seen from below, are treated *en bloc*.

The faces show the same largeness of style. The little dimple which gives such sweetness to the corners of the mouth, and the tiny depression in the lobe of the ear, are in fact, circular cavities as large as saucers. The nose measures 3 feet and a half in length; the mouth, so delicately curved, is about the same in width; even the sensitive nostril, which looks ready to expand with the breath of life, exceeds 8 inches in length. The ear (which is placed high, and is well detached from the head) measures 3 feet and 5 inches from top to tip.

A recent writer,* who brings sound practical knowledge to bear upon the subject, is of opinion that the
Egyptian sculptors did not even "point" their work
beforehand. If so, then the marvel is only so much
the greater. The men who, working in so coarse and
friable a material, could not only give beauty and
finish to heads of this size, but could with barbaric
tools hew them out *ab initio* from the natural rock,
were the Michael Angelos of their age.

It has already been said that the last Rameses to
the southward is the best preserved. His left arm
and hand are injured, and the head of the uræus
sculptured on the front of the pschent is gone; but
with these exceptions the figure is as whole, as fresh
in surface, as sharp in detail, as on the day it was
completed. The next is shattered to the waist. His
head lies at his feet, half buried in sand. The third
is nearly as perfect as the first; while the fourth has
lost not only the whole beard and the greater part of
the uræus, but has both arms broken away, and a big,
cavernous hole in the front of the body. From the
double-crowns of the two last, the top ornament is

---

* *L'absence de points fouillés*, la simplification voulue, la restriction des
détails et des ornements à quelques sillons plus ou moins hardis, l'engorge-
ment de toutes les parties délicates, démontrent que les Egyptiens étaient
loin d'avoir des procédés et des facilités inconnus."—*La Sculpture Egyptienne*, par EMILE SOLDI, p. 48.
  "Un fait qui nous parait avoir dû entraver les progrès de la sculpture,
c'est l'habitude probable des sculpteurs ou entrepreneurs égyptiens d'entre-
prendre le travail à même sur la pierre, sans avoir préalablement cherché
le modèle en terre glaise, comme on le fait de nos jours. Une fois le modèle
fini, on le moule et on le reproduit mathématiquement définitive. Ce pro-
cédé a toujours été employé dans les grandes époques de l'art; et il ne nous
a pas semblé qu'il ait jamais été en usage en Egypte."—*Ibid.*, p. 82.
  M. Soldi is also of opinion that the Egyptian sculptors were ignorant of
many of the most useful tools known to the Greek, Roman, and modern sculptors, such as the emery-tube, the diamond-point, etc. etc.

also missing. It looks a mere knob; but it measures eight feet in height.

Such an effect does the size of these four figures produce on the mind of the spectator, that he scarcely observes the fractures they have sustained. I do not remember to have even missed the head and body of the shattered one, although nothing is left of it above the knees. Those huge legs and feet covered with ancient inscriptions, * some of Greek, some of Phœnician origin, tower so high above the heads of those who look at them from below, that one scarcely thinks of looking higher still.

The figures are naked to the waist, and clothed in the usual striped tunic. On their heads they wear the double-crown, and on their necks rich collars of cabochon drops cut in very low relief. The feet are bare of sandals, and the arms of bracelets; but in the front of the body, just where the customary belt and buckle would come, are deep holes in the stone, such as might have been made to receive rivets, supposing the belts to have been made of bronze or gold. On the breast, just below the necklace, and on the upper part of each arm, are cut in magnificent ovals, between

---

* On the left leg of this colossus is the famous Greek inscription discovered by Messrs. Bankes and Salt. It dates from the reign of Psammetichus I., and purports to have been cut by a certain Damearchon, one of the 240,000 Egyptian troops of whom it is related by Herodotus (Book II. chaps. 29, 30) that they deserted because they were kept in garrison at Syene for three years without being relieved. The inscription, as translated by Colonel Leake, is thus given in Rawlinson's Herodotus (vol. II. p. 37):—
"King Psamatichus having come to Elephantine, those who were with Psamatichus, the son of Theocles, wrote this. They sailed, and came to above Kerkis, to where the river rises . . . the Egyptian Amasis. . . . The writer is Damearchon the son of Amœbichus, and Pelephus Pelekos, the son of Udamus." The king Psamatichus here named has been identified with the Psamtik I. of the inscriptions. It was in his reign, and not as it has sometimes been supposed, in the reign of Psammetichus II., that the great military defection took place.

four and five feet in length, the ordinary cartouches of
the king. These were probably tattooed upon his person in the flesh.

Some have supposed that these statues were originally coloured, and that the colour may have been
effaced by the ceaseless shifting and blowing of the
sand. Yet the drift was probably at its highest when
Burckhardt discovered the place in 1813; and on the
two heads that were still above the surface, he seems
to have observed no traces of colour. Neither can the
keenest eye detect any vestige of that delicate film of
stucco which with the Egyptians invariably prepared
their surfaces for painting. Perhaps the architects were
for once content with the natural colour of the sandstone, which is here very rich and varied. It happéns
also that the colossi come in a light-coloured vein of
the rock, and so sit relieved against a darker background. Towards noon, when the level of the façade
has just passed into shade and the sunlight still strikes
upon the statues, the effect is quite startling. The
whole thing, which is then best seen from the island,
looks like a huge onyx-cameo cut in high relief.

A statue of Ra,* to whom the temple is dedicated,
stands some twenty feet high in a niche over the doorway, and is supported on either side by a bas-relief
portrait of the king in an attitude of worship. Next
above these comes a superb hieroglyphic inscription

---

* *Ra*, a solar divinity, generally represented with the head of a hawk,
and the sun-disk on his head. "*Ra* veut dire *faire, disposer; c'est, en
effet, le dieu Ra qui a disposé, organisé le monde, dont la matière lui a été
donnée par Ptah."—P. PIERRET: *Dictionnaire d'Archéologie Egyptienne.*

"Ra est une autre des intelligences démiurgiques. Ptah avait créé le
soleil; le soleil, a son tour, est *le créateur des êtres, animaux et hommes.*
Il est à l'hémisphère supérieure ce qu'Osiris est à l'hémisphère inférieure.
Ra s'incarne à Héliopolis."—A, MARIETTE; *Notice des Monuments à Boulak,*
p. 123.

reaching across the whole front; above the inscription, a band of royal cartouches; above the cartouches, a frieze of sitting apes; above the apes, last and highest, some fragments of a cornice. The height of the whole may have been somewhat over a hundred feet. Wherever it has been possible to introduce them as decoration, we see the ovals of the king. Under those sculptured on the platforms and over the door, I observed the neck-lace, or collar ( ), which, in conjunction with the sign known as the determinative of metals, signifies gold (Nub); but when represented, as here, without the determinative, stands for Nubia, the Land of Gold. This addition, which I do not remember to have seen elsewhere in connection with the cartouches of Rameses II.,* is here used in a heraldic sense, as signifying the sovereignty of Nubia.

The relative position of the two Temples of Aboo Simbel has been already described—how they are excavated in two adjacent mountains and divided by a cataract of sand. The front of the small Temple lies parallel to the course of the Nile, here flowing in a north-easterly direction. The façade of the Great Temple is cut in the flank of the mountain, and faces due east. Thus the colossi, towering above the shoulder of the sand-drift, catch, as it were, a side view of the small Temple and confront vessels coming up the river. As for the sand-drift, it curiously resembles the glacier of the Rhone. In size, in shape, in position, in all but colour and substance, it is the same. Pent in be-

---

* An instance occurs, however, in a small inscription sculptured on the rocks of the Island of Sehayl in the First Cataract, which records the second panegyry of the reign of Rameses II.—See *Récueil des Monuments*, etc.; Brugsch, vol. II., Planche LXXXII., Inscription No. 6.

tween the rocks at top, it opens out like a fan at bottom. In this its inevitable course, is slants downward across the façade of the Great Temple. For ever descending, drifting, accumulating, it wages the old stealthy war; and, unhasting, unresting, labours grain by grain to fill the hollowed chambers, and bury the great statues, and wrap the whole Temple in a winding-sheet of golden sand, so that the place thereof shall know it no more.

It had very nearly come to this when Burckhardt went up (A.D. 1813). The top of the doorway was then thirty feet below the surface. Whether the sand will ever reach that height again, must depend on the energy with which it is combated. It can only be cleared as it accumulates. To avert it is impossible. Backed by the illimitable wastes of the Libyan desert, the supply from above is inexhaustible. Come it must; and come it will, to the end of time.

The drift rose to the lap of the northernmost colossus and half-way up the legs of the next, when the Philæ lay at Aboo Simbel. The doorway was clear, however, almost to the threshold, and the sand inside was not more than two feet deep in the first hall. The whole façade, we were told, had been laid bare, and the interior swept and garnished, when the Empress of the French, after opening the Suez Canal in 1869, went up the Nile as far as the Second Cataract. By this time, most likely, that yellow carpet lies thick and soft in every chamber, and is fast silting up the doorway again.

How well I remember the restless excitement of our first day at Aboo Simbel! While the morning was yet cool, the Painter and the Writer wandered to and

fro, comparing and selecting points of view, and super-
intending the pitching of their tents. The Painter
planted his on the very brink of the bank, face to face
with the colossi and the open doorway. The Writer
perched some forty feet higher on the pitch of the
sandslope; so getting a side-view of the façade, and a
peep of distance looking up the river. To fix the tent
up there was no easy matter. It was only by sinking
the tent-pole in a hole filled with stones, that it could
be trusted to stand against the steady push of the
north wind, which at this season is almost always
blowing.

Meanwhile the travellers from the other Dahabeeyahs were tramping backwards and forwards between
the two Temples; filling the air with laughter, and
waking strange echoes in the hollow mountains. As
the day wore on, however, they returned to their boats,
which one by one spread their sails and bore away for
Wady Halfeh.

When they were fairly gone and we had the mar-
vellous place all to ourselves, we went to see the
Temples.

The smaller one, though it comes first in order of
sailing, is generally seen last; and seen therefore to
disadvantage. To eyes fresh from the "Abode of Ra,"
the "Abode of Hathor" looks less than its actual size;
which is in fact but little inferior to that of the Temple
at Derr. A first hall, measuring some 40 feet in length
by 21 in width, leads to a transverse corridor, two
side-chambers, and a sanctuary 7 feet square, at the
upper end of which are the shattered remains of a
cow-headed statue of Hathor. Six square pillars, as at
Derr, support what, for want of a better word, one

must call the ceiling of the hall; though the ceiling is
in truth the superincumbent mountain.

   In this arrangement, as in the general character of
the bas-relief sculptures which cover the walls and pillars, there is much simplicity, much grace, but nothing
particularly new.   The façade, on the contrary, is a
daring innovation. Here the whole front is but a frame
for six recesses, from each of which a colossal statue,
erect and life-like, seems to be walking straight out
from the heart of the mountain.   These statues, three
to the right and three to the left of the doorway, stand
thirty feet high, and represent Rameses II. and Nofreari,
his queen.   Mutilated as they are, the male figures are
full of spirit, and the female figures full of grace.   The
Queen wears on her head the disk of Hathor and the
ostrich feathers of royalty.   The King is crowned with
the pschent, and with a fantastic helmet adorned with
plumes and horns.   They have their children with
them; the Queen her daughters, the King his sons—
infants of ten feet high, whose heads just reach to
the parental knee.

   The walls of these six recesses, as they follow the
slope of the mountain, form massive buttresses, the
effect of which is wonderfully bold in light and shadow.
The doorway gives the only instance of a porch that
we saw in either Egypt or Nubia.   The superb hieroglyphs that cover the faces of these buttresses and the
front of this porch are cut half-a-foot deep into the
rock, and are so large that they can be read from the
island in the middle of the river.   The tale they tell
—a tale retold, in many varied turns of old Egyptian
style upon the architraves within—is singular and interesting.

"Rameses, the Strong in Truth, the Beloved of Ammon," says the outer legend, "made this divine Abode * for his royal wife, Nofreari, whom he loves." The legend within, after enumerating the titles of the King, records that "his royal wife who loves him, Nofreari the Beloved of Maut, constructed for him this Abode in the mountain of the Pure Waters." On every pillar, in every act of worship pictured on the walls, even in the sanctuary, we find the names of Rameses and Nofreari "coupled and inseparable." In this double dedication, and in the unwonted tenderness of the style, one seems to detect traces of some event, perhaps of some anniversary, the particulars of which are lost for ever. It may have been a meeting; it may have been a parting; it may have been a prayer answered, or a vow fulfilled. We see, at all events, that Rameses and Nofreari desired to leave behind them an imperishable record of the affection which united them on earth, and which they hoped would reunite them in Amenti. What more do we need to know? We see that the Queen was fair; ** that the

* Though dedicated by Rameses to Nofreari, and by Nofreari to Rameses, this Temple was placed, primarily, under the patronage of Hathor, the supreme type of divine maternity. She is represented by Queen Nofreari, who appears on the façade as the mother of six children, and adorned with the attributes of the goddess. A Temple to Hathor would also be, from a religious point of view, the fitting pendant to a Temple of Ra. M. Mariette, in his *Notice des Monuments à Boulak*, remarks of Hathor that her functions are still but imperfectly known to us. "Peut-être était-elle à Ra ce que Maut est à Ammon, le récipient où le dieu s'engendre lui-même pour l'éternité."

** It is not often that one can say of a female head in an Egyptian wall-painting that it is beautiful; but in these portraits of the Queen, many times repeated upon the walls of the first Hall of the Temple of Hathor, there is, if not positive beauty according to our western notions, much sweetness and much grace. The name of *Nofreari* means Perfect, Good, or Beautiful Companion. That the word *Nofre* or *Nefer* should mean both Good and Beautiful —in fact, that Beauty and Goodness should be synonymous terms—is not merely interesting as it indicates a lofty philosophical standpoint, but as it reveals, perhaps, the latent germ of that doctrine which was hereafter to be

King was in his prime. We divine the rest; and the
poetry of the place at all events is ours. Even in these
barren solitudes there is wafted to us a breath from
the shores of old romance. We feel that Love once
passed this way, and that the ground is still hallowed
where he trod.

We hurried on to the Great Temple, without waiting to examine the lesser one in detail. A solemn
twilight reigned in the first hall, beyond which all was
dark. Eight colossi, four to the right and four to the
left, stand ranged down the centre, bearing the mountain on their heads. Their height is twenty-five feet.
With hands crossed on their breasts, they clasp the
flail and crook; emblems of majesty and dominion.
It is the attitude of Osiris, but the face is the face
of Rameses II. Seen by this dim light, shadowy,
mournful, majestic, they look as if they remembered
the past.

Beyond the first hall lies a second hall supported
on four square pillars; beyond this again, a transverse
chamber, the walls of which are covered with coloured
bas-reliefs of various Gods; last of all, the sanctuary.
Here, side by side, sit four figures larger than life—
Phthah, Ammon Ra, Ra, and Rameses deified. Before
them stands an altar, in shape a truncated pyramid,
cut from the solid rock. Traces of colour yet linger

taught with such brilliant results in the Alexandrian Schools. It is remarkable
that the word for Truth and Justice (*Ma*) was also one and the same.

There is often a quaint significance about Egyptian proper names which
reminds one of the names that came into favour in England under the Com-
monwealth. Take for instance *Bak-en Khonsu*, Servant-of-Khons; *Pa-du-
amen*, the Gift of Ammon; *Renpitnofre*, Good-year; *Noub-en Tekh*, Worth-
her-Weight-in-Gold (both women's names); and *Hor-mes-out'-a-Shu*, Horus-
son-of-the-Eye-of-Shu—which last, as a tolerably long compound, may claim
elationship with Praise - God-Barebones, Hew - Agag - in Pieces - before - the-
Lord, etc. etc.

on the garments of the statues; while in the walls on
either side are holes and grooves such as might have
been made to receive a screen of metal-work.

The air in the sanctuary was heavy with an acrid
smoke, as if the priests had been burning some strange
incense and were only just gone. For this illusion we
were indebted to the visitors who had been there before us. They had lit the place with magnesian wire;
the vapour of which lingers long in these unventilated
vaults.

To settle down then and there to a steady investigation of the wall-sculptures was impossible. We did
not attempt it. Wandering from hall to hall, from
chamber to chamber; now trusting to the faint gleams
that straggled in from without, now stumbling along
by the light of a bunch of candles tied to the end of
a stick, we preferred to receive those first impressions
of vastness, of mystery, of gloomy magnificence, which
are the more profound for being somewhat vague and
general.

Scenes of war, of triumph, of worship, passed before our eyes like the incidents of a panorama. Here
the King, borne along at full gallop by plumed steeds
gorgeously caparisoned, draws his mighty bow and
attacks a battlemented fortress. The besieged, some
of whom are transfixed by his tremendous arrows, sup-
plicate for mercy. They are evidently Assyrian. Their
skin is yellow; and they wear the long hair and beard,
the fillet, the rich robe, fringed cape, and embroidered
baldric with which we are familiar in the Nineveh
sculptures. A man driving off cattle in the foreground
looks as if he had stepped out of one of the tablets in
the British Museum. Rameses meanwhile towers, swift

5*

and godlike, above the crowd. His coursers are of such immortal strain as were the coursers of Achilles. His sons, his whole army, chariot and horse, follow headlong at his heels. All is movement and the splendour of battle.

Farther on, we see the King returning in state, preceded by his prisoners of war. Tied together in gangs, they stagger as they go, with heads thrown back and hands uplifted. These, however, are not Assyrians, but Abyssinians and Nubians, so true to the type, so thick-lipped, flat-nosed, and woolly-headed, that only the pathos of the expression saves them from being ludicrous. It is naturalness pushed to the verge of caricature.

A little farther still, and we find Rameses leading a string of these captives into the presence of Ammon Ra, Maut, and Khons—Ammon Ra weird and unearthly, with his blue complexion and towering plumes; Maut wearing the crown of Upper Egypt; Khons by a subtle touch of flattery depicted with the features of the King. Again, to right and left of the entrance, Ramses, thrice the size of life, slays a group of captives of various nations. To the left Ammon Ra, to the right Phra Harmachis, * approve and accept the sacrifice. In the second hall we see, as usual, the procession of the sacred bark. Pthah, Khem, and Pasht, gorgeous in many-coloured garments, gleam dimly, like figures in faded tapestry, from the walls of the transverse corridor.

But the wonder of Aboo Simbel is the huge subject on the north side of the Great Hall. This is a monster

---

* Phra, or Ra Harmachis, also called Har-em-Khou-ti, personifies the sun in his diurnal course from the eastern to the western horizon.

battle-piece which covers an area of 57 feet and 7 inches in length, by 25 feet 4 inches in height, and contains over 1100 figures. Even the heraldic cornice of cartouches and asps which runs round the rest of the ceiling is omitted on this side, so that the wall is literally filled with the picture from top to bottom.

Fully to describe this huge design would take many pages. It is a picture-gallery in itself. It represents not a single action but a whole campaign. It sets before us, with Homeric simplicity, the pomp and circumstance of war, the incidents of camp life, and the accidents of the open field. We see the enemy's city with its battlemented towers and triple moat; the besiegers' camp and the pavilion of the king; the march of infantry; the shock of chariots; the hand-to-hand melée; the flight of the vanquished; the triumph of the Pharaoh; the bringing in of the prisoners; the counting of the hands of the slain. A great river winds through the picture from end to end, and almost surrounds the invested city. The king in his chariot pursues a crowd of fugitives along the bank. Some are crushed under his wheels; some plunge into the water and are drowned. * Behind him, a moving wall of shields and spears, advances with rhythmic step the serried phalanx; while yonder, where the fight is thickest, we see chariots overturned, men dead and dying, and riderless horses making for the open. Meanwhile the besieged send out mounted scouts, and the country folk drive their cattle to the hills.

A grand frieze of chariots charging at full gallop divides the subject lengthwise, and separates the Egyptian camp from the field of battle. The camp is

* See chap. VIII., pp. 181-2, vol. I.

square, and enclosed, apparently, in a palisade of
shields. It occupies less than one sixth part of the
picture, and contains about a hundred figures. Within
this narrow space the artist has brought together an
astonishing variety of incidents. The horses feed in
rows from a common manger, or wait their turn and
impatiently paw the ground. Some are lying down.
One, just unharnessed, scampers round the enclosure.
Another, making off with the empty chariot at his
heels, is intercepted by a couple of grooms. Other
grooms bring buckets of water slung from the shoulders
on wooden yokes. A wounded officer sits apart, his
head resting on his hand; and an orderly comes in
haste to bring him news of the battle. Another, hurt
apparently in the foot, is having the wound dressed by
a surgeon. Two detachments of infantry, marching
out to reinforce their comrades in action, are met at
the entrance to the camp by the royal chariot returning from the field. Rameses drives before him some
fugitives, who are trampled down, seized, and despatched upon the spot. In one corner stands a row
of objects that look like joints of meat; and near them
are a small altar and a tripod brazier. Elsewhere, a
couple of soldiers, with a big bowl between them, sit
on their heels and dip their fingers in the mess,
precisely as every Fellah does to this day. Meanwhile
it is clear that Egyptian discipline was strict, and that
the soldier who transgressed was as abjectly subject to
the rule of stick as his modern descendant. In no
less than three places do we see this time-honoured
institution in full operation, the superior officer ener-
getically flourishing his staff; the private taking his
punishment with characteristic disrelish. In the middle

of the camp, watched over by his keeper, lies Rameses' tame lion; while close against the royal pavilion a
hostile spy is surprised and stabbed by the officer on
guard. The pavilion itself is very curious. It is
evidently not a tent but a building, and was probably
an extemporaneous construction of crude brick. It has
four arched doorways, and contains in one corner an
object like a cabinet, with two sacred hawks for supporters. This object, which is in fact almost identical
with the hieroglyphic emblem used to express a royal
panegyry or festival, stands, no doubt, for the private
oratory of the King. Five figures kneel before it in
adoration.

To enumerate all or half the points of interest in
this amazing picture would ask altogether too much
space. Even to see it, with time at command and all
the help that candles and magnesian torches can give,
is far from easy. The relief is unusually low, and the
surface, having originally been covered with stucco, is
purposely roughened all over with tiny chisel-marks,
which painfully confuse the details. Nor is this all.
Owing to some kind of saline ooze in that part of the
rock, the stucco has not only peeled off, but the actual
surface is injured. It seems to have been eaten away,
just as iron is eaten by rust. A few patches adhere,
however, in places, and retain the original colouring.
The river is still covered with blue and white zigzags,
to represent water; some of the fighting groups are
yet perfect; and two very beautiful royal chariots, one of
which is surmounted by a richly ornamented parasol-
canopy, are as fresh and brilliant as ever.

The horses throughout are excellent. The chariot
frieze is almost Panathenaic in its effect of multitudi-

nous movement; while the horses in the camp of
Rameses, for naturalness and variety of treatment, are
perhaps the best that Egyptian art has to show. It is
worth noting also that a horseman, that *rara avis*,
occurs some four or five times in different parts of the
picture.

The scene of the campaign is laid in Syria. The
river of blue and white zigzags is the Orontes;* the
city of the besieged is Kadesh or Kades;** the enemy
are the Kheta. The whole is, in fact, a grand picture-
epic of the events immortalised in the poem of
Pentaour—that poem which M. de Rougé has described as "a sort of Egyptian Iliad." The comparison would, however, apply to the picture with greater
force than it applies to the poem. Pentaour, who was
in the first place a courtier, and in the second place a
poet, has sacrificed everything to the prominence of
his central figure. He is intent upon the glorification
of the King; and his poem, which is a mere pæan of
praise, begins and ends with the prowess of Rameses
Mer-Ammon. If, then, it is to be called an Iliad, it is
an Iliad from which everything that does not immediately concern Achilles is left out. The picture, on
the contrary, though it shows the hero in combat and
in triumph, and always of colossal proportions, yet has
space for a host of minor characters. The episodes in
which these characters appear are essentially Homeric.
The spy is surprised and slain, as Dolon was slain by
Ulysses. The men feast, and fight, and are wounded,

---

* In Egyptian, *Aaranatu.*
** In Egyptian, *Kateshu.* " Aujourd'hui encore il existe une ville de Kades
près d'une courbe de l'Oronte dans le voisinage de Homs." *Leçons de M. de
Rougé, Professées au Collége de France.* See MÉLANGES D'ARCHÉOLOGIE,
Egyp. and Assyr., vol. II. p. 269. The bend of the river is actually given in
the bas-reliefs.

just like the long-haired sons of Achaia; while their
horses, loosed from the yoke, eat white barley and oats

"Hard by their chariots, waiting for the dawn."

Like Homer, too, the artist of the battle-piece is careful
to point out the distinguishing traits of the various
combatants. The Kheta go three in a chariot; the
Egyptians only two. The Kheta wear a moustache
and scalp-lock; the Egyptians pride themselves on "a
clean shave," and cover their bare heads with pon-
derous wigs. The Sardinian contingent cultivate their
own thick hair, whiskers, and mustachios; and their
features are distinctly European. They also wear the
curious helmet, surmounted by a ball and two spikes,
by which they may always be recognised in the sculptures. These Sardinians appear only in the border-
frieze, next the floor. The sand had drifted up just at
that spot, and only the top of one fantastic helmet was
visible above the surface. Not knowing in the least to
what this might belong, we set the men to scrape
away the sand; and so, quite by accident, uncovered
the most curious and interesting group in the whole
picture. The Sardinians * (in Egyptian Shardana)
seem to have been naturalised prisoners of war drafted

---

* "La légion *S'ardana* de l'armée de Ramses II. provenait d'une première
descente de ces peuples en Égypte. 'Les *S'ardaina* qui étaient des prison-
niers de sa majesté,' dit expressément le texte de Karnak, au commencement
du poëme de *Pentaour*. Les archéologues ont remarqué la richesse de leur
costume et de leurs armures. Les principales pièces de leur vêtements
semblent couverts de broderies. Leur bouclier est une rondache : ils portent
une longue et large épée de forme ordinaire, mais on remarque aussi dans leurs
mains une épée d'une longueur démesurée. Le casque des S'ardana est très
caractéristique; sa forme est arrondie, mais il est surmonté d'une tige qui sup-
porte une boule de métal. Cet ornement est accompagné de deux cornes en
forme de croissant. . . . Les S'ardana de l'armée Égyptienne ont seulement
des favoris et des moustaches coupés très courts."—*Mémoire sur les Attaques
Dirigées contre l'Égypte*, etc. etc. E. DE ROUGÉ. *Revue Archéologique,*
vol. XVI. pp. 90, 91.

into the ranks of the Egyptian army; and are the first
European people whose name appears on the monuments.

There is but one hour in the twenty-four at which
it is possible to form any idea of the general effect of
this vast subject; and that is at sunrise. Then only
does the pure day stream in through the doorway, and
temper the gloom of the side-aisles with light reflected
from the sunlit floor. The broad divisions of the picture and the distribution of the masses may then be
dimly seen. The details, however, require candle-light,
and can only be studied a few inches at a time.
Even so, it is difficult to make out the upper groups
without the help of a ladder. Salame, mounted on a
chair and provided with two long sticks lashed together, could barely hold his little torch high enough
to enable the Writer to copy the inscription on the
middle tower of the fortress of Kades.

It is fine to see the sunrise on the front of the
Great Temple; but something still finer takes place on
certain mornings in the year, in the very heart of the
mountain. As the sun comes up above the eastern
hill-tops, one long, level beam strikes through the doorway, pierces the inner darkness like an arrow, pene-
trates to the sanctuary, and falls like fire from heaven
upon the altar at the feet of the Gods.

No one who has watched for the coming of that
shaft of sunlight can doubt that it was a calculated
effect, and that the excavation was directed at one
especial angle in order to produce it. In this way
Ra,* to whom the temple was dedicated, may be said to

---

* *Ra*, ou quelquefois Horus. C'est le dieu solaire par excellence."—A. MA-
RIETTE. *Notice des Monuments à Boulak*, p. 123. See also footnote at p. 60.
of this vol. It will be seen by the above that M. Mariette, who certainly knows
more than any one in the world about the Egyptian Pantheon, admits that Ra

have entered in daily, and by a direct manifestation of his presence to have approved the sacrifices of his worshippers.

I need scarcely say that we did not see half the wall-sculptures or even half the chambers, that first afternoon at Aboo Simbel. We rambled to and fro, lost in wonder, and content to wonder, like rustics at a fair. We had, however, ample time to come again and again, and learn it all by heart. The Writer went in constantly, and at all hours; but most frequently at the end of the day's sketching, when the rest were walking or boating in the cool of the late afternoon.

It is a wonderful place to be alone in—a place in which the very darkness and silence are old, and in which Time himself seems to have fallen asleep. Wandering to and fro among these sculptured halls, like a shade among shadows, one seems to have left the world behind; to have done with the teachings of the present; to belong one's self to the past. The very Gods assert their ancient influence over those who question them in solitude. Seen in the fast-deepening gloom of evening, they look instinct with supernatural life. There were times when I should scarcely have been surprised to hear them speak—to see them rise from their painted thrones and come down from the walls. There were times when I felt I believed in them.

There was something so weird and awful about the place, and it became so much more weird and awful the farther one went in, that I rarely ventured beyond

and Horus are identical. This is important, and shows that the work of sim-plification foreseen by Ampère is now begun in earnest. The day is, perhaps, approaching when Khons will also be recognised as a form of Ra, Hathor as a version of Isis, etc. etc.

the first hall when quite alone. One afternoon, however, when it was a little earlier, and therefore a little
lighter, than usual, I went to the very end, and sat at
the feet of the Gods in the sanctuary. All at once (I
cannot tell why, for my thoughts just then were far
away) it flashed upon me that a whole mountain hung
—ready, perhaps, to cave in—above my head. Seized
by a sudden panic such as one feels in dreams, I tried
to run; but my feet dragged, and the floor seemed to
sink under them. I felt I could not have called for
help, though it had been to save my life. It is un-
necessary, perhaps, to add that the mountain did not
cave in, and that I had my fright for nothing. It
would have been a grand way of dying, all the same;
and a still grander way of being buried.

My visits to the Great Temple were not always so
dramatic. I sometimes took Salame, who smoked
cigarettes when not on active duty, or held a candle
while I sketched patterns of cornices, head-dresses of
Kings and Gods, designs of necklaces and bracelets,
heads of captives, and the like. Sometimes we explored the side-chambers. Of these there are eight;
pitch-dark, and excavated at all kinds of angles. Two
or three are surrounded by stone benches cut in the
rock; and in one the hieroglyphic inscriptions are part
cut, part sketched in black and left unfinished. As
this temple is entirely the work of Rameses II., and
betrays no sign of having been added to by any of his
successors, these evidences of incompleteness would seem
to show that the King died before the work was ended.

I was always under the impression that there were
secret places yet undiscovered in these dark chambers,
and Salame and I were always looking for them. At

Denderah, at Edfoo, at Medinet Haboot, at Philæ,* there have been found crypts in the thickness of the walls and recesses under the pavements, for the safe-keeping of treasure in time of danger. The rock-cut temples must also have had their hiding-places; and these would doubtless take the form of concealed cells in the walls, or under the floors of the side-chambers.

To come out from these black holes into the twi-light of the Great Hall and see the landscape set, as it were, in the ebon frame of the doorway, was alone worth the journey to Aboo Simbel. The sun being at such times in the west, the river, the yellow sand-island, the palms and tamarisks opposite, and the mountains of the eastern desert, were all flooded with a glory of light and colour to which no pen or pencil could possibly do justice. Not even the mountains of Moab in Holman Hunt's "Scapegoat" were so warm with rose and gold.

Thus our days passed at Aboo Simbel; the workers working; the idlers idling; strangers from the outer world now and then coming and going. The heat on shore was great, especially in the sketching-tents; but the north breeze blew steadily every day from about an hour after sunrise till an hour before sunset, and on board the Dahabeeyah it was always cool.

The Happy Couple took advantage of this good wind to do a good deal of boating, and by judiciously timing their excursions, contrived to use the tail of the day's breeze for their trip out, and the strong arms of four good rowers to bring them back again. In this

---

* A rich treasure of gold and silver rings was found by Ferlini, in 1834, immured in the wall of one of the pyramids of Merõe, in Upper Nubia. See *Lepsius's Letters*, translated by L. and J. HORNER, Bohn, 1853, p. 151.

way they managed to see the little rock-cut Temple of
Ferayg, which the rest of us unfortunately missed. On
another occasion they paid a visit to a certain Sheyhk
who lived at a village about two miles south of Aboo
Simbel. He was a great man, as Nubian magnates go.
His name was Hassan Ebn Rashwan el Kasheff, and
he was a grandson of that same old Hassan Kasheff
who was vice-regent of Nubia in the days of Burckhardt and Belzoni. He received our Happy Couple
with distinguished hospitality, killed a sheep in their
honour, and entertained them for more than three
hours. The meal consisted of an endless succession
of dishes, all of which, like that bugbear of our childhood, the hated Air with Variations, went on repeat-
ing the same theme under a multitude of disguises;
and, whether roast, boiled, stewed or minced, served
on skewers, smothered in rice, or drowned in sour
milk, were always mutton *au fond.*

We now despaired of ever seeing a crocodile; and
but for a trail that our men discovered on the island
opposite, we should almost have ceased to believe that
there were crocodiles in Egypt. The marks were quite
fresh when we went to look at them. The creature
had been basking high and dry in the sun, and this
was the point at which he had gone down again to
the river. The damp sand at the water's edge had
taken the mould of his huge fleshy paws, and even of
the jointed armour of his tail, though this last impression was somewhat blurred by the final rush with
which he had taken to the water. I doubt if Robinson
Crusoe, when he saw the famous footprint on the shore,
was more excited than we of the Philæ at sight of this
genuine and undeniable trail.

As for the Idle Man, he flew at once to arms and made ready for the fray. He caused a shallow grave to be dug for himself a few yards from the spot; then went and lay in it for hours together, morning after morning, under the full blaze of the sun,—flat, patient, alert,—with his gun ready cocked, and a Pall Mall Budget up his back. It was not his fault if he narrowly escaped sunstroke, and had his labour for his reward. That crocodile was too clever for him, and took care never to come back.

Our sailors, meanwhile, though well pleased with an occasional holiday, began to find Aboo Simbel monotonous. As long as the Bagstones stayed, the two crews met every evening to smoke, and dance, and sing their quaint roundelays together. But when rumours came of wonderful things already done this winter above Wady Halfeh—rumours that represented the Second Cataract as a populous solitude of crocodiles — then our faithful consort slipped away one morning before sunrise, and the Philæ was left companionless.

At this juncture, seeing that the men's time hung heavy on their hands, our Painter conceived the idea of setting them to clean the face of the northernmost Colossus, still disfigured by the plaster left on it when the great cast* was taken by Mr. Hay some fifty years

* This cast, the property of the British Museum, is placed over a door leading to the library at the end of the northern Vestibule, opposite the staircase. I was informed by the late Mr. Bonomi that the mould was made by Mr. Hay, who had with him an Italian assistant, picked up in Cairo. They took with them some barrels of plaster and a couple of ladders, and contrived, with such spars and poles as belonged to the Dahabeeyah, to erect a scaffolding and a matted shelter for the plasterman. The Colossus was at this time buried up to its chin in sand, which made their task so much the easier. When the mould of the head was brought to England, it was sent to Mr. Bonomi's studio, together with a mould of the head of the Colossus at Mitrahenny, a mould of the apex of the fallen obelisk at Karnak, and moulds of the wall-sculptures at

before. This happy thought was promptly carried into
effect. A scaffolding of spars and oars was at once
improvised, and the men, delighted as children at play,
were soon swarming all over the huge head, just as the
carvers may have swarmed over it in the days when
Rameses was king.

All they had to do was to remove any small lumps
that might yet adhere to the surface, and then tint the
white patches with coffee. This they did with bits of
sponge tied to the ends of sticks; but Reïs Hassan, as
a mark of dignity, had one of the Painter's old brushes,
of which he was immensely proud.

It took them three afternoons to complete the job;
and we were all sorry when it came to an end. To
see Reïs Hassan artistically touching up a gigantic
nose almost as long as himself; Riskalli and the
cook-boy staggering to and fro with relays of coffee,
brewed "thick and slab" for the purpose; Salame
perched cross-legged, like some complacent imp, on
the towering rim of the great pschent overhead; the
rest chattering and skipping about the scaffolding like
monkeys, was, I will venture to say, a sight more
comic than has ever been seen at Aboo Simbel before
or since.

Rameses' appetite for coffee was prodigious. He
consumed I know not how many gallons a day. Our
cook stood aghast at the demand made upon his stores.

Bayt-el-Welly. Mr. Bonomi superintended the casting and placing of all these
in the Museum about three years after the moulds were made. This was at
the time when Mr. Hawkins held the post of Keeper of Antiquities. I mention
these details, not simply because they have a special interest for all who are
acquainted with Aboo Simbel, but because a good deal of misapprehension has
prevailed on the subject, some travellers, attributing the disfigurement of the
head to Lepsius, others to the Crystal Palace Company, and so forth. Even
so careful a writer as the late Miss Martineau ascribes it, on hearsay, to
Champollion.

Never before had he been called upon to provide for a guest whose mouth measured three feet and a half in width.

Still, the result justified the expenditure. The coffee proved a capital match for the sandstone; and though it was not possible wholly to restore the uniformity of the original surface, we at least succeeded in obliterating those ghastly splotches, which for so many years have marred this beautiful face as with the unsightliness of leprosy.

What with boating, fishing, lying in wait for crocodiles, cleaning the colossus, and filling reams of thin letter paper to friends at home, we got through the first week quickly enough—the Painter and the Writer working hard, meanwhile, in their respective ways; the Painter on his big canvas in front of the Temple; the Writer shifting her little tent as she listed.

Now, although the most delightful occupation in life is undoubtedly sketching, it must be admitted that the sketcher at Aboo Simbel works under difficulties. Foremost among these comes the difficulty of position. The great Temple stands within about twenty-five yards of the brink of the bank, and the lesser Temple within as many feet; so that to get far enough from one's subject is simply impossible. The present Writer sketched the small Temple from the deck of the Dahabeeyah; there being no point of view obtainable on shore.

Next comes the difficulty of colour. Everything, except the sky and the river, is yellow—yellow, that is to say, "with a difference;" yellow ranging through every gradation of orange, maize, apricot, gold, and buff. The mountains are sandstone; the Temples are

sandstone; the sandslope is powdered sandstone from
the sandstone desert. In all these objects, the scale
of colour is necessarily the same. Even the shadows,
glowing with reflected light, give back tempered repeti-
tions of the dominant hue. Hence it follows that he
who strives, however humbly, to reproduce the facts of
the scene before him, is compelled, *bon gré*, *mal gré*,
to execute what some of our young painters would
now-a-days call a Symphony in Yellow.

Lastly, there are the minor inconveniences of sun,
sand, wind, and flies. The glare from above and the
glare from below are alike intolerable. Dazzled, blinded,
unable to even look at his subject without the aid of
smoke-coloured glasses, the sketcher whose tent is
pitched upon the sandslope over against the great
Temple, enjoys a foretaste of cremation. When the
wind blows from the north (which at this time of the
year is almost always,) the heat is less distressing,
but the sand is maddening. It fills your hair, your
eyes, your water-bottles; silts up your colour-box; dries
into your skies; and reduces your Chinese white to
a gritty paste the colour of salad-dressing. As for
the flies, they have a morbid appetite for water-colours.
They follow your wet brush along the paper, leave
their legs in the yellow ochre, and plunge with avidity
into every little pool of cobalt as it is mixed ready for
use. Nothing disagrees with them; nothing poisons
them—not even olive-green.

It was a delightful time, however—delightful alike
for those who worked and those who rested—and
these small troubles counted for nothing in the scale.
Yet it was pleasant, all the same, to break away for a
day or two, and be off to Wady Halfeh.

CHAPTER XVII.

The Second Cataract.

A FRESH breeze, a full sail, and the consciousness
of a holiday well earned, carried us gaily along from
Aboo Simbel to Wady Halfeh.　We started late in the
afternoon of the first day, made about twelve miles before the wind dropped, and achieved the remaining
twenty-eight miles before noon the next day.　It was
our last trip on the Nile under canvas.　At Wady
Halfeh the Philæ was doomed to be dismantled.　The
big sail that had so long been our pride and delight
would there be taken down, and our good boat, her
grace and swiftness gone at one fell swoop, would become a mere lumbering barge, more suggestive of civic
outings on the Thames than of Cleopatra's galley.

For some way beyond Aboo Simbel, the western
bank is fringed by a long line of volcanic mountains,
as much alike in height, size, and shape, as a row of
martello towers.　They are divided from one another
by a series of perfectly uniform sand-drifts; while on
the rounded top of each mountain, thick as the cur-
rants on the top of a certain cake, known to school-
boys by the endearing name of "black-caps," lies a
layer of the oddest black stones in the world.　Having
more than once been to the top of the rock of Abshek
(which is the first large mountain of the chain, and
strewn in the same way) we recognised the stones, and
knew what they were like.　In colour they are purplish

6*

black, tinged here and there with dull red. They ring
like clinkstone when struck, and in shape are most
fantastic. L. picked up some like petrified bunches
of grapes. Others are twisted and writhen like the
Vesuvian lava of 1871. They lie loose upon the surface, and are of all sizes; some being as small as cur-
rants, and others as large as quartern loaves. Speaking as one having no kind of authority, I should say
that these stones are unquestionably of fiery parentage.
One seems to see how, boiling and bubbling in a state
of fusion, they must have been suddenly checked by
contact with some cooler medium.

Where the chain ends, about three or four miles
above Aboo Simbel, the view widens, and a host of
outlying mountains are seen scattered over an immense
plain reaching for miles into the western desert. On
the eastern bank, Kalat Adda,* — a huge, rambling

* " A castle, resembling in size and form that of Ibrim; it bears the name
of Kalat Adda; it has been abandoned many years, being entirely surrounded
by barren rocks. Part of its ancient wall, similar in construction to that of
Ibrim, still remains. The habitations are built partly of stone, and partly of
bricks. On the most elevated spot in the small town, eight or ten gray granite
columns of small dimensions lie on the ground, with a few capitals near them
of clumsy Greek architecture."—Burckhardt's *Travels in Nubia*, 1819, p. 38.
In a curious Arabic history of Nubia written in the tenth century A.D. by
one Abdallah ben Ahmed ben Solaïm of Assouan, fragments of which are preserved in the great work of Makrizy, quoted by Burckhardt and E. Quatremere
(see footnote, p. 281. Vol. I.), there occurs the following remarkable passage:—
" In this province (Nubia) is situated the city of Bedjrash, capital of Maris, the
fortress of Ibrim, and another place called Adwa, which has a port, and is,
they say, the birthplace of the sage Lokman and of Dhoul Noun. There
is to be seen there a magnificent Birbeh"—("On y voit un *Berba* mag-
nifique").—*Mémoires Géographiques sur l'Egypte*, etc. E. QUATREMERE,
Paris 1811; vol. II. p. 8.
If Adwa and Adda are one and the same, it is possible that in this
passage we find preserved the only comparatively modern indication of
some great rock-cut temple, the entrance to which is now entirely covered
by the sand. It is clear that neither Aboo Simbel (which is on the opposite
bank, and some three or four miles north of Adda) nor Ferayg (which is
also some way off, and quite a small place) can here be intended. That
another temple exists somewhere between Aboo Simbel and Wady Halfeh,
and is yet to be discovered, seems absolutely certain from the tenor of a large

Roman citadel, going to solitary ruin, on the last water-washed precipice to the left—brings the opposite range to a like end, and abuts on a similar plain, also scattered over with detached peaks. The scene here is desolately magnificent. A large island covered with palms divides the Nile in two branches, each of which looks as wide as the whole river. An unbounded distance opens away to the silvery horizon. On the banks there is no verdure; neither is there any sign of human toil. Nothing lives, nothing moves, save the wind and the river.

Of all the strange peaks we have yet seen, the mountains hereabout are the strangest. Alone or in groups, they start up here and there from the deserts on both sides, like the pieces on a chess-board. They are for the most part conical; but they are not extinct craters, such as are the volcanic cones of Korosko and Dakkeh. Seeing how they all rose to about the same

stela sculptured on the rock a few paces north of the smaller temple at Aboo Simbel. This stela, which is one of the most striking and elaborate there, represents an Egyptian gateway surmounted by the winged globe, and shows Rameses II. enthroned and receiving the homage of a certain Prince, whose name, as translated by Rosellini, is Rameses-Neniscti-Habai. The inscription, which is in sixteen columns and perfectly preserved, records the titles and praises of the King, and states how "he hath made a monumental abode for Horus, his father, Lord of Ha'm, excavating in the bowels of the rock of Ha'm to make him a habitation of many ages." We know nothing of the Rock of Ha'm (rendered Sciam by Rosellini), but it should no doubt be sought somewhere between Aboo Simbel and Wady Halfeh. "Qual sito precisamente dinotisi in questo nome di Sciam, io non saprei nel presente stato delle cose determinare: credo peraltro secondo varie luoghi delle iscrizioni che lo ricordano, che fosse situato sull' una o l'altra sponda del Nilo, nel paese compreso tra Wadi-halfa e Ibsambul, o poco oltre. E qui dovrebbe trovarsi il nominato speco di Horus, fino al presente occulto a noi."—ROSELLINI, Letterpress to *Monumento Storici*, vol. III., part II. p. 184. It would hence appear that the Rock of Ha'm is mentioned in other inscriptions.

The distance between Aboo Simbel and Wady Halfeh is only forty miles, and the likely places along the banks are but few. Would it not the discovery of this lost Temple be an enterprise worthier the ambition of tourists, than the extermination of such few crocodiles as yet linger north of the Second Cataract?

height, and were alike capped with that mysterious *couche* of shining black stones, the Writer could not help fancying that, like the isolated Rocher de Corneille and Rocher de St. Michel at Puy, they might be but fragments of a rocky crust, rent and swept away at some infinitely remote period of the world's history, and that the level of their present summits might represent perhaps the ancient level of the plain.

As regards form, they are weird enough for the wildest geological theories. All taper more or less towards the top. One is four-sided, like a pyramid; another, in shape a truncated cone, looks as if crowned with a pagoda summer-house; a third seems to be surmounted by a mosque and cupola; a fourth is scooped out in tiers of arches; a fifth is crowned, apparently, with a cairn of piled stones; and so on with variations as endless as they are fantastic. A geologist might perhaps account for these caprices by showing how fire, and earthquake, and deluge, had here succeeded each other; and how, after being first covered with volcanic stones and then split into chasms, the valleys thus opened had by and by been traversed by torrents which wore away the softer parts of the rock and left the harder standing.

Some way beyond Kalat Adda, when the Aboo Simbel range and the palm island have all but vanished in the distance, and the lonely peak, called the Mountain of the Sun (Gebel esh-Shems), has been left far behind, we come upon a new wonder—namely, upon two groups of scattered tumuli, one on the eastern, one on the western bank. Not volcanic forms these; not even accidental forms, if one may venture to form an opinion from so far off. They are of various sizes;

some little, some big; all perfectly round and smooth, and covered with a rich greenish-brown alluvial soil. How did they come there? Who made them? What did they contain? The Roman ruin close by—the 240,000* deserters who must have passed this way—the Egyptian and Ethiopian armies that certainly poured their thousands along these very banks, and that might have fought many a battle on this open plain, suggest all kinds of possibilities, and fill one's head with visions of buried arms, and jewels, and cinerary urns. We are more than half-minded to stop the boat and land that very moment; but are content on second thoughts with promising ourselves that we will at least excavate one of the smaller hillocks on our way back.

And now, the breeze freshening and the Dahabeeyah tearing gallantly along, we leave the tumuli behind and enter upon a still more desolate region, where the mountains recede farther than ever, and the course of the river is interrupted by perpetual sandbanks.

On one of these sandbanks, just a few yards above the edge of the water, lay a log of drift-wood, apparently a battered old palm trunk, with some remnants of broken branches yet clinging to it; such an object, in short, as my American friends would very properly call a "snag."

Our pilot leaned forward on the tiller, put his finger to his lip, and whispered:—

"Crocodilo!"

The Painter, the Idle Man, the Writer, were all on deck, and not one believed him. They had seen too

---

* See footnote, p. 59 of this vol.

many of these snags already, and were not going to
let themselves again be excited about nothing.

The pilot pointed to the cabin where L. and the
Little Lady were indulging in that minor vice called
afternoon tea.

"Sittèh!" said he, "call Sittèh! Crocodilo!"

We examined the object through our glasses. We
laughed the pilot to scorn. It was the worst imitation
of a crocodile that we had yet seen.

All at once the palm-trunk lifted up its head,
cocked its tail, found its legs, set off running, wriggling,
undulating down the slope with incredible rapidity,
and was gone before we could utter an exclamation.

We three had a bad time when the other two came
up and found that we had seen our first crocodile
without them.

A sandbank which we passed next morning was
scored all over with fresh trails, and looked as if it
had been the scene of a crocodile-parliament. There
must have been at least twenty or thirty members present at the sitting; and the freshness of the marks
showed that they had only just dispersed.

A keen and cutting wind carried us along the last
thirty miles of our journey. We had supposed that
the farther south we penetrated, the hotter we should
find the climate; yet now, strange to say, we were
shivering in seal-skins, under the most brilliant sky in
the world, and in a latitude more southerly than that
of Mecca or Calcutta. It was some compensation, however, to run at full speed past the dullest of Nile
scenery, seeing only sandbanks in the river; sand-hills
and sand-flats on either hand; a disused shadoof or a
skeleton boat rotting at the water's edge; a wind-

tormented Dôm-palm struggling for existence on the brink of the bank.

At a fatal corner about six miles below Wady Halfeh, we passed a melancholy flotilla of dismantled Dahabeeyahs—the Fostat, the Zenobia, the Alice, the Mansoorah—all alike weather-bound and laid up helplessly against the wind. The Mansoorah, with Captain and Mrs. E. on board, had been three days doing these six miles: at which rate of progress they might reasonably hope to reach Cairo in about a year and a month.

The palms of Wady Halfeh, blue with distance, came into sight at the next bend; and by noon the Philæ was once more moored alongside the Bagstones under a shore crowded with cangias, covered with bales and packing cases, and, like the shores of Mahatta and Assouan, populous with temporary huts. For here it is that traders going by water embark and disembark on their way to and fro between Dongola and the First Cataract.

There were three Temples—or at all events three ancient Egyptian buildings—once upon a time on the western bank over against Wady Halfeh. Now there are a few broken pillars, a solitary fragment of brick pylon, some remains of a flight of stone steps leading down to the river, and a wall of enclosure overgrown with wild pumpkins. These ruins, together with a rambling native Khan and a noble old sycamore, form a picturesque group backed by amber sand-cliffs, and mark the site of a lost city* belonging to the early days of Usurtasen III.

* "Un Second Temple, plus grand, mais tout aussi détruit que le précédent, existe un peu plus au sud, c'était le grand temple de la ville Égyptienne

The Second, or Great Cataract, begins a little way above Wady Halfeh and extends over a distance of many miles. It consists, like the First Cataract, of a succession of rocks and rapids, and is skirted for the first five miles or so by the sand-cliff ridge which, as I have said, forms a background to the ruins just opposite Wady Halfeh. This ridge terminates abruptly in the famous precipice known as the Rock of Abooseer. Only adventurous travellers bound for Dongola or Khartoom go beyond this point; and they, for the most part, take the shorter route across the desert from Korosko. L. and the Writer would fain have hired camels and pushed on as far as Semneh; which is a matter of only two days' journey from Wady Halfeh, and, for people provided with sketching tents, is one of the easiest of inland excursions.

One may go to the Rock of Abooseer by land or by water. The Happy Couple and the Writer took two native boatmen versed in the intricacies of the Cataract; and went in the felucca. L. and the Painter preferred donkeying. Given a good breeze from the right quarter, there is, as regards time, but little to choose between the two routes. No one, however, who has approached the Rock of Abooseer by water, and seen it rise like a cathedral front from the midst of that labyrinth of rocky islets—some like clusters of basaltic columns, some crowned with crumbling ruins, some bleak and bare, some green with wild pome-granate trees—can doubt which is the more pic-turesque.

de *Béhéni*, qui exista sur cet emplacement, et qui d'après l'étendu des débris de poteries répandus sur la plaine aujourd'hui déserte, parait avoir été assez grande."—Champollion, *Lettres écrites d'Égypte*, etc., ed. 1868; Letter IX.

Landing among the tamarisks at the foot of the
cliff, we come to the spreading skirts of a sand-drift
steeper and more fatiguing to climb than the sand-
drift at Aboo Simbel. We do climb it, however, though
somewhat sulkily, and finding the donkey-party perched
upon the top, are comforted with draughts of ice-cold
lemonade, brought in a goollah from Wady Halfeh.

The summit of the rock is a mere ridge, steep and
overhanging towards east and south, and carved all
over with autographs in stone. Some few of these are
interesting; but for the most part they record only the
visits of the illustrious-obscure. We found Belzoni's
name; but looked in vain for the signatures of Burckhardt, Champollion, Lepsius, and Ampère.

Owing to the nature of the ground and the singular
clearness of the atmosphere, the view from this point
seemed to me to be the most extensive I had ever
looked upon. Yet the height of the rock of Abooseer
is comparatively insignificant. It would count but as
a mole-hill, if measured against some Alpine summits
of my acquaintance. I doubt whether it is as lofty as
even the Great Pyramid. It is, however, a giddy place
to look down from, and seems higher than it is.

It is hard, now that we are actually here, to realise
that this is the end of our journey. The Cataract—an
immense multitude of black and shining islets, among
which the river, divided into hundreds of separate
channels, spreads far and wide for a distance, it is
said, of more than sixteen miles,—foams at our feet.
Foams, and frets, and falls; gushing smooth and strong
where its course is free; murmuring hoarsely where it
is interrupted; now hurrying; now loitering; here ed-
dying in oily circles; there lying in still pools unbroken

by a ripple; everywhere full of life, full of voices; everywhere shining to the sun. Northwards, where it winds away towards Aboo Simbel, we see all the fantastic mountains of yesterday on the horizon. To the east, still bounded by out-liers of the same disconnected chain, lies a rolling waste of dark and stony wilderness, trenched with innumerable valleys through which flow streams of sand. On the western side, the continuity of the view is interrupted by the ridge that ends with Abooseer. Southwards, the Libyan desert reaches away in one vast undulating plain; tawny, arid, monotonous; all sun; all sand; lit here and there with arrowy flashes of the Nile. Farthest of all, pale but distinct, on the outermost rim of the world, rise two mountain summits, one long, one dome-like. Our Nubians tell us that these are the mountains of Dongola. Comparing our position with that of the Third Cataract as it appears upon the map, we come to the conclusion that these ghost-like silhouettes are the summits of Mount Fogo * and Mount Arambo — two apparently parallel mountains situated on opposite sides of the river about ten miles below Hannek, and consequently about 145 miles, as the bird flies, from the spot on which we are standing.

In all this extraordinary panorama, so wild, so weird, so desolate, there is nothing really beautiful, except the colour. But the colour is transcendent. Never, even in Egypt, have I seen anything so tender, so transparent, so harmonious. I shut my eyes, and it all comes before me. I see the amber of the sands; the pink and pearly mountains; the Cataract rocks, all

* Mount Fogo, as shown upon Keith Johnston's map of Egypt and Nubia, would seem to be identical with the Ali Bersi of Lepsius.

black and purple and polished; the dull gray palms that cluster here and there upon the larger islands; the vivid verdure of the tamarisks and pomegranates; the Nile, a greenish brown flecked with yeasty foam; over all, the blue and burning sky, permeated with light, and palpitating with sunshine.

I made no sketch. I felt that it would be ludicrous to attempt it. And I feel now that any endeavour to put the scene into words is a mere presumptuous effort to describe the indescribable. Words are useful instruments; but, like the etching needle and the burin, they stop short at form. They cannot translate colour.

If a traveller pressed for time asked me whether he should or should not go as far as the Second Cataract, I think I should recommend him to turn back from Aboo Simbel. The trip must cost four days; and if the wind should happen to be unfavourable either way, it may cost six or seven. The forty miles of river that have to be twice traversed are the dullest on the Nile; the Cataract is but an enlarged and barren edition of the Cataract between Assouan and Philæ; and the great view, as I have said, has not that kind of beauty which attracts the general tourist.

It has an interest, however, beyond and apart from that of beauty. It rouses one's imagination to a sense of the greatness of the Nile. We look across a world of desert, and see the river still coming from afar. We have reached a point at which all that is habitable and familiar comes abruptly to an end. Not a village, not a bean-field, not a shadoof, not a sakkieh, is to be seen in the plain below. There is no sail on those dangerous waters. There is no moving creature on

those pathless sands. But for the telegraph wires *
stalking, ghost-like, across the desert, it would seem as
if we had touched the limit of civilisation, and were
standing on the threshold of a land unexplored.

Yet for all this, we feel as if we were at only the
beginning of the mighty river. We have journeyed
well-nigh a thousand miles against the stream; but
what is that to the distance which still lies between us
and the Great Lakes? And how far beyond the Great
Lakes must we seek for the Source that is even yet
undiscovered?

We stayed at Wady Halfeh but one night, and
paid but one visit to the Cataract. We saw no crocodiles, though they are still plentiful among these rocky
islets. The M. B.'s, who had been here a week, were
full of crocodile stories, and of Alfred's deeds of arms.
He had stalked and shot a monster, two days before
our arrival; but the creature had rushed into the water
when hit, waving its tail furiously above its head, and
had neither been seen nor heard of since.

Like Achilles, the crocodile has but one vulnerable
spot; and this is a small unarmoured patch behind the
forearm. He will take a good deal of killing even
there unless the bullet finds its way to a vital part, or
is of the diabolical kind called "explosive." Even
when mortally wounded, he seldom drops on the spot.
With his last strength, he rushes to the water and dies
at the bottom.

After three days the carcase rises and floats, and
our friends were now waiting in order that Alfred
might bag his big game. Too often, however, the poor

* The wires in 1874 reached to Khartoom. They are now carried, I believe, as far as Sennar.

brute either crawls into a hole, or, in his agony, becomes entangled among weeds and comes up no more.
For one crocodile bagged, a dozen regain the river,
and after lingering miserably under water, die out of
sight and out of reach of the sportsman.

While we were climbing the Rock of Abooseer, our
men were busy taking down the big sail and preparing
the Philæ for her long and ignominious journey down
stream. We came back to find the mainyard laid
along like a roof-tree above our heads; the sail rolled
up in a huge ball and resting on the roof of the
kitchen; the small aftersail and yard hoisted on the
mainmast; the oars lashed six on each side; and the
lower deck a series of yawning chasms, every alternate
plank being taken up so as to form seats and standing
places for the rowers.

Thus dismantled, the Dahabeeyah becomes, in
fact, a galley. Her oars are now her chief motive
power; and a crew of steady rowers (having always the
current in their favour) can do thirty miles a day.
When, however, a good breeze blows from the south,
the small sail and the current are enough to carry the
boat well along; and then the men reserve their
strength for rowing by night, when the wind has
dropped. Sometimes, when it is a dead calm and the
rowers need rest, the Dahabeeyah is left to her own
devices, and floats with the stream—now waltzing
ludicrously in the middle of the river; now drifting
sidewise like Mr. Winkle's horse; now sidling up to
the east bank; now changing her mind and blundering
over to the west; making upon an average about a
mile and a half or two miles an hour, and presenting
a pitiful spectacle of helpless imbecility. At other

times, however, the head wind blows so hard that
neither oars nor current avail; and then there is nothing for it but to lie under the bank and wait for
better times.

This was our sad case in going back to Aboo
Simbel. Having struggled with no little difficulty
through the first five-and-twenty miles, we came to a
dead lock about half-way between Faras and Gebel
esh-Shems. Carried forward by the stream, driven
back by the wind, buffeted by the waves, and bumped
incessantly by the rocking to and fro of the felucca,
our luckless Philæ, after oscillating for hours within the
space of a mile, was run at last into a sheltered nook,
and there left in peace till the wind should change or
drop.

Imprisoned here for a day and a half, we found
ourselves, fortunately, within reach of the tumuli which
we had already made up our minds to explore. Making first for those on the east bank, we took with us
in the felucca four men to row and dig, a fire-shovel,
a small hatchet, an iron bar, and a large wicker basket,
which were the only implements we possessed. What
we wanted both then and afterwards, and what no
Dahabeeyah should ever be without, were two or three
good spades, a couple of picks, and a crowbar.

Climbing to the top of one of the highest of these
hillocks, we began by surveying the ground. The
desert here is firm to the tread, flat, compact, and
thickly strewn with pebbles. Of the fine yellow sand
which characterises the Libyan bank, there is little to
be seen, and that little lies like snow in drifts and
clefts and hollows, as if carried thither by the wind.
The tumuli, however, are mounded of pure alluvial

mould, smooth, solid, and symmetrical. We counted
thirty-four of all sizes, from five to about five-and-thirty
feet in height, and saw at least as many more on the
opposite side of the river.

Selecting one of about eight feet high, we then set
the sailors to work; and although it was impossible,
with so few men and such insufficient tools, to cut
straight through the centre of the mound, we at all
events succeeded in digging down to a solid sub-
stratum of lumps of crude clay, evidently moulded by
hand.

Whether these formed only the foundation of the
tumulus, or concealed a grave excavated below the
level of the desert, we had neither time nor means to
ascertain. It was something, at all events, to have
convinced ourselves that the mounds were artificial. *

As we came away, we met a Nubian peasant trudg-
ing northwards. He was leading a sorry camel; had a
white cockerel under his arm; and was followed by a
frightened woman, who drew her shawl over her face
and cowered behind him, at sight of the Ingleezeh.

We asked the man what the mounds were, and
who made them; but he shook his head, and said they
had been there "from old time." We then inquired
by what name they were known in these parts; to
which, urging his camel forward, he replied hesitat-
ingly that they had a name, but that he had forgotten it.

Having gone a little way, however, he presently

* On referring to Col. H. Vyse's *Voyage into Upper Egypt*, etc., I see
that he also opened one of these tumuli, but "found no indication of an artificial construction." I can only conclude that he did not carry his excavation
low enough. As it is difficult to suppose the tumuli made for nothing, I cannot
help believing that they would repay a more systematic investigation.

turned back, saying that he now remembered all about
it, and that they were called "The Horns of Yackma."

More than this we could not get from him. Who
Yackma was, or how he came to have horns, or why
his horns should take the form of tumuli, was more
than he could tell or we could guess.

We gave him a small backsheesh, however, in return for this mysterious piece of information, and went
our way with all possible speed; intending to row
across and see the mounds on the opposite bank before
sunset. But we had not calculated upon the difficulty
of either threading our way among a chain of sandbanks, or going at least two miles farther north, so as
to get round into the navigable channel at the other
side. We of course tried the shorter way, and after
running aground some three or four times, had to give
it up, hoist our little sail, and scud homewards as fast
as the wind would carry us.

The coming back thus, after an excursion in the
felucca, is one of the many pleasant things that one
has to remember of the Nile. The sun has set; the
afterglow has faded; the stars are coming out. Lean-
ing back with a satisfied sense of something seen or
done, one listens to the old dreamy chant of the
rowers, and to the ripple under the keel. The palms,
meanwhile, glide past, and are seen in bronzed relief
against the sky. Presently the big boat, all glittering
with lights, looms up out of the dusk. A cheery voice
hails from the poop. We glide under the bows. Half-
a-dozen smiling brown faces bid us welcome, and as
many pairs of brown hands are outstretched to help
us up the side. A savoury smell is wafted from the

kitchen; a pleasant vision of the dining-saloon, with table ready spread and lamps ready lit, flashes upon us through the open doorway. We are at home once more. Let us eat, drink, rest, and be merry; for to-morrow the hard work of sight-seeing and sketching begins again.

———

CHAPTER XVIII.

Discoveries at Aboo Simbel.

WE came back to find a fleet of Dahabeeyahs ranged along the shore at Aboo Simbel, and no less than three sketching tents in occupation of the ground. One of these, which happened to be pitched on the precise spot vacated by our Painter, was courteously shifted to make way for the original tenant; and in the course of a couple of hours, we were all as much at home as if we had not been away for half-a-day.

Here, meanwhile, was our old acquaintance the "Fostat" with her party of gentlemen; yonder the "Zenobia," all ladies; the little "Alice" with Sir J. C. and Mr. W. on board; the "Sirena," flying the stars and stripes; the "Mansoorah," bound presently for the Fayoom. To these were next day added the "Ebers," with a couple of German savants; and the "Bagstones," welcome back from Wady Halfeh.

What with arrivals and departures, exchange of visits, exhibitions of sketches, and sociabilities of various kinds, we had now quite a gay time. The Philæ gave a dinner-party and fantasia under the very noses of the colossi, and every evening there was drumming and howling enough among the assembled crews to raise the ghosts of Rameses and all his Queens. This was pleasant enough while it lasted; but when the strangers dropped off one by one, and at the end of three days we were once more alone, I think we were not sorry. The place was, somehow, too solemn for

"Singing, laughing, ogling, and all that."

It was by comparing our watches with those of the travellers whom we met at Aboo Simbel, that we now found out how hopelessly our timekeepers and theirs had gone astray. We had been altering ours continually ever since leaving Cairo; but the sun was as continually putting them wrong again, so that we had lost all count of the true time. The first words with which we now greeted a new comer were—"Do you know what o'clock it is?" To which the stranger as invariably replied that it was the very question he was himself about to ask. The confusion became at last so great that, finding we had about eleven hours of day to thirteen of night, we decided to establish an arbitrary canon; so we called it seven when the sun rose, and six when it set, which answered every purpose.

It was between two and four o'clock, according to this time of ours, that the Southern Cross was now visible every morning. It is undoubtedly best seen at Aboo Simbel. The river is here very wide, and just where the constellation rises there is an opening in the mountains on the eastern bank, so that these four fine stars, though still low in the heavens, are seen in a free space of sky. If they make, even so, a less magnificent appearance than one has been led to expect, it is probably because we see them from too low a point of view. To say that a constellation is foreshortened sounds absurd; yet that is just what is the matter with the Southern Cross at Aboo Simbel. Viewed at an angle of about 30⁰, it necessarily looks distort and

dim. If seen burning in the zenith, it would no doubt
come up to the level of its reputation.

It was now the fifth day after our return from
Wady Halfeh, when an event occurred that roused us
to an unwonted pitch of excitement, and kept us at
high pressure throughout the rest of our time.

The day was Sunday; the date February 16th,
1874; the time, according to Philæ reckoning, about
eleven a.m., when the Painter, enjoying his seventh
day's holiday after his own fashion, went strolling about
among the rocks. He happened to turn his steps
southwards, and, passing the front of the Great Temple,
climbed to the top of a little shapeless mound of fallen
cliff, and sand, and crude-brick wall, just against the
corner where the mountain slopes down to the river.
Immediately round this corner, looking almost due
south, and approachable by only a narrow ledge of
rock, are two votive tablets sculptured and painted,
both of the thirty-eighth year of Rameses II. We had
seen these from the river as we came back from Wady
Halfeh, and had remarked how fine the view must be
from that point. Beyond the fact that they are
coloured, and that the colour upon them is still bright,
there is nothing remarkable about these inscriptions.
There are many such at Aboo Simbel. Our Painter
did not, therefore, come here to examine the tablets;
he was attracted solely by the view.

Turning back presently, his attention was arrested
by some much mutilated sculptures on the face of the
rock, a few yards nearer the south buttress of the
Temple. He had seen these sculptures before—so, indeed, had I, when wandering about that first day in
search of a point of view—without especially remark-

ing them. The relief was low; the execution slight; and the surface so broken away that only a few confused outlines remained.

The thing that now caught the Painter's eye, however, was a long crack running transversely down the face of the rock. It was such a crack as might have been caused, one would say, by blasting.

He stooped—cleared the sand away a little with his hand—observed that the crack widened—poked in the point of his stick; and found that it penetrated to a depth of two or three feet. Even then, it seemed to him to stop, not because it encountered any obstacle, but because the crack was not wide enough to admit the thick end of the stick.

This surprised him. No mere fault in the natural rock, he thought, would go so deep. He scooped away a little more sand; and still the cleft widened. He introduced the stick a second time. It was a long palm-stick like an alpenstock, and it measured about five feet in length. When he probed the cleft with it this second time, it went in freely up to where he held it in his hand—that is to say, to a depth of quite four feet.

Convinced now that there was some hidden cavity in the rock, he carefully examined the surface. There were yet visible a few hieroglyphic characters and part of two cartouches, as well as some battered outlines of what had once been figures. The heads of these figures were gone (the face of the rock, with whatever may have been sculptured upon it, having come away bodily at this point), while from the waist downwards, they were hidden under the sand. Only some hands and arms, in short, could be made out.

They were the hands and arms, apparently, of four figures; two in the centre of the composition, and two at the extremities. The two centre ones, which seemed to be back to back, probably represented gods; the outer ones, worshippers.

All at once, it flashed upon the Painter that he had seen this kind of group many a time before—*and generally over a doorway.*

Feeling sure now that he was on the brink of a discovery, he came back; fetched away Salame and Mehemet Ali; and, without saying a syllable to any one, set to work with these two to scrape away the sand at the spot where the crack widened.

Meanwhile the luncheon bell having rung thrice, we concluded that the Painter had rambled off some-where into the desert; and so sat down without him. Towards the close of the meal, however, came a pen-cilled note, the contents of which ran as follows:—

"Pray come immediately—I have found the en-trance to a tomb. Please send some sandwiches— A. M'C."

To follow the messenger at once to the scene of action, was the general impulse. In less than ten minutes we were there, asking breathless questions, peeping in through the fast-widening aperture, and helping to clear away the sand.

All that Sunday afternoon, heedless of possible sun-stroke, unconscious of fatigue, we toiled upon our hands and knees, as for bare life, under the burning sun. We had all the crew up, working like tigers. Every one helped; even the dragoman and the two maids. More than once, when we paused for a mo-

ment's breathing space, we said to each other:—"If
those at home could see us, what would they say!"

And now, more than ever, we felt the need of implements. With a spade or two and a wheelbarrow, we
could have done wonders; but with only one small
fire-shovel, a birch broom, a couple of charcoal baskets,
and about twenty pairs of hands, we were poor indeed.
What was wanted in means, however, was made up in
method. Some scraped away the sand; some gathered
it into baskets; some carried the baskets to the edge
of the cliff, and emptied them into the river. The Idle
Man distinguished himself by scooping out a channel
where the slope was steepest; which greatly facilitated
the work. Emptied down this shoot and kept continually going, the sand poured off in a steady stream like
water.

Meanwhile the opening grew rapidly larger. When
we first came up—that is, when the Painter and the
two sailors had been working on it for about an hour
—we found a hole scarcely as large as one's hand,
through which it was just possible to catch a dim
glimpse of painted walls within. By sunset, the top of
the doorway was laid bare, and where the crack ended
in a large triangular fracture, there was an aperture
about a foot and a half square, into which Mehemet
Ali was the first to squeeze his way. We passed him
in a candle and a box of matches; but he came out
again directly, saying that it was a most beautiful
Birbeh, and quite light within.

The Writer wriggled in next. She found herself
looking down from the top of a sandslope, into a small
square chamber. This sand-drift, which here rose to
within a foot and a half of the top of the doorway,

was heaped to the ceiling in the corner behind the door,
and thence sloped steeply down, completely covering
the floor. There was light enough to see every detail
distinctly—the painted frieze running round just under
the ceiling; the bas-relief sculptures on the walls, gorgeous with unfaded colour; the smooth sand, pitted
near the top, where Mehemet Ali had trodden, but un-
disturbed elsewhere by human foot; the great gap in
the middle of the ceiling, where the rock had given
way; the fallen fragments on the floor, now almost
buried in sand.

Satisfied that the place was absolutely fresh and
untouched, the Writer crawled out, and the others, one
by one, crawled in. When each had seen it in turn, the
opening was barricaded for the night; the sailors being
forbidden to enter it, lest they should injure the decorations.

That evening was held a solemn council, whereat it
was decided that Talhamy and Reïs Hassan should go
to-morrow to the nearest village, there to engage the
services of fifty able-bodied natives. With such help, we
calculated that the place might easily be cleared in two
days. If it was a tomb, we hoped to discover the entrance to the mummy pit below; if but a small chapel,
or Speos, like those at Ibrim, we should at least have
the satisfaction of seeing all that it contained in the
way of sculptures and inscriptions.

This was accordingly done; but we worked again
next morning just the same till mid-day. Our native
contingent, numbering about forty men, then made their
appearance in a rickety old boat, the bottom of which
was half full of water.

They had been told to bring implements; and they

did bring such as they had—two broken oars to dig with, some baskets, and a number of little slips of planking which, being tied between two pieces of rope and drawn along the surface, acted as scrapers, and were useful as far as they went. Squatting in double file from the entrance of the Speos to the edge of the cliff, and to the burden of a rude chant propelling these improvised scrapers, the men began by clearing a path to the doorway. This gave them work enough for the afternoon. At sunset, when they dispersed, the path was scooped out to a depth of four feet, like a miniature railway cutting between embankments of sand.

Next morning came the Sheykh in person, with his two sons and a following of a hundred men. This was so many more than we had bargained for, that we at once foresaw a scheme to extort money. The Sheykh, however, proved to be that same Rashwan Ebn Hassan el Kashef, by whom the Happy Couple had been so hospitably entertained about a fortnight before; we therefore received him with honour, invited him to luncheon, and, hoping to get the work done quickly, set the men on in gangs under the superintendence of Reïs Hassan and the head sailor.

By noon, the door was cleared down to the threshold, and the whole south and west walls were laid bare to the floor.

We now found that the débris which blocked the north wall and the centre of the floor was not, as we had at first supposed, a pile of fallen fragments, but one solid boulder which had come down bodily from above. To remove this was impossible. We had no tools to cut or break it, and it was both wider and

higher than the doorway. Even to clear away the
sand which rose behind it to the ceiling would have
taken a long time, and have caused inevitable injury
to the paintings around. Already the brilliancy of
the colour was marred where the men had leaned
their backs, all wet with perspiration, against the
walls.

Seeing, therefore, that three-fourths of the decorations were now uncovered, and that behind the fallen
block there appeared to be no subject of great size or
importance, we made up our minds to carry the work
no further.

Meanwhile, we had great fun at luncheon with our
Nubian Sheykh—a tall, well-featured man with much
natural dignity of manner. He was well dressed, too,
and wore a white turban most symmetrically folded; a
white vest buttoned to the throat; a long loose robe of
black serge; an outer robe of fine black cloth with
hanging sleeves and a hood; and on his feet, white
stockings and scarlet morocco shoes. When brought
face to face with a knife and fork, his embarrassment
was great. He was, it seemed, too grand a personage
to feed himself. He must have a "feeder;" as the
great man of the Middle Ages had a "taster." Talhamy
accordingly, being promoted to this office, picked out
choice bits of mutton and chicken with his fingers,
dipped pieces of bread in gravy, and put every morsel
into our guest's august mouth, as if the said guest were
a baby.

The sweets being served, the Little Lady, L., and
the Writer took him in hand, and fed him with all
kinds of jams and preserved fruits. Enchanted with
these attentions, the poor man ate till he could eat no

longer; then laid his hand pathetically over the region
next his heart, and cried for mercy. After luncheon,
he smoked his chibouque, and coffee was served. Our
coffee did not please him. He tasted it, but immediately returned the cup, telling the waiter with a
grimace, that the berries were burned and the coffee
weak. When, however, we apologised for it, he
protested with Oriental insincerity that it was excellent.

To amuse him was easy, for he was interested in
everything; in L.'s field-glass, in the Painter's accordion,
in the piano, and the lever corkscrew. With some Eau-
de-Cologne he was also greatly charmed, rubbing it on
his beard and inhaling it with closed eyes, in a kind of
rapture. To make talk was, as usual, the great difficulty. When he had told us that his eldest son was
Governor of Derr; that his youngest was five years of
age; that the dates of Derr were better than the dates
of Wady Halfeh; and that the Nubian people were very
poor, he was at the end of his topics. Finally, he re-
quested us to convey a letter from him to Lord D——,
who had entertained him on board his Dahabeeyah the
year before. Being asked if he had brought his letter
with him, he shook his head, saying:—"Your dragoman shall write it."

So paper and a reed-pen were produced, and Talhamy wrote to dictation as follows:—

"God have care of you. I hope you are well. I
am sorry not to have had a letter from you since you
were here. Your brother and friend,
RASHWAN EBN HASSAN EL KASHEF."

A model letter this; brief, and to the point.

Our urbane and gentlemanly Sheykh was, however, not quite so charming when it came to settling time. We had sent at first for fifty men, and the price agreed upon was five piastres, or about a shilling English, for each man per day. In answer to this call, there first came forty men for half a day; then a hundred men for a whole day, or what was called a whole day; so making a total of six pounds due for wages. But the descendant of the Kashefs would hear of nothing so commonplace as the simple fulfilment of a straightfor- ward contract. He demanded full pay for a hundred men for two whole days, a gun for himself, and a liberal backsheesh in cash. Finding he had asked more than he had any chance of getting, he conceded the question of wages, but stood out for a game-bag and a pair of pistols. Finally, he was obliged to be content with the six pounds for his men, and for himself two pots of jam, two boxes of sardines, a bottle of eau-de-Cologne, a box of pills, and half-a-sovereign.

By four o'clock he and his followers were gone, and we once more had the place to ourselves. So long as they were there it was impossible to do anything, but now, for the first time, we fairly entered into possession of our newly-found treasure.

All the rest of that day, and all the next day, we spent at work in and about the Speos. L. and the Little Lady took their books and knitting there, and made a little drawing-room of it. The Writer copied paintings and inscriptions. The Idle Man and the Painter took measurements and surveyed the ground round about, especially endeavouring to make out the plan of certain fragments of wall, the foundations of which were yet traceable.

A careful examination of these ruins, and a little clearing of the sand here and there, led to further discoveries.   They found that the Speos had been approached by a large outer hall built of sun-dried brick, with one principal entrance facing the Nile, and two side-entrances facing northwards. The floor was buried deep in sand and débris, but enough of the walls remained above the surface to show that the ceiling had been vaulted and the side-entrances arched.

The southern boundary wall of this hall, when the surface sand was removed, appeared to be no less than 20 feet in thickness. This was not in itself so wonderful, there being instances of ancient Egyptian crude-brick walls which measure 30 feet in thickness; but it was astounding as compared with the north, east, and west walls, which measured only 3 feet. Deeming it impossible that this mass could be solid throughout, the Idle Man set to work with a couple of sailors to probe the centre part of it, and it soon became evident that there was a hollow space about three feet in width running due east and west down not quite exactly the middle of the structure.

All at once the Idle Man thrust his fingers into a skull!

This was such an amazing and unexpected incident, that for the moment he said nothing, but went on quietly displacing the sand and feeling his way under the surface.   The next instant his hand came in contact with the edge of a clay bowl, which he carefully withdrew.   It measured about four inches in diameter, was hand-moulded, and full of caked sand.   He now proclaimed his discoveries, and all ran to help in the work. Soon a second and smaller skull was turned up, then another bowl, and then, just under the place from which the bowls were taken, the bones of two skeletons all detached, perfectly desiccated, and apparently complete. The remains were those of a child and a small grown person—probably a woman. The teeth were sound; the bones wonderfully delicate and brittle. As for the little skull (which had fallen apart at the sutures), it was pure and fragile in texture as the cup of a water-lily.

We laid the bones aside as we found them, examining every handful of sand, in the hope of discovering something that might throw light upon the burial. But in vain. We found not a shred of clothing, not a bead, not a coin, not the smallest vestige of anything that could help one to judge whether the interment had taken place a hundred years ago or a thousand.

We now called up all the crew, and went on excavating downwards into what seemed to be a long and narrow vault measuring some fifteen feet by three.

After-reflection convinced us that we had stumbled upon a chance Nubian grave, and that the bowls (which at first we absurdly dignified with the name of cinerary urns) were but the usual water-bowls placed at the heads of the dead. But we were in no mood for reflection at the time. We made sure that the Speos was a mortuary chapel; that the vault was a vertical pit leading to a sepulchral chamber; and that at the bottom of it we should find . . . . who could tell what? Mummies, perhaps, and sarcophagi, and funereal gods, and jewels, and papyri, and wonders without end! That these uncared-for bones should be laid in the mouth of such a pit, scarcely occurred to us as an incongruity. Supposing them to be Nubian remains, what then? If a modern Nubian at the top, why not an ancient Egyptian at the bottom?

As the work of excavation went on, however, the vault was found to be entered by a steep inclined plane. Then the inclined plane turned out to be a flight of much worn and very shallow stairs. These led down to a small square landing, some twelve feet below the surface, from which landing an arched door-way* and passage opened into the fore-court of the Speos. Our sailors had great difficulty in excavating this part, in consequence of the weight of superincumbent sand and débris on the side next the Speos. By shoring up the ground, however, they were enabled completely to clear the landing, which was curiously paved with cones of rude pottery like the bottoms of amphoræ. These cones, of which we took out some twenty-eight or thirty, were not in the least like the celebrated funereal cones found so abundantly at Thebes. They bore no stamp, and were much shorter and more lumpy in shape. Finally, the cones being all removed, we came to a compact and solid floor of baked clay.

The Painter, meanwhile, had also been at work. Having traced the circuit and drawn out a ground-plan, he came to the conclusion that the whole mass adjoining the southern wall of the Speos was in fact composed of the ruins of a pylon, the walls of which were seven feet in thickness, built in regular string-

---

* It was long believed that the Egyptians were ignorant of the principle of the arch. This, however, was not the case. There are brick arches of the time of Rameses II. behind the Ramesseum at Thebes, and elsewhere. Still, arches are rare in Egypt. We filled in and covered the arch again, and the greater part of the staircase, in order to preserve the former.

courses of moulded brick, and finished at the angles
with the usual *torus*, or round moulding. The super-
structure, with its chambers, passages, and top cornice,
was gone; and this part with which we were now concerned was merely the basement, and included the
bottom of the staircase.

The Painter's ground-plan demolished all our hopes
at one fell swoop. The vault was a vault no longer.
The staircase led to no sepulchral chamber. The
brick floor hid no secret entrance. Our mummies
melted into thin air, and we were left with no ex-
cuse for carrying on the excavations. We were mortally disappointed. In vain we told ourselves that the
discovery of a large brick pylon, the existence of which
had been unsuspected by preceding travellers, was an
event of greater importance than the finding of a tomb.
We had set our hearts on the tomb; and I am afraid
we cared less than we ought for the pylon.

Having traced thus far the course of the excavations and the way in which one discovery led step by
step to another, I must now return to the Speos, and,
as accurately as I can, describe it, not only from my
notes made on the spot, but by the light of such ob-
servations as I afterwards made among structures of
the same style and period. I must, however, premise
that, not being able to go inside while the excavators
were in occupation, and remaining but one whole day
at Aboo Simbel after the work was ended, I had but
short time at my disposal. I would gladly have made
coloured copies of all the wall-paintings; but this was
impossible. I therefore was obliged to be content with
transcribing the inscriptions and sketching a few of the
more important subjects.

The rock-cut chamber which I have hitherto described as a Speos, and which we at first believed to
be a tomb, was in fact neither the one nor the other.
It was the adytum of a partly-built, partly-excavated
monument coeval in date with the Great Temple. In
certain points of design this monument resembles the
contemporary Speos of Bayt el Welly. It is evident,
for instance, that the outer halls of both were originally vaulted; and the much mutilated sculptures over
the doorway of the excavated chamber at Aboo Simbel
are almost identical in subject and treatment with those
over the entrance to the excavated parts of Bayt el
Welly. As regards general conception, the Aboo Simbel monument comes under the same head with the
contemporary Temples of Derr, Gerf Hossayn, and
Wady Sabooah; being in a mixed style which combines
excavation with construction. This style seems to have
been peculiarly in favour during the reign of Rameses II.

Situated at the south-eastern angle of the rock, a
little way beyond the façade of the Great Temple, this
rock-cut adytum and hall of entrance face S.E. by E.,
and command much the same view that is commanded
higher up by the Temple of Hathor. The adytum, or
excavated Speos, measures 21 feet $2\frac{1}{2}$ inches in breadth
by 14 feet 8 inches in length. The height from floor
to ceiling is about 12 feet. The doorway measures 4
feet $3\frac{1}{2}$ inches in width; and the outer recess for the
doorframe, 5 feet. Two large circular holes, one in the
threshold and the other in the lintel, mark the place of
the pivot on which the door once swung.

It is not very easy to measure the outer hall in its
present ruined and encumbered state; but as nearly as
we could judge, its dimensions are as follows:—Length

8*

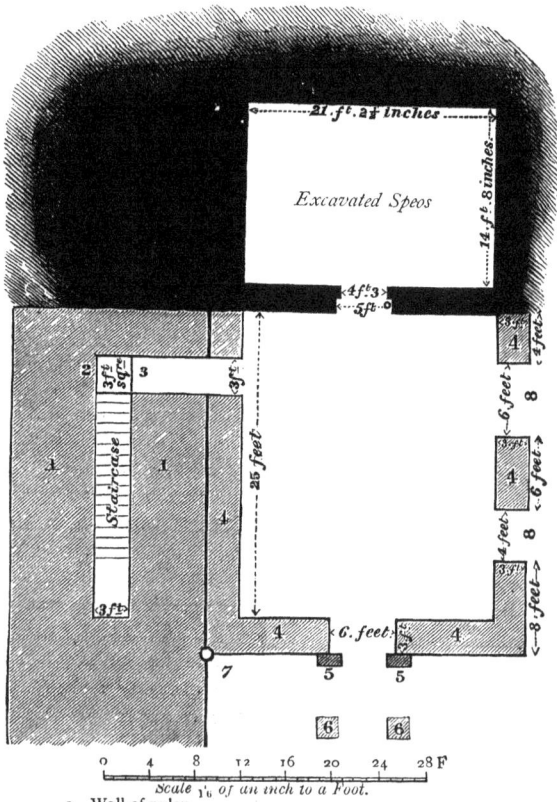

Scale $\frac{1}{10}$ of an inch to a Foot.

1. Wall of pylon.
2. Square landing.
3. Arched doorway and passage leading to vaulted hall.
4. Walls of outer hall or pronaos.
5. Door-jambs.
6. Stone hawks on pedestals.
7. Torus of pylon.
8. Arched entrances in N. wall of pronaos.

25 feet; width $22\frac{1}{2}$ feet; width of principal entrance facing the Nile, 6 feet; width of two side entrances, 4 feet and 6 feet respectively; thickness of crude-brick walls, 3 feet. Engaged in the brickwork on either side of the principal entrance to this hall are two stone door-jambs; and some six or eight feet in front of these, there originally stood two stone hawks on hiero-glyphed pedestals. One of these hawks we found *in situ*, the other lay some little distance off, and the Painter (suspecting nothing of these after-revelations) had used it as a post to which to tie one of the main ropes of his sketching tent. A large hieroglyphed slab, which I take to have formed part of the door, lay overturned against the side of the pylon some few yards nearer the river.

So far as we could see, there was no stone revête-ment upon the inner side of the walls of the pronaos. If anything of the kind ever existed, some remains of it would probably be found by thoroughly clearing the area; an interesting enterprise for any who may have leisure to undertake it.

I have now to speak of the decorations of the ady-tum, the walls of which, from immediately under the ceiling to within three feet of the floor, are covered with religious subjects elaborately sculptured in bas-relief, coated as usual with a thin film of stucco, and coloured with a richness for which I know no parallel, except in the tomb of Seti I.* at Thebes. Above the level of the drifted sand, this colour was as brilliant in tone, and as fresh in surface, as on the day when it was transferred to those walls from the palette of the

* Commonly known as Belzoni's Tomb.

painter. All below that level, however, was dimmed and damaged.

The ceiling is surrounded by a frieze of cartouches supported by sacred asps; each cartouche, with its supporters, being divided from the next by a small sitting figure. These figures, in other respects uniform, wear the symbolic heads of various gods—the cow-head of Hathor, the ibis-head of Thoth, the hawk-head of Horus, the jackal head of Anubis, etc. etc. The cartouches contain the ordinary style and title of Rameses II. (Ra-user-ma Sotep-en-Ra Rameses Mer-amen), and are surmounted by a row of sun-disks. Under each sitting god is depicted the phonetic hieroglyph signifying *Mer*, or Beloved. By means of this device, the whole frieze assumes the character of a connected legend, and describes the king not only as beloved of Ammon, but as Rameses beloved of Hathor, of Thoth, of Horus—in short, of each God depicted in the series.

These Gods excepted, the frieze is almost identical in design with the frieze in the first hall of the great Temple.

WEST WALL.*

The West, or principal wall, facing the entrance, is divided into two large subjects, each containing two figures the size of life. In the division to the right, Rameses II. worships Ra; in the division to the left, he worships Ammon Ra; thus following the order ob-

---

* I write of these walls, for convenience, as N., S., E., and W., as one is so accustomed to regard the position of buildings parallel with the river; but the present monument, as it is turned slightly southward round the angle of the rock, really stands S.E. by E., instead of east and west like the large Temple.

served in the other two temples, where the subjects relating to Ammon Ra occupy the left half, and the subjects relating to Ra occupy the right half, of each
structure.   An upright ensign surmounted by an exquisitely drawn and coloured head of Horus Aroëris
separates these two subjects.*   In the subject to the
right, Rameses, wearing the red and white pschent,
presents an offering of two small aryballos vases without handles. The vases are painted blue, and are probably intended to represent lapis lazuli; a substance
much prized by the ancient Egyptians, and known to
them by the name of *khesbet*. The King's necklace,
armlets, and bracelets are also blue. Ra sits enthroned,
holding in one hand the crux ansata (⚱) and in the
other the greyhound-headed ** sceptre of the Gods.
He is hawk-headed, and crowned with the sun-disk
and asp. His flesh is painted bright Venetian red. He
wears a pectoral ornament; a rich necklace of alternate
vermilion and black drops; and a golden-yellow belt
studded with red and black stones. The throne, which
stands on a blue platform, is painted in stripes of red,
blue, and white.   The platform is decorated with a
row of gold-coloured stars and tau-crosses picked out
with red.   At the foot of this platform, between the
God and the King, stands a small altar, on which are

---

* Horus Aroëris.—"Celui-ci, qui semble avoir été frère d'Osiris, porte une
tête d'épervier coiffée du pschent.   Il est presque complètement identifié avec
le soleil dans la plupart des lieux où il était adoré, et il en est de même très
souvent pour Horus, fils d'Isis."—*Notice Sommaire des Monuments du Louvre*,
1873.   DE ROUGÉ.   In the present instance, this God seems to have been
identified with Ra.
** " Le sceptre à tête de lévrier, nommé à tort sceptre à tête de coucoupha,
était porté par les dieux."—*Dic. d'Arch. Égyptienne:* P. PIERROT; Paris,
1875.

placed the usual blue lotus with red stalk, and a spouted vessel in form not unlike a coffee-pot.

To the left of the Horus ensign, seated back-to-back with Ra upon a similar throne, sits Ammon Ra— of all Egyptian Gods the most terrible to look upon— with his blue-black complexion, his corselet of golden chain-armour, and his head-dress of towering plumes.* Here the wonderful preservation of the surface enabled one to see by what means the ancient artists were wont to produce this singular blue-black effect of colour. It was evident that the flesh of the God had first been laid in with dead black, and then coloured over with a dry, powdery cobalt-blue, through which the black remained partially visible. He carries in one hand the crux ansata, and in the other the greyhound-headed sceptre.

To him advances the King, his right hand uplifted, and in his left a small basket containing a votive statuette that may represent Ma, the Goddess of Truth and Justice. If so, however, it is Ma shorn of her dis-

---

* Ammon of the blue complexion is the most ancient type of this God. He here represents divine royalty, in which character his title is:—"Lord of the Heaven, of the Earth, of the Waters, and of the Mountains." "Dans ce rôle de roi du monde, Amon a les chairs peintes en bleu pour indiquer sa nature céleste; et lorsqu'il porte le titre de Seigneur des Trônes, il est représenté· assis, la couronne en tête: d'ordinaire il est debout."—*Étude des Monuments de Karnak.* DE ROUGÉ. *Mélanges d'Archéologie*, vol. I. 1873.

There were almost as many varieties of Ammon in Egypt as there are varieties of the Madonna in Italy or Spain. There was an Ammon of Thebes, an Ammon of Elephantine, an Ammon of Coptos, an Ammon of Chemmis (Panopolis), an Ammon of the Resurrection, Ammon of the Dew, Ammon of the Sun (Ammon Ra), Ammon Self-created, etc. etc. Ammon and Khem were doubtless identical.   It is an interesting fact that our English words, chemical, chemist, chemistry, etc., which the dictionaries derive from the Arabic *al-kimia*, may be traced back a step farther to the Panopolitan name of this most ancient God of the Egyptians, Khem (Gr. Pan; Latin, Priapus), the deity of plants and herbs and of the creative principle.   A cultivated Egyptian would, doubtless, have regarded all these Ammons as merely local or symbolical types of a single deity.

tinctive feather, and holding the jackal-headed staff instead of the customary crux ansata.

As portraiture, there is not much to be said for any of these heads of Rameses II. The features bear a certain resemblance to the well-known profile of the King; but the effect altogether is formal and unsatisfactory. The action of the figure is, however, graceful and animated, and displays in all its purity the firm and flowing line of Egyptian draughtsmanship.

The dress of the King is very rich in colour; the mitre-shaped casque being of a vivid cobalt-blue* picked out with gold-colour; the belt, necklace, armlets, and bracelets, of gold, studded apparently with precious stones; the apron, green and gold. Over the King's head hovers the sacred vulture, emblem of Maut, holding in her claws a kind of scutcheon upon which is depicted the crux ansata.

---

* The material of this blue helmet, so frequently depicted on the monuments, *may* have been the Homeric Kuanos, about which so much doubt and conjecture have gathered, and which Mr. Gladstone supposes to have been a metal. — (See *Juventus Mundi*, chap. xv. p. 532.) A paragraph in *The Academy* (June 8, 1876) gives the following particulars of certain perforated lumps of a "blue metallic substance," discovered at Hissarlik by Dr. Schliemann, and there found lying under the copper shields to which they had probably been attached. "An analytical examination by Landerer (Berg. Hüttenm. Zeitung, xxxiv. 430) has shown them to be sulphide of copper. The art of colouring the metal was known to the coppersmiths of Corinth, who plunged the heated copper into the fountain of Peirene. It appears not impossible that this was a sulphur spring, and that the blue colour may have been given to the metal by plunging it in a heated state into the water and converting the surface into copper sulphide."

It is to be observed that the Pharaohs are almost always represented wearing this blue helmet in the battle-pieces, and that it is frequently studded with gold rings. It must therefore have been of metal. If not of sulphuretted copper, it may have been made of steel, which, in the well-known instance of the butcher's sharpener, as well as in representations of certain weapons, is always painted blue upon the monuments.

SOUTH WALL.

The subjects represented on this wall are as
follows:—

1. Rameses, life-size, presiding over a table of offerings. The king wears upon his head the *klaft*, or
head-cloth, striped gold and white, and decorated with
the uræus. The table is piled in the usual way with
flesh, fowl, and flowers. The surface being here quite
perfect, the details of these objects are seen to be
rendered with surprising minuteness. Even the tiny
black feather-stumps of the plucked geese are given
with the fidelity of Chinese art; while a red gash in
the breast of each shows in what way it was slain for
the sacrifice. The loaves are shaped precisely like the
so-called "cottage-loaves" of to-day, and have the same
little depression in the top, made by the baker's finger.
Lotus and papyrus blossoms in elaborate bouquet-
holders crown the pile.

2. Two tripods of light and elegant design, containing flowers.

3. The Bari, or sacred boat, painted gold-colour,
with the usual veil half-drawn across the naos, or
shrine; the prow of the boat being richly carved,
decorated with the Uta* or symbolic eye, and preceded by a large fan of ostrich feathers. The boat is
peopled with small black figures, one of which kneels
at the stern; while a sphinx couchant, with black body

---

* "This eye, called *uta*, was extensively used by the Egyptians both as
the pendant or ornament of a necklace during life, and as a Sepulchral amulet.
It represented the eye of a cow, especially that of the cow-form of the goddess
Athor, supposed to be the mother of the sun," etc. etc.—*Guide to First and
Second Egyptian Rooms*. S. BIRCH.

M. Grébaut, in his translation of a hymn to Ammon Ra, observes:—"Le
soleil marchant d'Orient en Occident éclaire de ses deux yeux les deux régions
du Nord et du Midi."—*Révue d'Arch.* vol. xxv. 1873; p. 387.

and human head, keeps watch at the prow. The
sphinx symbolises the king.

On this wall, in a space between the sacred boat
and the figure of Rameses, occurs a hieroglyphed inscription in ten vertical columns, sculptured in high
relief and elaborately coloured. For a translation of

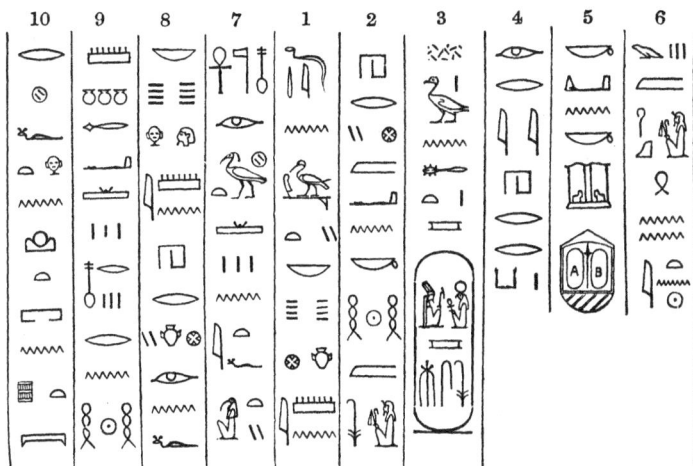

NOTE.—This inscription reads according to the
numbering of the columns, beginning at 1 and reading
to the right; then resuming at 7 and reading to the
left. The spaces lettered A B in the lowest figure of
column 5 are filled in with the two cartouches of
Rameses II.

this inscription I am indebted to the courtesy of
Dr. Birch.

INSCRIPTION ON SOUTH WALL,
translated by S. Birch, Esq., LL.D. F.S.A., etc. etc.

Says Thoth, Lord of Sesen* resident in the midst
of Amenheri**—I give thee a long time to rule over
the upper and lower country, Son of my Race, Beloved
Rameses, Beloved of Amen, and to perform all thy
wishes. I give thee to celebrate the millions festivals
of thirty years*** of the king Ra-user-Ma, Approved of
the Sun, Rameses Beloved of Amen, as ruler of the
orbit of the Solar disk. The living, perfect God,
giving glory to his father Thoth, Lord of Sesen, Resident in Amenheri, he made great and good monuments for ever in face of the Horizon of Heaven.

The meaning of which is that Thoth, addressing
Rameses II., then living and reigning, promises him
a long life and many anniversaries of his jubilee, in
return for the works made in his (Thoth's) honour at
Aboo Simbel and elsewhere.

NORTH WALL.

At the upper end of this wall is depicted a life-
sized female figure wearing an elaborate blue head-

---

* *Sesen*—Ashmoon or Hermopolis.
** *Amenheri*—Aboo Simbel.
*** According to M. P. Pierret, these panegyries, or festivals of thirty years,
were religious jubilees in celebration of each *thirtieth* anniversary of the accession of the reigning Pharaoh. There are however instances of panegyries
bearing dates at variance with this reckoning; as for instance there is record
of a panegyry of the XVIIIth year of Pepi, as well as of panegyries of the
years XXXIV. and XXXVII. of Rameses II.

dress surmounted by a disk and two ostrich feathers. She holds in her right hand the crux ansata, and in her left the jackal-headed sceptre. This not being the sceptre of a goddess, and the head-dress resembling that of the Queen as represented on the façade of the Temple of Hathor, I conclude we have here a portrait of Nofre-ari, corresponding to the portrait of Rameses on the opposite wall. Near her stands a table of offerings, on which, among other objects, are placed four vases of a rich blue colour traversed by bands of yellow. They perhaps represent the kind of glass known as the false murrhine.* Each of these vases contains an object like a pine, the ground-colour of which is deep yellow, patterned over with scale-like subdivisions in vermilion. We took them to represent grains of maize pyramidally piled.

Lastly, a pendant to that on the opposite wall, comes the sacred Bari. It is, however, turned the reverse way, with its prow towards the east; and it rests upon an altar, in the centre of which are the cartouches of Rameses II. and a small hieroglyphed inscription, thus translated by S. Birch, Esq., LL.D., etc.

INSCRIPTION ON NORTH WALL,

"Beloved by Amen Ra, King of the Gods resident in the Land of Kenus."**

Beyond this point, at the end nearest the N.E. corner of the chamber, the piled sand conceals what-

---

* There are, in the British Museum, some bottles and vases of this description, dating from the eighteenth dynasty; see Case E, *Second Egyptian Room*. They are of dark blue translucent glass, veined with waving lines of opaque white and yellow.

** *Kenus* — Nubia.

ever else the wall may contain in the way of decoration.

EAST WALL.

If the east wall is decorated like the others (which
may be taken for granted), its tableaux and inscriptions are hidden behind the sand which here rises to
the ceiling. The doorway also occurs in this wall,
occupying a space 4 feet 3½ inches in width on the
inner side.

One of the most interesting incidents connected
with the excavation of this little adytum remains yet
to be told.

I have described the female figure at the upper end
of the north wall, and how she holds in her right hand
the crux ansata and in her left the jackal-headed
sceptre. The hand that holds the crux hangs by her
side; the hand that holds the sceptre is half raised.
Close under this upraised hand, at a height of between
three and four feet from the actual level of the floor,
there were visible upon the uncoloured surface of the
original stucco several lines of free-hand writing. This
writing was laid on, apparently, with the brush, and
the ink, if ever it had been black, had now become
brown. Five long lines and three shorter lines were
uninjured. Below these were traces of other fragmentary lines, almost obliterated by the sand.

We knew at once that this quaint faint writing must
be in either the hieratic or demotic hand. We could
distinguish, or thought we could distinguish, in it vague
outlines of forms already familiar to us in the hieroglyphs
—abstracts, as it were, of birds and snakes and boats.

There could be no doubt, at all events, that the thing was curious; and we set it down in our own minds as the writing of either the architect or decorator of the place.

Anxious to make, if possible, an exact facsimile of this inscription, the Writer copied it three times. Of the last and best of these copies I am so fortunate as to be able to give a translation from the learned pen of Dr. Birch.

HIERATIC INSCRIPTION
N. Wall of Speos.

Translated by S. Birch Esq., LL.D., &c. &c.

. . . . thy son having . . . . thou hast conquered the worlds at once Ammon Ra Harmachis* the God at the first time,** who gives life, health, and a time of many praises to the groom . . . . of the Khen,*** son of the Royal son of Cush,† Opener of the road, Maker of transport boats, Giver of instructions to his Lord . . . . Amenshaa . . . .

We all know how difficult it is to copy correctly in a language of which one is ignorant; and the tiniest curve or dot omitted, is, I am told, fatal to the sense of these ancient characters. In the present instance, notwithstanding the care with which the transcript was made, there must still have been errors; for it has been found undecipherable in places; and in these places there occur inevitable lacunæ.

---

* *i.e.* Ammon Ra, the Sun-God, in conjunction or identification with Har-em-axu, or Horus-on-the-Horizon, another Solar Deity.
** The primæval God.
*** Inner-place, or sanctuary.
† Ethiopia.

Enough, however, remains to show that the lines were written, not as we had supposed by the artist, but by a distinguished visitor, whose name unfortunately is illegible. This visitor was a son of the Prince of Cush, or as it is literally written, the Royal Son of Cush; that being the official title of the Governor of Ethiopia.* As there were certainly eight governors of Ethiopia during the reign of Rameses II. (and perhaps more, whose names have not reached us), it is impossible even to hazard a guess at the parentage of our visitor. We gather, however, that he was sent hither to construct a road; also that he built transport boats; and that he exercised priestly functions in that part of the Temple which was inaccessible to all but dignitaries of the sacerdotal order.

Site, inscriptions, and decorations taken into account, there yet remains this question to be answered: —

What was the nature and character of the monument just described?

It adjoined a pylon, and, as we have seen, it consisted of a vaulted pronaos in crude brick, and an adytum excavated in the rock. On the walls of this

* M. Chabas observes that Governors of Ethiopia bore this title, even though they did not themselves belong to the family of the Pharaoh (see *Antiquité Hist.* p. 141).

It is a curious fact that one of the Governors of Ethiopia during the reign of Rameses II. was called Mes, or Messou, signifying son, or child—which by some Egyptologists has been identified with *Moses*. Now the Moses of the Bible was adopted by Pharaoh's daughter, "became to her as a son," was instructed in the wisdom of the Egyptians, and married a Cushite woman, black but comely. It would perhaps be too much to speculate on the possibility of his having held the office of Governor, or Royal Son of Cush. M. Maspero, however, who has honoured me. with his views on this subject, is of opinion that the Egyptians, having the sound of *sh* in their own language, would not have transcribed as *Messore* or *Mosa* a name which they had heard pronounced as *Moshu* by the Hebrews.

adytum are depicted various Gods with their attributes, votive offerings, and portraits of the King performing acts of adoration. The Bari, or ark, is also represented upon the north and south walls of the adytum. These are unquestionably the ordinary features of a temple.

On the other hand, there must be noted certain objections to these premises. It seemed to us that the pylon was built first, and that the S. boundary wall of the pronaos, being a subsequent erection, was supported against the slope of the pylon as far as where the spring of the vaulting began. Besides which, the pylon would have been a disproportionately large adjunct to a little monument the entire length of which, from the doorway of the pronaos to the west wall of the adytum, was less than 47 feet. We therefore concluded that the pylon belonged to the large temple, and was erected at the side, instead of in front of the façade, on account of the very narrow space between the mountain and the river.*

The pylon at Kom Ombo is, probably for the same reason, placed at the side of the Temple and on a lower level. To those who might object that a brick pylon would hardly be attached to a Temple of the first class, I would observe that the remains of a similar pylon are still to be seen at the top of what was once the landing-place leading to the Great Temple at Wady Halfeh. It may, therefore, be assumed that this little monument, although connected with the pylon by means of a doorway and staircase, was an excrescence of later date.

* At about an equal distance to the N. of the Great Temple, on the verge of the bank, is a shapeless block of brick ruin, which might possibly, if investigated, turn out to be the remains of a second pylon corresponding to this which we partially uncovered to the S.

Being an excrescence, however, was it, in the strict sense of the word, a Temple?

Even this seems to be doubtful. In the adytum there is no trace of any altar—no fragment of stone dais or sculptured image—no granite shrine, as at Philæ —no sacred recess, as at Denderah. The standard of Horus Aroëris occupies the centre place upon the wall facing the entrance, and occupies it, not as a tutelary divinity, but as a decorative device to separate the two large subjects already described. Again, the Gods represented in these subjects are Ra and Ammon Ra, the tutelary Gods of the Great Temple; but if we turn to the dedicatory inscription on page 124 we find that Thoth, whose image never occurs at all upon the walls* (unless as one of the little Gods in the cornice), is really the presiding deity of the place. It is he who welcomes Rameses and his offerings; who acknowledges the "glory" given to him by his beloved son; and who, in return for the great and good monuments erected in his honour, promises the king that he shall be given "a long time to rule over the upper and lower country."

Now Thoth was, *par excellence*, the God of Letters. He is styled the Lord of Divine Words; the Lord of the Sacred Writings; the Spouse of Truth. He personifies the Divine Intelligence. He is the patron of art and science; and he is credited with the invention of the alphabet. In one of the most interesting of Champollion's letters from Thebes,** he relates how, in the fragmentary ruins of the western extremity of the

* He may, however, be represented on the North wall, where it is covered by the sand-heap.
** Letter XIV. p. 235. *Nouvelle Ed.* Paris, 1868.

Ramesseum, he found a doorway adorned with the figures of Thoth and Saf; Thoth as the God of Literature, and Saf inscribed with the title of Lady President of the Hall of Books. At Denderah there is a chamber especially set apart for the sacred writings, and sculptured all over its walls with a catalogue raisonnée of the manuscript treasures of the Temple. At Edfoo a kind of closet built up between two of the pillars of the Hall of Assembly, was reserved for the same purpose. Every Temple, in short, had its library; and as the Egyptian books — being written on papyrus or leather, rolled up, and stored in coffers—occupied but little space, the rooms appropriated to this purpose were generally small.

It is Dr. Birch's opinion that our little monument may have been the library of the Great Temple of Aboo Simbel. This being the case, the absence of an altar, and the presence of Ra and Ammon Ra in the two principal tableaux, are sufficiently accounted for. The tutelary deity of the Great Temple and the patron deity of Rameses II. would naturally occupy, in this subsidiary structure, the same places that they occupy in the principal one; while the library, though in one sense the domain of Thoth, is still under the protection of the gods of the Temple to which it is an adjunct.

I do not believe we once asked ourselves how it came to pass that the place had remained hidden all these ages long; yet its very freshness proved how early it must have been abandoned. If it had been open in the time of the successors of Rameses II., they would probably, as elsewhere, have interpolated inscriptions and cartouches, or have substituted their

9*

own cartouches for those of the founder. If it had
been open in the time of the Ptolemies and Cæsars,
travelling Greeks and learned Romans, and strangers
from Byzantium and the cities of Asia Minor, would
have cut their names on the door-jambs and scribbled
ex-votos on the walls. If it had been open in the
days of Nubian Christianity, the sculptures would have
been coated with mud, and washed with lime, and
daubed with pious caricatures of St. George and the
Holy Family. But we found it intact — as perfectly
preserved as a tomb that had lain hidden under the
rocky bed of the desert. For these reasons I am inclined to think that it became inaccessible while
Rameses yet lived. There can be little doubt that a
wave of earthquake passed, during his reign, along
the left bank of the Nile, beginning possibly above
Wady Halfeh, and extending at least as far north as
Gerf Hossayn. Such a shock might have wrecked the
Temple at Wady Halfeh, as it dislocated the pylon of
Wady Sabooah, and shook the built-out porticoes of
Derr and Gerf Hossayn; which last four Temples, as
they do not, I believe, show signs of having been
added to by later Pharaohs, may be supposed to have
been abandoned in consequence of the ruin that had
befallen them. Here, at all events, it shook the mountain of the Great Temple, cracked one of the Osiride
columns of the First Hall,* shattered one of the four

* That this shock of earthquake occurred during the lifetime of Rameses II.,
seems to be proven by the fact that, where the Osiride column is cracked across,
a wall has been built up to support the two last pillars to the left at the upper
end of the great hall, on which wall is a large stela covered with an elaborate
hieroglyphic inscription, dating from the xxxvth year, and the 13th day of the
month of Tybi, *of the reign of Rameses II.* The right arm of the external
colossus, to the right of the great doorway, has also been supported by the
introduction of an arm to his throne, built up of square blocks; this being the
only arm to any of the thrones. Miss Martineau detected a restoration of part

great Colossi, more or less injured the other three,
flung down the great brick pylon, reduced the pronaos
of the library to a heap of ruin, and not only brought
down part of the ceiling of the excavated adytum, but
rent open a vertical fissure in the rock, some 20 or
25 feet in length.

With so much irreparable damage done to the
Great Temple, and with so much that was reparable
calling for immediate attention, it is no wonder that
these brick buildings were left to their fate.   The
priests would have rescued the sacred books from
among the ruins, and then the place would have been
abandoned.

So much by way of conjecture.   As hypothesis,
however, a sufficient reason is perhaps suggested for
the wonderful state of preservation in which the little
chamber had been handed down to the present time.
A rational explanation is also offered for the absence
of later cartouches, of Greek and Latin ex-votos, of
Christian emblems, and of subsequent mutilation of
every kind.   For, save that one contemporary visitor
—the son of the Royal Son of Cush—the place contained, when we opened it, no record of any passing
traveller; no defacing autograph of tourist, archæologist,
or scientific explorer.   Neither Belzoni nor Champollion
had found it out.   Even the sharp eyes of the terrible
Lepsius had passed it by.

It happens sometimes that hidden things, which in
themselves are easy to find, escape detection because

of the lower jaw of the northernmost colossus, and also of a part of the dress of
one of the Osiride statues in the great hall.   I have in my possession a photo-
graph taken at a time when the sand was several feet lower than at present,
which shows that the right leg of the northernmost colossus is also a restoration
on a gigantic scale, being built up, like the throne-arm, in great blocks.

no one thinks of looking for them.   But such was
not the case in this present instance.   Search had
been made here again and again; and even quite
recently.

It seems that when the Khedive entertains distinguished guests and sends them in gorgeous Dahabeeyahs up the Nile, he grants them a virgin mound,
or so many square feet of a famous necropolis; lets
them dig as deep as they please; and allows them to
keep whatever they may find.   Sometimes he sends
out scouts to beat the ground; and then a tomb is
found and left unopened, and the illustrious visitor is
allowed to discover it.   When the scouts are unlucky,
it may even sometimes happen that an old tomb is
re-stocked; carefully closed up; and then, with all
the charm of unpremeditation, re-opened a day or two
after.

Now Sheykh Rashwan Ebn Hassan el Kashef told
us that in 1869, when the Empress of the French was
at Aboo Simbel, and again when the Prince and
Princess of Wales came up the Nile after the Prince's
illness, he received strict orders to find some hitherto
undiscovered tomb,* in order that the Khedive's
guests might have the satisfaction of opening it.   But,
he added, although he left no likely place untried
among the rocks and valleys on both sides of the
river, he could find nothing.   To have unearthed such
a Birbeh as this, would have done him good service
with the Government, and have ensured him a splendid
backsheesh from Prince or Empress.   As it was, he

---

* There are tombs in some of the ravines behind the Temples, which,
however, we did not see.

got reprimanded for want of diligence, and he even believed himself to be out of favour to this day.

I may here mention—in order to have done with this subject—that besides being buried outside to a depth of about eight feet, the adytum had been partially filled inside by a gradual infiltration of sand from above. This can only have accumulated at the time when the old sand-drift was at its highest. That drift, sweeping in one unbroken line across the front of the Great Temple, must at one time have risen here to a height of twenty feet above the present level. From thence the sand had found its way down the perpendicular fissure already mentioned. In the corner behind the door, the sand-pile rose to the ceiling, in shape just like the deposit at the bottom of an hour-glass. I am informed by the Painter that when the top of the doorway was found and an opening first effected, the sand poured out *from within*, like water escaping from an opened sluice.

Here, then, is positive proof (if proof were needed) that we were first to enter the place, at all events since the time when the great sand-drift rose as high as the top of the fissure.

The Painter wrote his name and ours, with the date (February 16th, 1874) on a space of blank wall over the inside of the doorway; and this was the only occasion upon which any of us left our names upon an Egyptian monument. On arriving at Korosko, where there is a post-office, he also dispatched a letter to the "Times," briefly recording the facts here related. That letter, which appeared on the 18th of March following, is reprinted in the Appendix at the end of this volume.

I am told that our names have been partially effaced, and that the wall-paintings which we had the happiness of admiring in all their beauty and freshness, are already much injured. Such is the fate of every Egyptian monument, great or small. The tourist carves it all over with names and dates, and in some instances with caricatures. The student of Egyptology, by taking wet paper "squeezes," sponges away every vestige of the original colour. The "collector" buys and carries off everything of value that he can get; and the Arab steals for him. The work of destruction, meanwhile, goes on apace. There is no one to prevent it; there is no one to discourage it. Every day, more inscriptions are mutilated — more tombs are rifled — more paintings and sculptures are defaced. The Louvre contains a full-length portrait of Seti I., cut out bodily from the walls of his sepulchre in the Valley of the Tombs of the Kings. The Museums of London, of Berlin, of Turin, of Florence, are rich in spoils which tell their own lamentable tale. When science leads the way, is it wonderful that ignorance should follow?

CHAPTER XIX.

Back through Nubia.

THERE are fourteen Temples between Aboo Simbel and Philæ; to say nothing of grottoes, tombs, and other ruins. As a rule, people begin to get tired of Temples about this time, and vote them too plentiful. Meek travellers go through them as a duty; but the greater number rebel. Our Happy Couple, I grieve to say, went over to the majority. Dead to shame, they openly proclaimed themselves bored. They even skipped several Temples.

For myself, I was never bored by them. Though they had been twice as many, I should not have wished them fewer. Miss Martineau tells how, in this part of the river, she was scarcely satisfied to sit down to break-fast without having first explored a Temple; but I could have breakfasted, dined, supped on Temples. My appetite for them was insatiable, and grew with what it fed upon. I went over them all. I took notes of them all. I sketched them every one.

I may as well say at once that I shall reproduce but few of those notes. If, surrounded by their local associations, these ruins fail to interest many who travel far to see them, it is not to be supposed that they would interest readers at home. Here and there, per-haps, might be one who would care to pore with me over every broken sculpture; to spell out every half-legible cartouche; to trace through Greek and Roman influences (which are nowhere more conspicuous than in these Nubian buildings) the slow deterioration of the Egyptian style. But the world for the most part reserves itself, and rightly, for the great epochs and the great names of the past; and because it has not yet had too much of Karnak, of Aboo Simbel, of the Pyramids, it sets slight store by those minor monuments which record the periods of foreign rule, and the decline of native art.

For these reasons, therefore, I propose to dismiss very briefly many places upon which I bestowed hours of delightful labour.

We left Aboo Simbel just as the moon was rising on the evening of the 18th of February, and dropped down with the current for three or four miles before mooring for the night. At six next morning the men began rowing; and at half-past eight, the heads of the Colossi were still looking placidly after us across a ridge of intervening hills. They were then more than five miles distant in a direct line; but every feature was still distinct in the early daylight. I went up again and again, as long as they remained in sight, and bade good-bye to them at last with that same heartache which comes of a farewell view of the Alps.

When I say that we were seventeen days getting from Aboo Simbel to Philæ, and that we had the wind against us from sunrise till sunset almost every day, it will be seen that our progress was of the slowest. To those who were tired of Temples, and to the crew who were running short of bread, these long days of lying up under the bank, or of rocking to and fro in the middle of the river, were dreary enough.

Slowly but surely, however, the hard-won miles go

by. Sometimes the barren desert hems us in to right
and left, with never a blade of green between the rock
and the river. Sometimes, as at Tosko*, we come
upon an open tract, where there are palms, and castor-
berry plantations, and corn-fields alive with quail. The
Idle Man goes ashore at Tosko with his gun, while the
Little Lady and the Writer climb a solitary rock about
200 feet above the river. The bank shelves here, and
a crescent-like wave of inundation, about three miles in
length, overflows it every season. From this height one
sees exactly how far the wave goes, and how it must
make a little bay when it is there. Now it is a bay of
barley, full to the brim, and rippling with the breeze.
Beyond the green comes the desert; the one defined
against the other as sharply as water against land. The
desert looks wonderfully old beside the young green of
the corn, and the Nile flows wide among sandbanks,
like a tidal river near the sea. The village, squared off
in parallelograms, like a cattle-market, lies mapped out
below. A field-glass shows that the houses are simply
cloistered courtyards roofed with palm-thatch; the
sheykh's house being larger than the rest, with the usual
open space and spreading sycamore in front. There are
women moving to and fro in the courtyards, and husbandmen in the castor-berry patches. A funeral with a
train of wailers goes out presently towards the burial-
ground on the edge of the desert. The Idle Man, a
slight figure with a veil twisted round his hat, wades,
half-hidden, through the barley, signalling his whereabouts every now and then by a puff of white smoke. A
cargo-boat, stripped and shorn, comes floating down the

---

* Tosko is on the eastern bank, and not, as in Keith Johnston's map, on
the west.

river, making no visible progress. A native felucca, carrying one tattered brown sail, goes swiftly up with the wind at a pace that will bring her to Aboo Simbel before nightfall. Already she is past the village; and those black specks yonder, which we had never dreamed were crocodiles, have slipped off into the water at her approach. And now she is far in the distance—that glowing, illimitable distance, traversed by long silvery reaches of river, and ending in a vast flat, so blue and aerial that, but for some three or four notches of purple peaks on the horizon, one could scarcely discern the point at which land and sky melt into each other.

Ibrim comes next; then Derr; then Wady Sabooah. At Ibrim, as at Derr, there are "fair" families, whose hideous light hair and blue eyes (grafted on brown-black skins) date back to Bosnian forefathers of 360 years ago. These people give themselves airs, and are the *haute noblesse* of the place. The men are lazy and quarrelsome. The women trail longer robes, wear more beads and rings, and are altogether more unattractive and castor-oily than any we have seen elsewhere. They keep slaves, too. We saw these unfortunates trotting at the heels of their mistresses, like dogs. Knowing slavery to be officially illegal in the dominions of the Khedive, the M. B.s applied to a dealer, who offered them an Abyssinian girl for ten pounds. This useful article— warranted a bargain—was to sweep, wash, milk, and churn; but was not equal to cooking. The M.B.s, it is needless to add, having verified the facts, retired from the transaction.

At Derr we pay a farewell visit to the Temple; and

at Amada, arriving towards close of day, see the great
view for the last time in the glory of sunset.

And now, though the north wind blows persistently,
it gets hotter every day. The crocodiles like it, and
come out to bask in the sunshine. Called up one morning in the middle of breakfast, we see two—a little
one and a big one—on a sandbank near by. The men
rest upon their oars. The boat goes with the stream.
No one speaks; no one moves. Breathlessly and in dead
silence, we drift on till we are close beside them. The
big one is rough and black, like the trunk of a London
elm, and measures full eighteen feet in length. The
little one is pale and greenish, and glistens like glass.
All at once, the old one starts, doubles itself up for a
spring, and disappears with a tremendous splash. But
the little one, apparently unconscious of danger, lifts its
tortoise-like head, and eyes us sidewise. Presently some
one whispers; and that whisper breaks the spell. Our
little crocodile flings up its tail, plunges down the bank,
and is gone in a moment.

The crew could not understand how the Idle Man,
after lying in wait for crocodiles at Aboo Simbel, should
let this rare chance pass without a shot. But we had
heard since then of so much indiscriminate slaughter at
the Second Cataract, that he was resolved to bear no
part in the extermination of those old historic reptiles.
That a sportsman should wish for a single trophy is not
unreasonable; but that scores of crack shots should go
up every winter, killing and wounding these wretched
brutes at an average rate of from twelve to eighteen
per gun, is mere butchery, and cannot be too strongly
reprehended. Year by year, the creatures become shyer
and fewer; and the day is probably not far distant when

a crocodile will be as rarely seen below Semneh as it
is now rarely seen below Assouan.

The thermometer stands at 85⁰ in the saloon of the
Philæ, when we come one afternoon to Wady Sabooah,
where there is a solitary Temple drowned in sand. It
was approached once by an avenue of sphinxes and
standing colossi, now shattered and buried. The roof
of the pronaos, if ever it was roofed, is gone. The inner
halls and the sanctuary—all excavated in the rock—
are choked and impassable. Only the propylon stands
clear of sand; and that, massive as it is, looks as if
one touch of a battering-ram would bring it to the
ground. Every huge stone in it is loose. Every block
in the cornice seems tottering in its place. In all this,
we fancy we recognise the work of our Aboo Simbel
earthquake. *

At Wady Sabooah we see a fat native. The fact
claims record, because it is so uncommon. A stalwart
middle-aged man, dressed in a tattered kilt and carrying a palm-staff in his hand, he stands before us the
living double of the famous wooden statue at Boulak.
He is followed by his two wives and three or four
children, all bent upon trade. The women have
trinkets, the boys a live chameleon and a small stuffed
crocodile for sale. While the Painter is bargaining for
the crocodile and L. for a nose-ring, the Writer makes

---

* This is one of the Temples erected by Rameses the Great, and, I believe, not added to by any of his successors. The colossi, the Osiride columns,
the sphinxes (now battered out of all human semblance) were originally made
in his image. The cartouches are all his, and in one of the inner chambers
there is a list of his little family. All these chambers were accessible till three
or four years ago, when a party of German travellers carried off some sculptured tablets of great archæological interest; since when the entrance has been
sanded up by order of Mariette Bey. See also, with regard to the probable
date of the earthquake at this place, chap. XVIII. p. 132 of this volume.

acquaintance with a pair of self-important hoopoes, who live in the pylon and evidently regard it as a big nest of their own building. They sit observing me curiously while I sketch, nodding their crested polls and chattering disparagingly, like a couple of critics. By and by comes a small black bird with a white breast, and sings deliciously. It is like no little bird that I have ever seen before; but the song that it pours so lavishly from its tiny throat is as sweet and brilliant as a canary's.

Powerless against the wind, the Dahabeeyah lies idle day after day in the sun. Sometimes, when we chance to be near a village, the natives squat on the bank, and stare at us for hours together. The moment any one appears on deck, they burst into a chorus of "Backsheesh!" There is but one way to get rid of them, and that is to sketch them. The effect is instantaneous. With a good sized block and a pencil, a whole village may be put to flight at a moment's notice. If on the other hand one wishes for a model, the difficulty is insuperable. The Painter tried in vain to get some of the women and girls (not a few of whom were really pretty) to sit for their portraits. I well remember one haughty beauty, shaped and draped like a Juno, who stood on the bank one morning, scornfully watching all that was done on deck. She carried a flat basket back-handed; and her arms were covered with bracelets, and her fingers with rings. Her little girl, in a Madame Nubia fringe, clung to her skirts, half wondering, half frightened. The Painter sent out an ambassador plenipotentiary to offer her anything from sixpence to half-a-sovereign, if she would only stand like that for half-an-hour. The manner of her refusal was grand. She drew her shawl over her face, took her child's hand, and stalked away like an offended goddess. The Writer, meanwhile, hidden behind a curtain, had snatched a tiny sketch from the cabin-window.

On the western bank, somewhere between Wady Sabooah and Maharrakeh, in a spot quite bare of vegetation, stand the ruins of a fortified town which is neither mentioned by Murray nor entered in the maps. It is built high on a base of reddish rock, and commands the river and the desert. The Painter and Writer explored it one afternoon, in the course of a long ramble. Climbing first a steep slope strewn with masonry, we came to the remains of a stone gateway. Finding this impassable, we made our way through a breach in the battlemented wall, and thence up a narrow road down which had been poured a cataract of *débris*. Skirting a ruined postern at the top of this road, we found ourselves in a close labyrinth of vaulted arcades built of crude brick and lit at short intervals by openings in the roof. These strange streets—for they were streets—were lined on either side by small dwellings built of crude brick on stone foundations. We went into some of the houses—mere ruined courts and roofless chambers, in which were no indications of hearths or staircases. In one lay a fragment of stone column about 14 inches in diameter. The air in these ancient streets was foul and stagnant, and the ground was everywhere heaped with fragments of black, red, and yellowish pottery, like the shards of Elephantine and Philæ. A more desolate place in a more desolate situation I never saw. It looked as if it had been besieged, sacked, and abandoned, a thousand years ago;

which is probably under the mark, for the character of
the pottery would seem to point to the period of
Roman occupation. Noting how the brick superstruc-
tures were reared on apparently earlier masonry, we
concluded that the beginnings of this place were probably Egyptian, and the later work Roman or Coptic.
The marvel was that any town should have been built
in so barren a spot, there being not so much as an
inch-wide border of lentils for a mile or more between
the river and the desert.

Having traversed the place from end to end, we
came out through another breach on the westward
side, and, thinking to find a sketchable point of view
inland, struck down towards the plain. In order to
reach this, one first must skirt a deep ravine which
divides the rock of the citadel from the desert. Following the brink of this ravine to the point at which
it falls into the level, we found to our great surprise that we were treading the banks of an extinct
river.

It was full of sand now; but beyond all question
it had once been full of water. It came, evidently,
from the mountains over towards the north-west. We
could trace its windings for a long way across the
plain, thence through the ravine, and on southwards
in a line parallel with the Nile. Here, beneath our
feet, were the water-worn rocks through which it had
fretted its way; and yonder, half-buried in sand, were
the boulders it had rounded and polished, and borne
along in its course. I doubt, however, if when it was
a river of water, this stream was half as beautiful as
now, when it is a river of sand. It was turbid then,
no doubt, and charged with sediment. Now it is more

golden than Pactolus, and covered with ripples more playful and undulating than were ever modelled by Canaletti's pencil.

Supposing yonder town to have been founded in the days when the river was a river, and the plain fertile and well watered, the mystery of its position is explained. It was protected in front by the Nile, and in the rear by the ravine and the river. But how long ago was this? Here apparently was an independent stream, taking its rise among the Libyan mountains. It dated back, consequently, to a time when those barren hills collected and distributed water—that is to say, to a time when it used to rain in Nubia. And that time must have been before the rocky barrier broke down at Silsilis, in the old days when the land of Cush flowed with milk and honey.*

It would rain even now in Nubia, if it could. That same evening when the sun was setting, we saw a fan-like drift of dappled cloud miles high above our heads, melting, as it seemed, in fringes of iridescent vapour. We could distinctly see those fringes forming, wavering, and evaporating; unable to descend as rain because dispersed at a high altitude by radiated heat from the desert. This, with one exception, was the only occasion on which I saw clouds in Nubia.

Coming back, we met a solitary native, with a string of beads in his hand and a knife up his sleeve. He followed us for a long way, volunteering a but half-intelligible story about some unknown Birbeh** in the

---

* Not only near this nameless town, but in many other parts between Aboo Simbel and Philæ, we found the old alluvial soil lying as high as from 20 to 30 feet above the level of the present inundations.
** Ar. *Birbeh*, Temple.

desert. We asked where it was, and he pointed up the course of our unknown river.

"You have seen it?" said the Painter.

"Marrat keteer" (many times).

"How far is it?"

"One day's march in the hagger" (desert).

"And have no Ingleezeh ever been to look for it?"

He shook his head at first, not understanding the question; then looked grave, and held up one finger.

Our stock of Arabic was so small, and his so interlarded with Kensee, that we had great difficulty in making out what he said next. We gathered, however, that some Howadji, travelling alone and on foot, had gone in search of this Birbeh, and never came back. Was he lost? Was he killed?—Who could say?

"It was a long time ago," said the man with the beads. "It was a long time ago, and he took no guide with him."

We would have given much to trace the river to its source, and search for this unknown Temple in the desert. But it is one of the misfortunes of this kind of travelling that one cannot easily turn aside from the beaten track. The hot season is approaching; the river is running low; the daily cost of the Dahabeeyah is exorbitant; and in Nubia, where little or nothing can be bought in the way of food, the dilatory traveller risks starvation. It was something, however, to have seen with one's own eyes that the Nile, instead of flowing for a distance of 1200 miles unfed by any

10*

affluent, had here received the waters of a tributary.*

To those who have a South breeze behind them, the Temples must now follow in quick succession. We, however, achieved them by degrees, and rejoiced when our helpless Dahabeeyah lay within rowing reach of anything worth seeing. Thus we pull down one day to Maharrakeh—in itself a dull ruin; but picturesquely desolate. Seen as one comes up the bank on landing, two parallel rows of columns stand boldly up against the sky, supporting a ruined entablature. In the foreground, a few stunted Dôm-palms starve in an arid soil. The barren desert closes in the distance.

We are beset here by an insolent crowd of savage-looking men and boys, and impudent girls with long frizzy hair and Nubian fringes, who pester us with beads and pebbles; dance, shout, slap their legs and clap their hands in our faces; and pelt us when we go away. One ragged warrior brandishes an antique brass-mounted firelock full six feet long in the barrel, and some of the others carry slender spears.

The Temple—a late Roman structure—would seem to have been wrecked by earthquake before it was completed. The masonry is all in the rough—pillars as they came from the quarry; capitals blocked out, waiting for the carver. These unfinished ruins—of which every stone looks new, as if the work was still in progress—affect one's imagination strangely. On a

---

* "The Nile receives its last tributary, the Atbara, in Lat. 17° 42′ N., at the northern extremity of the peninsular tract anciently called the island of Meröe, and thence flows N. (a single stream without the least accession) through 12 degrees of latitude; or, following its winding course, at least 1200 miles, to the sea."—*Blackie's Imperial Gazetteer*, 1861. A careful survey of the country would probably bring to light the dry beds of many more such tributaries as the one described above.

fallen wall South of the portico, the Idle Man detected some remains of a Greek inscription;* but for hiero-glyphic characters, or cartouches by which to date the building, we looked in vain.**

Dakkeh comes next in order; then Gerf Hossayn, Dendoor, and Kalabsheh. Arriving at Dakkeh soon after sunrise, we find the whole population—screaming, pushing, chattering, laden with eggs, pigeons, and gourds for sale—drawn up to receive us. There is a large sand island in the way here; so we moor about a mile above the Temple.

We first saw the twin pylons of Dakkeh some weeks ago from the deck of the Philæ, and we then likened them to the majestic towers of Edfoo. Approaching them now by land, we are surprised to find them so small. It is a brilliant, hot morning; and our way lies by the river, between the lentil slope and the castor-berry patches. There are flocks of pigeons flying low overhead; barking dogs and crowing cocks in the vil-lage close by; and all over the path, hundreds of

* Of this wall, Burckhardt notices that "it has fallen down, apparently from some sudden and violent concussion, as the stones are lying on the ground in layers, as when placed in the wall; a proof that they must have fallen all at once."—*Travels in Nubia:* Ed. 1819, p. 100. But he has not observed the in-scription, which is in large characters, and consists of three lines on three sepa-rate layers of stones. The Idle Man copied the original upon the spot, which copy has since been identified with an ex-voto of a Roman soldier published in Boeckh's *Corpus Inscr. Grac.*, of which the following is a translation:—
"The vow of Verecundus the soldier, and his most pious parents and Gaius his little brother, and the rest of his brethren."
** A clue, however, might possibly be found to the date. There is a rudely sculptured tableau—the only piece of sculpture in the place—on a detached wall near the standing columns. It represents Isis worshipped by a youth in a short toga. Both figures are lumpish and ill-modelled; and Isis, seated under a conventional fig-tree, wears her hair erected in stiff rolls over the forehead, like a diadem. It is the face and stiffly-dressed hair of Marciana, the sister of Trajan, as shown upon the well-known coin engraved in Smith's *Dic. of Greek and Roman Biography*, vol. II. p. 939. Maharrakeh is the Hiera Sycaminos, or Place of the Sacred Fig-tree, where ends the Itinerary of Antoninus.

beetles—real, live scarabs, black as coal and busy as
ants—rolling their clay pellets up from the water's
edge to the desert. If we were to examine a score or
so of these pellets, we should here and there find one
that contained no eggs; for it is a curious fact that the
scarab-beetle makes and rolls her pellet, whether she
has an egg to deposit or not. The female beetle,
though assisted by the male, is said to do the heavier
share of the pellet-rolling; and if evening comes on
before her pellet is safely stowed away, she will sleep
holding it with her feet all night, and resume her
labour in the morning. *

The Temple here—begun by an Ethiopian king
named Arkaman (Ergamenes), about whom Diodorus
Siculus has a long story to tell, and carried on by the
Ptolemies and Cæsars—stands in a desolate open space
to the north of the village, and is approached by an
avenue, the walls of which are constructed with blocks
from some earlier building. The whole of this avenue
and all the waste ground for three or four hundred
yards round about the Temple, is not merely strewn
but piled with fragments of pottery, pebbles, and large
smooth stones of porphyry, alabaster, basalt, and a kind
of marble like verde antico. These stones are puzzling.
They look as if they might be fragments of statues
that had been rolled and polished by ages of friction
in the bed of a torrent. Among the potsherds we find
some inscribed fragments, like those of Elephantine.**

* See "*The Scarabæus Sacer*" by C. Woodrooffe, B.A.—a paper (based on
notes by the late Rev. C. Johns) read before the Winchester and Hampshire
Scientific and Literary Society, Nov. 8, 1875. *Privately printed.*
** See Chap. X. p. 233, vol. I. Dakkeh (the Pselcis of the Greeks and Romans.
the Pselk of the Egyptians) was at one time regarded as the confine of Egypt
and Ethiopia, and would seem to have been a great military station. The in-

Of the Temple I will only say that, as masonry, it is better put together than any work of the XVIIIth or XIXth dynasties with which I am acquainted. The sculptures, however, are atrocious. Such mis-shapen hieroglyphs; such dumpy, smirking goddesses; such clownish kings in such preposterous head-dresses, we have never seen till now. The whole thing, in short, as regards sculpturesque style, is the Ptolemaic out-Ptolemied.

Rowing round presently to Kobban—the river running wide, with the sand island between—we land under the walls of a huge crude-brick structure, black with age, which at first sight looks quite shapeless; but which proves to be an ancient Egyptian fortress, buttressed, towered, loopholed, finished at the angles with the invariable moulded torus, and surrounded by a deep dry moat, which is probably yet filled each summer by the inundation.

Now of all rare things in the valley of the Nile, a purely secular ruin is the rarest; and this, with the exception of some foundations of dwellings here and there, is the first we have seen. It is very, very old; as old certainly as the days of Thothmes III., whose name is found on some scattered blocks about a quarter of a mile away, and who built two similar fortresses at Semneh, thirty-five miles above Wady Halfeh. It may even be a thousand years older still, and date from the time of Amenemhat III., whose name is also found

scribed potsherds here are chiefly receipts and accounts of soldiers' pay. The walls of the Temple outside, and of the chambers within, abound also in free-hand graffiti, most of which are written in red ink. We observed some that appeared to be trilingual. The Writer copied one which is supposed by Dr. Birch to be in Ethiopian Demotic, and is apparently a name; and another in rude characters which appear to be quite unknown.

on a stela near Kobban.* For here was once an
ancient city, when Pselcis (now Dakkeh) was but a
new suburb on the opposite bank. The name of this
ancient city is lost, but it is by some supposed to be
identical with the Metacompso of Ptolemy.** As the
suburb grew, the mother town declined, and in time,
the suburb became the city, and the city became the
suburb. The scattered blocks aforesaid, together with

* " Less than a quarter of a mile to the south are the ruins of a small sandstone Temple with clustered columns; and on the way, near the village, you
pass a stone stela of Amenemha III., mentioning his eleventh year."—*Murray's
Handbook for Egypt*, p. 481. M. Maspero, writing of Usertasen III., says,
"Son fils et successeur, Amenemhat III., fit construire en face de Pselkis une
forteresse importante."—*Hist. Ancienne des Peuples de l'Orient*. Chap. III.
p. 113.
    At Kobban also was found the famous stela of Rameses II., called the
Stela of Dakkeh; see chap. XIV. pp. 32-35 of this volume. In this inscription,
a cast from which is at the Louvre, Rameses II. is stated to have caused an
artesian well to be made in the desert between this place and Gebel Oellaky,
in order to facilitate the working of the gold mines of those parts.
    ** "According to Ptolemy, Metachompso should be opposite Pselcis, where
there are extensive brick ruins. If so, Metachompso and Contra Pselcis must
be the same town."—*Topography of Thebes*, etc.; Sir G. Wilkinson. Ed. 1835,
p. 488. M. Vivien de St. Martin is, however, of opinion that the island of
Derar, near Maharrakeh, is the true Metachompso. See *Le Nord de l'Afrique*,
section VI. p. 161. Be this as it may, we at all events know of one great siege
that this fortress sustained, and of one great battle fought beneath its walls.
"The Ethiopians," says Strabo, "having taken advantage of the withdrawal
of part of the Roman forces, surprised and took Syene, Elephantine, and Philæ,
enslaved the inhabitants, and threw down the statues of Cæsar. But Petronius,
marching with less than 10,000 infantry and 800 horse against an army of
30,000 men, compelled them to retreat to Pselcis. He then sent deputies to
demand restitution of what they had taken, and the reasons which had induced
them to begin the war. On their alleging that they had been ill treated by the
nomarchs, he answered that these were not the sovereigns of the country—but
Cæsar. When they desired three days for consideration and did nothing which
they were bound to do, Petronius attacked and compelled them to fight. They
soon fled, being badly commanded and badly armed, for they carried large
shields made of raw hides, and hatchets for offensive weapons. Part of the
insurgents were driven into the city, others fled into the uninhabited country,
and such as ventured upon the passage of the river escaped to a neighbouring
island, where there were not many crocodiles, on account of the current. . . .
Petronius then attacked Pselcis, and took it."—STRABO's *Geography*, Bohn's
translation, 1857, vol. III., pp. 267-8. This island to which the insurgents fled
may have been the large sand island which here still occupies the middle of
the river, and obstructs the approach to Dakkeh. Or they may have fled to
the island of Derar, seven miles higher up. Strabo does not give the name of
the island.

the remains of a small Temple, yet mark the position of the elder city.

The walls of this most curious and interesting fortress have probably lost much of their original height. They are in some parts 30 feet thick, and nowhere less than 20. Vertical on the inside, they are built at a buttress-slope outside, with additional shallow buttresses at regular distances. These last, as they can scarcely add to the enormous strength of the original wall, were probably designed for effect. There are two entrances to the fortress; one in the centre of the north wall, and one in the south. We enter the enclosure by the last-named, and find ourselves in the midst of an immense parallelogram measuring about 450 feet from east to west, and perhaps 300 feet from north to south.

All within these bounds is a wilderness of ruin. The space looks large enough for a city, and contains what might be the *débris* of a dozen cities. We climb huge mounds of rubbish; skirt cataracts of broken pottery; and stand on the brink of excavated pits, honeycombed forty feet below with brick foundations. Over these mounds and at the bottom of these pits, swarm men, women, and children, filling and carrying away basket-loads of rubble. The dust rises in clouds. The noise, the heat, the confusion, are indescribable. One pauses, bewildered, seeking in vain to discover in this mighty maze any indication of a plan. It is only by an effort that one gradually realises how the place is but a vast shell, and how all these mounds and pits mark the site of what was once a huge edifice rising tower above tower to a central keep, such as we see represented in the battle-subjects of Aboo Simbel and Thebes.

That towered edifice and central keep—quarried,
broken up, carried away piecemeal, reduced to powder,
and spread over the land as manure—has now disappeared almost to its foundations. Only the well in
the middle of the enclosure, and the great wall of circuit, remain. That wall is doomed, and will by and
by share the fate of the rest. The well, which must
have been very deep, is choked with rubbish to the
brim. Meanwhile, in order to realise what the place
in its present condition is like, one need but imagine
how the Tower of London would look if the whole of
the inner buildings—White Tower, Chapel, Armoury,
Governor's Quarters and all—were levelled in shapeless ruin, and only the outer walls and moat were left.

Built up against the inner side of the wall of circuit are the remains of a series of massive towers, the
tops of which, as they are even now, strangely enough,
shorter than the external structure, can never have
communicated with the battlements, unless by ladders.
The finest of these towers, together with a magnificent
fragment of wall, faces the eastern desert.

Going out by the N. entrance, we find the sides of
the gateway, and even the steps leading down into the
moat, in perfect preservation; while at the base of the
great wall, on the outer side facing the river, there yet
remains a channel or conduit about two feet square,
built and roofed with stone, which in Murray is described as a water-gate.

The sun is high, the heat is overwhelming, the
felucca waits; and we turn reluctantly away, knowing
that between here and Cairo we shall see no more
curious relic of the far-off past than this dismantled
stronghold. It is a mere mountain of unburnt brick;

altogether unlovely; admirable only for the gigantic
strength of its proportions; pathetic only in the abject-
ness of its ruin. Yet it brings the lost ages home to
one's imagination in a way that no Temple could ever
bring them. It dispels for a moment the historic
glamour of the sculptures, and compels us to remember
those nameless and forgotten millions, of whom their
rulers fashioned soldiers in time of war, and builders
in time of peace.

Our adventures by the way are few and far between;
and we now rarely meet a Dahabeeyah. Birds are
more plentiful than when we were in this part of the
river a few weeks ago. We see immense flights of
black and white cranes congregated at night on the
sandbanks; and any number of quail may be had for
the shooting. It is matter for rejoicing when the Idle
Man goes out with his gun and brings home a full
bag; for our last sheep was killed before we started
for Wady Halfeh, and our last poultry ceased cackling
at Aboo Simbel.

One morning early, we see a bride taken across
the river in a big boat full of women and girls, who
are clapping their hands and shrilling the tremulous
zaghareet. The bride—a chocolate beauty with magnificent eyes—wears a gold brow-pendant and nose-ring,
and has her hair newly plaited in hundreds of tails,
finished off at the ends with mud pellets daubed with
yellow ochre. She stands surrounded by her companions, proud of her finery, and pleased to be stared
at by the Ingleezeh.

About this time, also, we see one night a wild sort
of festival going on for some miles along both sides
of the river. Watch-fires break out towards twilight,

first on this bank, then on that; becoming brighter and more numerous as the darkness deepens. By and by, when we are going to bed, we hear sounds of drumming on the Eastern bank, and see from afar a torchlight procession and dance. The effect of this dance of torches—for it is only the torches that are visible—is quite diabolic. The lights flit and leap as if they were alive; circling, clustering, dispersing, bobbing, poussetting, pursuing each other at a gallop, and whirling every now and then through the air, like rockets. Late as it is, we would fain put ashore and see this orgy more nearly; but Reïs Hassan shakes his head. The natives hereabout are said to be quarelsome; and if, as it is probable, they are celebrating the festival of some local saint, we might be treated as intruders.

Coming at early morning to Gerf Hossayn, we make our way up to the Temple, which is excavated in the face of a limestone cliff, a couple of hundred feet, perhaps, above the river. A steep path, glaring hot in the sun, leads to a terrace in the rock; the Temple being approached through the ruins of a built-out portico and an avenue of battered colossi. It is a gloomy place within—an inferior edition, so to say, of the Great Temple of Aboo Simbel; and of the same date. It consists of a first hall supported by Osiride pillars, a second and smaller hall with square columns; a smoke-blackened sanctuary; and two side-chambers. The Osiride colossi, which stand 20 feet high without the entablature over their heads or the pedestal under their feet, are thick-set, bow-legged, and mis-shapen. Their faces would seem to have been painted black originally; while those of the avenue outside have distinctly Ethiopian features. One seems to detect here, as at Derr and Wady Sabooah, the work of provincial sculptors; just as at Aboo Simbel one recognises the master-style of the artists of the Theban Ramesseum.

The side-chambers at Gerf Hossayn are infested with bats. These bats are the great sight of the place, and have their appointed showman. We find him waiting for us with an end of tarred rope, which he flings, blazing, into the pitch-dark doorway. For a moment we see the whole ceiling hung, as it were, with a close fringe of white, filmy-looking pendants. But it is only for a moment. The next instant the creatures are all in motion, dashing out madly in our faces like driven snow-flakes. We picked up a dead one afterwards, when the rush was over, and examined it by the outer daylight—a lovely little creature, white and downy, with fine transparent wings, and little pink feet, and the prettiest mousey mouth imaginable.

Bordered with dwarf palms, acacias, and henna-bushes, the cliffs between Gerf Hossayn and Dendoor stand out in detached masses so like ruins that sometimes we can hardly believe they are rocks. At Dendoor, when the sun is setting and a delicious gloom is stealing up the valley, we visit a tiny Temple on the western bank. It stands out above the river surrounded by a wall of enclosure, and consists of a single pylon, a portico, two little chambers, and a sanctuary. The whole thing is like an exquisite toy, so covered with sculptures, so smooth, so new-looking, so admirably built. Seeing them half by sunset, half by dusk, it matters not that these delicately-wrought bas-reliefs are of the Decadence school.* The rosy half-light of

* "C'est un ouvrage non achevé du temps de l'empereur Auguste. Quoi que peu important par son étendue, ce monument m'a beaucoup interessé,

an Egyptian after-glow covers a multitude of sins, and
steeps the whole in an atmosphere of romance.

Wondering what has happened to the climate, we
wake shivering next morning an hour or so before
break of day, and, for the first time in several weeks,
taste the old early chill upon the air. When the sun
rises, we find ourselves at Kalabsheh, having passed
the limit of the Tropic during the night. Henceforth,
no matter how great the heat may be by day, this chill
invariably comes with the dark hour before dawn.

The usual yelling crowd, with the usual beads,
baskets, eggs, and pigeons, for sale, greets us on the
shore at Kalabsheh. One of the men has a fine old
two-handed sword in a shabby blue velvet sheath, for
which he asks five Napoleons. It looks as if it might
have belonged to a crusader. Some of the women
bring buffalo-cream in filthy-looking black skins slung
round their waists like girdles. The cream is excellent; but the skins temper one's enjoyment of the
unaccustomed dainty.

There is a magnificent Temple here, and close by,
excavated in the cliff, a rock-cut Speos, the local name
of which is Bayt-el-Welly. The sculptures of this
famous Speos have been more frequently described
and engraved than almost any sculptures in Egypt.
The procession of Ethiopian tribute-bearers, the assault of the Amorite city, the Triumph of Rameses, are
familiar not only to every reader of Wilkinson, but to
every visitor passing through the Egyptian Rooms of
the British Museum *. Notwithstanding the casts that

puisqu'il est entièrement relatif à l'incarnation d'Osiris sous forme humaine, sur
la terre."—*Lettres écrites d'Égypte*, etc.: CHAMPOLLION. Paris, 1868, p. 126.
    * See Chapter XV. p. 46 of this volume.

have been taken from them, and the ill-treatment to
which they have been subjected by natives and visitors,
they are still beautiful. The colour of those in the
roofless courtyard, though so perfect when Mr. Bonomi
executed his admirable facsimiles, has now almost
entirely peeled off; but in the portico and inner
chambers it is yet brilliant. An emerald green Osiris,
a crimson Anubis, and an Isis of the brightest chrome
yellow, are astonishingly pure and forcible in quality.
As for the flesh-tones of the Anubis, this was I believe
the only instance I observed of a true crimson in
Egyptian pigments.

Between the Speos of Bayt-el-Welly and the neighbouring Temple of Kalabsheh there lies about half-a-
mile of hilly pathway and a gulf of 1400 years. Rameses ushers us into the presence of Augustus, and we
pass, as it were, from an oratory in the Great House
of Pharaoh to the presence chamber of the Cæsars.

But if the decorative work in the presence-chamber
of the Cæsars was anything like the decorative work in
the Temple of Kalabsheh, then the taste thereof was of
the vilest. Such a masquerade of deities; such striped
and spotted and cross-barred robes; such outrageous
head-dresses; such crude and violent colouring, * we
have never seen the like of. As for the goddesses,
they are gaudier than the dancing damsels of Luxor;
while the kings balance on their heads diadems com-
pounded of horns, moons, birds, balls, beetles, lotus-
blossoms, asps, vases, and feathers. The Temple however, is conceived on a grand scale. It is the Karnak
of Nubia. But it is a Karnak that has evidently been

* I observed mauve here, for the first and only time; and very brilliant
ultramarine. There are also traces of gilding on many of the figures.

visited by a shock of earthquake far more severe than
that which shook the mighty pillars of the Hypostyle
Hall and flung down the obelisk of Hatasu. From the
river, it looks like a huge fortress; but seen from the
threshold of the main gateway, it is a wilderness of
ruin. Fallen blocks, pillars, capitals, entablatures, lie
so extravagantly piled, that there is not one spot in all
those halls and courtyards upon which it is possible to
set one's foot on the level of the original pavement.
Here, again, the earthquake seems to have come before the work was completed. There are figures outlined on the walls, but never sculptured. Others have
been begun, but never finished. You can see where
the chisel stopped—you can even detect which was
the last mark it made on the surface. One traces
here, in fact, the four processes of wall-decoration. In
some places the space is squared off and ruled by the
mechanic; in others, the subject is ready drawn within
those spaces by the artist. Here the sculptor has
carried it a stage farther; yonder the painter has begun
to colour it.

More interesting, however, than aught else at Kalabsheh is the Greek inscription of Silco of Ethiopia.*
This inscription—made famous by the commentaries
of Niebuhr and Letronne—was discovered by M. Gau
in A.D. 1818. It consists of 21 lines very neatly written
in red ink, and it dates from the sixth century of the
Christian era. It commences thus:—

> I, Silco, puissant king of the Nubians and all the Ethiopians,
> I came twice as far as Talmis** and Taphis.***

* See Chapterr XII., p. 278 of vol. i.
** TALMIS: (Kalabsheh).
*** TAPHIS: (Tafah).

I fought against the Blemyes,* and God granted me the victory.
I vanquished them a second time; and the first time
I established myself completely with my troops.
I vanquished them, and they supplicated me.
I made peace with them; and they swore to me by their idols.
I trusted them; because they are a people of good faith.
Then I returned to my dominions in the Upper Country.
For I am a powerful king.
Not only am I no follower in the train of other kings,
But I go before them.
As for those who seek strife against me,
I give them no peace in their homes till they entreat my pardon.
For I am a lion on the plains, and a goat upon the mountains.
                    etc. etc. etc.

The historical value of this inscription is very great.
It shows that in the sixth century, while the native inhabitants of this part of the Valley of the Nile yet ad-
hered to the ancient Egyptian faith, the Ethiopians of
the south were professedly Christian.

The descendants of the Blemmys are a fine race;
tall, strong, and of a rich chocolate complexion. Strolling through the village at sunset, we see the entire population—old men sitting at their doors; young men
lounging and smoking; children at play. The women,
with glittering white teeth and liquid eyes, and a profusion of gold and silver ornaments on neck and brow,
come out with their little brown babies astride on hip
or shoulder, to stare as we go by. One sick old woman, lying outside her hut on a palm-wood couch,
raises herself for a moment on her elbow—then sinks
back with a weary sigh, and turns her face to the wall.
The mud dwellings here are built in and out of a
maze of massive stone foundations, the remains of

* Blemyes:—The Blemyes were a nomadic race of Berbers, supposed to
be originally of the tribe of Bilmas of Tibbous in the central desert, and settled
as early as the time of Eratosthenes in that part of the Valley of the Nile which
lies between the First and Second Cataracts. See *Le Nord de l'Afrique*, by
M. V. DE ST. MARTIN. Paris, 1863, Section III. p. 73.

buildings once magnificent. Some of these walls are
built in concave courses; each course of stones, that is
to say, being depressed in the centre, and raised at
the angles; which mode of construction was adopted
in order to offer less resistance when shaken by earthquake. *

We observe more foundations built thus, at Tafah,
where we arrive next morning. As the mason's work
at Tafah is of a late Roman date, it follows that earth-
quakes were yet frequent in Nubia at a period long
subsequent to the great shock of B.C. 27, mentioned by
Eusebius. Travellers are too ready to ascribe everything in the way of ruin to the fury of Cambyses and
the pious rage of the early Christians. Nothing, however, is easier than to distinguish between the damage
done to the monuments by the hand of man, and the
damage caused by subterraneous upheaval. Mutilation
is the rule in the one case; displacement in the other.
At Denderah, for example, the injury done is wholly
wilful; at Aboo Simbel, it is wholly accidental; at
Karnak, it is both wilful and accidental. As for Kalabsheh, it is clear that no such tremendous havoc
could have been effected by human means without the
aid of powerful rams, fire, or gunpowder; any of which
must have left unmistakeable traces.

At Tafah there are two little temples; one in picturesque ruin, one quite perfect, and now used as a
stable. There are also a number of stone foundations;
separate; quadrangular; subdivided into numerous small
chambers, and enclosed in boundary walls, some of
which are built in the concave courses just named.

* See *The Habitations of Man in all Ages.* V. LE DUC. Chap. IX. p. 93.

These substructions, of which the Painter counted eighteen, have long been the puzzle of travellers.*

Tafah is charmingly placed; and the seven miles which divide it from Kalabsheh—once, no doubt, the scene of a cataract—are perhaps the most picturesque on this side of Wady Halfeh. Rocky islets in the river; palm-groves, acacias, carobs, henna and castor-berry bushes, and all kinds of flowering shrubs, along the edges of the banks; fantastic precipices riven and pinnacled, here rising abruptly from the water's edge, and there from the sandy plain, make lovely sketches whichever way one turns. There are gazelles, it is said, in the ravines behind Tafah; and one of the natives—a truculent fellow in a ragged shirt and dirty white turban—tells how, at a distance of three hours up a certain glen, there is another Birbeh, larger than either of these in the plain, and a great standing statue taller than three men. Here, then, if the tale be true, is another ready-made discovery for whoever may care to undertake it.

This same native, having sold a necklace to the Idle Man and gone away content with his bargain, comes back by and by with half the village at his heels, requiring double price. This modest demand being refused, he rages up and down like a maniac; tears off his turban; goes through a wild manual exer-

* They probably mark the site of a certain Coptic monastery described in an ancient Arabic MS. quoted by E. Quatremere, which says that "in the town of Tafah there is a fine monastery of Ansoun. It is very ancient; but so solidly built, that after so great a number of years it still stands uninjured. Near this monastery, facing the mountain, are situated fifteen villages." See *Mémoires Hist. et Géographiques sur l'Egypte et la Nubie*, par E. QUATRE- MERE. Paris, 1811, vol. II. p. 55.

The monastery and the villages were, doubtless, of Romano-Egyptian con- struction in the first instance, and may originally have been a sacred College, like the sacred College at Philæ.

11*

cise with his spear; then sits down in stately silence, with his friends and neighbours drawn up in a semi-circle behind him.

This, it seems, is Nubian for a challenge. He has thrown down his gauntlet in form, and demands trial by combat. The noisy crowd, meanwhile, increases every moment. Reïs Hassan looks grave, fearing a possible fracas; and the Idle Man, who is reading the morning service down below (for it is on a Sunday morning) can scarcely be heard for the clamour out-side. In this emergency, it occurs to the Writer to send a message ashore informing these gentlemen that the Howadjis are holding mosque in the Dahabeeyah, and entreating them to be quiet till the hour of prayer is past. The effect of the message, strange to say, is instantaneous. The angry voices are at once hushed. The challenger puts on his turban. The assembled spectators squat in respectful silence on the bank. A whole hour goes by thus, so giving the storm time to blow over; and when the Idle Man reappears on deck, his would-be adversary comes forward quite pleasantly to discuss the purchase afresh.

It matters little how the affair ended; but I be-lieve he was offered his necklace back in exchange for the money paid, and preferred to abide by his bar-gain. It is as evidence of the sincerity of the reli-gious sentiment in the minds of a semi-savage people,* that I have thought the incident worth telling.

---

* "The peasants of Tafa relate that they are the descendants of the few Christian inhabitants of the city who embraced the Mahommedan faith when the country was conquered by the followers of the Prophet; the greater part of their brethren having either fled or been put to death on that event taking place. They are still called Oulad el Nusara, or the Christian progeny."— *Travels in Nubia:* BURCKHARDT. London 1819, p. 121.

We are now less than forty miles from Philæ; but the head wind is always against us, and the men's bread is exhausted, and there is no flour to be bought in these Nubian villages. The poor fellows swept out the last crumbs from the bottom of their bread-chest three or four days ago, and are now living on quarter-rations of lentil soup, and a few dried dates bought at Wady Halfeh. Patient and depressed, they crouch silently beside their oars, or forget their hunger in sleep. For ourselves, it is painful to witness their need, and still more painful to be unable to help them. Talhamy, whose own stores are at a low ebb, vows he can do nothing. It would take his few remaining tins of preserved meat to feed fifteen men for two days, and of flour he has barely enough for the Howadjis. Hungry? well, yes—no doubt they are hungry. But what of that? They are Arabs; and Arabs bear hunger as camels bear thirst. It is nothing new to them. They have often been hungry before—they will often be hungry again. Enough! It is not for the ladies to trouble themselves about such fellows as these!

Excellent advice, no doubt; but hard to follow. Not to be troubled, and not to do what little we can for the poor lads, is impossible. When that little means laying violent hands on Talhamy's reserve of eggs and biscuits, and getting up lotteries for prizes of chocolate and tobacco, that worthy evidently considers that we have taken leave of our wits.

Under a burning sky, we touch for an hour or two at Gertasseh, and then push on for Dabod. The lime-stone quarries at Gertasseh are full of votive sculptures and inscriptions; and the little ruin—a mere cluster of graceful columns supporting a fragment of cornice—

stands high on the brink of a cliff overhanging the river. Take it as you will, from above or below, looking North or looking South, it makes a charming sketch.

If transported to Dabod on that magic carpet of the fairy-tale, one would take it for a ruin on the "beached margent" of some placid lake in dreamland. It lies between two bends of the river, which here flows wide, showing no outlet and seeming to be girdled by mountains and palm-groves. The Temple is small and uninteresting; begun, like Dakkeh, by an Ethiopian king, and finished by Ptolemies and Cæsars. The one curious thing about it is a secret cell, most cunningly devised. Adjoining the sanctuary is a dark side-chamber; in the floor of the side-chamber is a pit, once paved over; in one corner of the pit is a man-hole opening into a narrow passage; and in the narrow passage are steps leading up to a secret chamber constructed in the thickness of the wall. We saw other secret chambers in other Temples;* but not one in which the old approaches were so perfectly preserved.

From Dabod to Philæ is but ten miles; and we are bound for Torrigoor, which is two miles nearer. Now Torrigoor is that same village at the foot of the beauti-

---

* In these secret chambers (the entrance to which was closed by a block of masonry so perfectly fitted as to defy detection) were kept, says M. Mariette, the images of gold and silver and lapis lazuli, the precious vases, the sistrums, the jewelled collars, and all the portable treasures of the Temples. We saw a somewhat similar pit and small chamber in a corner of the Temple of Dakkeh, and some very curious crypts and hiding places under the floor of the dark chamber to the E. of the Sanctuary at Philæ, all of course long since broken open and rifled. But we had strong reason to believe that the Painter discovered the whereabouts of a hidden chamber or passage to the W. of the Sanctuary, yet closed, with all its treasures probably intact. We had, however, no means of opening the wall, which is of solid masonry.

ful sand-drift, near which we moored on our way up the river; and here we are to stay two days, followed by at least a week at Philæ. No sooner, therefore, have we reached Torrigoor, than Reïs Hassan and three sailors start for Assouan to buy flour. Old Ali, Riskalli, and Moosa, whose homes lie in the villages round about, get leave of absence for a week; and we find ourselves reduced all at once to a crew of five, with only Khaleefeh in command. Five, however, are as good as fifty, when the Dahabeeyah lies moored and there is nothing to do; and our five, having succeeded in buying some flabby Nubian cakes and green lentils, are now quite happy. So the Painter pitches his tent at the top of the sand-drift; and the Writer sketches the ruined convent opposite; and L. and the Little Lady write no end of letters; and the Idle Man, with Mehemet Ali for a retriever, shoots quail; and everybody is satisfied.

Hapless Idle Man!—hapless, but homicidal. If he had been content to shoot only quail, and had not taken to shooting babies! What possessed him to do it? Not—not, let us hope—an ill-directed ambition, foiled of crocodiles! He went serene and smiling, with his gun under his arm, and Mehemet Ali in his wake. Who so light of heart as that Idle Man? Who so light of heel as that turbaned retriever? We heard our sportsman popping away presently in the barley. It was a pleasant sound, for we knew his aim was true. "Every shot," said we, "means a bird." We little dreamed that one of those shots meant a baby.

All at once, a woman screamed. It was a sharp, sudden scream, following a shot—a scream with a ring of horror in it. Instantly it was caught up from point to point, growing in volume and seeming to be echoed from every direction at once. At the same moment, the bank became alive with human beings. They seemed to spring from the soil—women shriek-ing and waving their arms; men running; all making for the same goal. The Writer heard the scream, saw the rush, and knew at once that a gun accident had happened.

A few minutes of painful suspense followed. Then Mehemet Ali appeared, tearing back at the top of his speed; and presently — perhaps five minutes later, though it seemed like twenty—came the Idle Man; walking very slowly and defiantly, with his head up, his arms folded, his gun gone, and an immense rabble at his heels.

Our scanty crew, armed with sticks, flew at once to the rescue, and brought him off in safety. We then learned what had happened.

A flight of quail had risen; and as quail fly low, skimming the surface of the grain and diving down again almost immediately, he had taken a level aim. At the instant that he fired, and in the very path of the quail, a woman and child who had been squatting in the barley, sprang up screaming. He at once saw the coming danger; and, with admirable presence of mind, drew the charge of his second barrel. He then hid his cartridge-box and hugged his gun, determined to hold it as long as possible. The next moment he was surrounded, overpowered, had the gun wrenched from his grasp, and received a blow on the back with a stone. Having captured the gun, one or two of the men let go. It was then that he shook off the rest, and came back to the boat. Mehemet Ali at the same time flew to call a rescue. He, too, came in for some hard knocks, besides having his shirt rent, and his turban torn off his head.

Here were we, meanwhile, with less than half our crew, a private war on our hands, no captain, and one of our three guns in the hands of the enemy. What a scene it was! A whole village, and apparently a very considerable village, swarming on the bank; all hurrying to and fro; all raving, shouting, gesticulating. If we had been on the verge of a fracas at Tafah, here we were threatened with a siege.

Drawing in the plank between the boat and the shore, we held a hasty council of war.

The woman being unhurt, and the child, if hurt at all, hurt very slightly, we felt justified in assuming an injured tone, calling the village to account for a case of cowardly assault, and demanding instant restitution of the gun. We accordingly sent Talhamy to parley with the head-man of the place and peremptorily demand the gun. We also bade him add—and this we regarded as a master-stroke of policy—that if due submission was immediately made, the Howadji, one of whom was a Hakeem, would permit the father to bring his child on board to have its hurts attended to.

Outwardly indifferent, inwardly not a little anxious, we waited the event. Talhamy's back being towards the river, we had the whole semicircle of swarthy faces full in view—bent brows, flashing eyes, glittering teeth; all anger, all scorn, all defiance. Suddenly the expression of the faces changed—the change beginning with those nearest the speaker, and spreading gradually outwards. It was as if a wave had passed over them. We knew then that our *coup* was made. Talhamy returned. The villagers crowded round their leaders, deliberating. Numbers now began to sit down; and when a Nubian sits down, you may be sure that he is no longer dangerous.

Presently—after perhaps a quarter of an hour—the gun was brought back uninjured, and an elderly man carrying a blue blundle appeared on the bank. The plank was now put across; the crowd was kept off; and the man with the bundle, and three or four others, were allowed to pass.

The bundle being undone, a little brown imp of about four years of age, with shaven head and shaggy scalp-lock, was produced. He whimpered at first, see-ing the strange white faces; but when offered a fig, forgot his terrors, and sat munching it like a monkey. As for his wounds, they were literally skin-deep, the shot having but slightly grazed his shoulders in four or five places. The Idle Man, however, solemnly sponged the scratches with warm water, and L. covered them with patches of sticking-plaister. Finally, the father was presented with a Napoleon; the patient was wrapped in one of his murderer's shirts; and the first act of the tragedy ended. The second and third acts were to come.

When the Painter and the Idle Man talked the affair over, they agreed that it was expedient, for the protection of future travellers, to lodge a complaint against the village; and this mainly on account of the treacherous blow dealt from behind, at a time when the Idle Man (who had not once attempted to defend himself) was powerless in the hands of a mob. They therefore went next day to Assouan; and the governor, charming as ever, promised that justice should be done. Meanwhile we moved the Dahabeeyah to Philæ, and there settled down for a week's sketching.

Next evening came a woful deputation from Torrigoor, entreating forgiveness, and stating that fifteen villagers had been swept off to prison.

The Idle Man explained that he no longer had anything to do with it; that the matter, in short, was in the hands of justice, and would be dealt with according to law. Hereupon the spokesman gathered up a handful of imaginary dust, and made believe to scatter it on his head.

"O dragoman!" he said, "tell the Howadji that there is no law but his pleasure, and no justice but the will of the Governor!"

Summoned next morning to give evidence, the Idle Man went betimes to Assouan, where he was received in private by the Governor and Moodeer. Pipes and coffee were handed, and the usual civilities exchanged. The Governor then informed his guest that fifteen men of Torrigoor had been arrested; and that fourteen of them unanimously identified the fifteenth as the one who struck the blow.

"And now," said the Governor, "before we send for the prisoners, it will be as well to decide on the sentence. What does his Excellency wish done to them?"

The Idle Man was puzzled. How could he offer an opinion, being ignorant of the Egyptian civil code? and how could the sentence be decided upon before the trial?

The Governor smiled serenely.

"But," he said, "this is the trial."

Being an Englishman, it necessarily cost the Idle

Man an effort to realise the full force of this explanation—an explanation which, in its sublime simplicity,
epitomised the whole system of the judicial administration of Egyptian law.   He hastened, however, to explain that he cherished no resentment against the
culprit or the villagers, and that his only wish was
to frighten them into a due respect for travellers in
general.

The Governor hereupon invited the Moodeer to
suggest a sentence; and the Moodeer—taking into consideration, as he said, his Excellency's lenient disposi-
tion—proposed to award to the fourteen innocent men
one month's imprisonment each; and to the real of-
fender two months' imprisonment, with a hundred and
fifty blows of the bastinado.

Shocked at the mere idea of such a sentence, the
Idle Man declared that he must have the innocent set
at liberty; but consented that the culprit, for the sake
of example, should be sentenced to the one hundred
and fifty blows—the punishment to be remitted after
the first few strokes had been dealt.   Word was now
given for the prisoners to be brought in.

The gaoler marched first, followed by two soldiers.
Then came the fifteen prisoners—I am ashamed to
write it!—chained neck to neck in single file.

One can imagine how the Idle Man felt at this
moment.

Sentence being pronounced, the fourteen looked as
if they could hardly believe their ears; while the fifteenth, though condemned to his one hundred and
fifty strokes ("seventy-five to each foot," specified the
Governor), was overjoyed to be let off so easily.

He was then flung down; his feet were fastened

soles uppermost; and two soldiers proceeded to execute
the sentence. As each blow fell, he cried:—"God save
the Governor! God save the Moodeer! God save the
Howadji!"

When the sixth stroke had been dealt, the Idle
Man turned to the Governor and formally interceded
for the remission of the rest of the sentence. The
Governor, as formally, granted the request; and the
prisoners, weeping for joy, were set at liberty.

The Governor, the Moodeer, and the Idle Man then
parted with a profusion of compliments; the Governor
protesting that his only wish was to be agreeable to
the English, and that the whole village should have
been bastinadoed, had his Excellency desired it.

We spent eight enchanted days at Philæ; and it so
happened, when the afternoon of the eighth came
round, that for the last few hours the Writer was alone
on the island. Alone, that is to say, with only a sailor
in attendance, which was virtually solitude; and Philæ
is a place to which solitude adds an inexpressible
touch of pathos and remoteness.

It has been a hot day, and there is dead calm on
the river. My last sketch finished, I wander slowly
round from spot to spot, saying farewell to Pharaoh's
Bed—to the Painted Columns—to every terrace, and
palm, and shrine, and familiar point of view. I peep
once again into the mystic chamber of Osiris. I see
the sun set for the last time from the roof of the
Temple of Isis. Then, when all that wondrous flush
of rose and gold has died away, comes the warm after-
glow. No words can paint the melancholy beauty of

Philæ at this hour. The surrounding mountains stand out jagged and purple against a pale amber sky. The Nile is glassy. Not a breath, not a bubble, troubles the inverted landscape. Every palm is twofold; every stone is doubled. The big boulders in mid-stream are reflected so perfectly that it is impossible to tell where the rock ends and the water begins. The Temples, meanwhile, have turned to a subdued golden bronze; and the pylons are peopled with shapes that glow with fantastic life, and look ready to step down from their places.

The solitude is perfect, and there is a magical stillness in the air. I hear a mother crooning to her baby on the neighbouring island—a sparrow twittering in its little nest in the capital of a column below my feet—a vulture screaming plaintively among the rocks in the far distance.

I look; I listen; I promise myself that I will remember it all in years to come—all these solemn hills, these silent colonnades, these deep, quiet spaces of shadow, these sleeping palms. Lingering till it is all but dark, I at last bid them farewell, fearing lest I may behold them no more.

CHAPTER XX.

Silsilis and Edfoo.

GOING, it cost us four days to struggle up from Assouan to Mahatta; returning, we slid down—thanks to our old friend the Sheykh of the Cataract—in one short, sensational half-hour. He came—flat-faced, fishy-eyed, fatuous as ever—with his head tied up in the same old yellow handkerchief, and with the same chibouque in his mouth. He brought with him a following of fifty stalwart Shellalees; and under his arm he carried a tattered red flag. This flag, on which were embroidered the crescent and star, he hoisted with much solemnity at the prow.

Consigned thus to the protection of the Prophet; windows and tambooshy * shuttered up; doors closed; breakables removed to a place of safety, and everything made snug, as if for a storm at sea, we put off from Mahatta at seven A.M. on a lovely morning in the middle of March. The Philæ, instead of threading her way back through the old channels, strikes across to the Libyan side, making straight for the Big-Bab—that formidable rapid which as yet we have not seen. All last night we heard its voice in the distance; now, at every stroke of the oars, that rushing sound draws nearer.

The Sheykh of the Cataract is our captain, and his men are our sailors to-day; Reïs Hassan and the crew

---

* *Ar.* Tambooshy—*i.e.*, saloon sky-light.

having only to sit still and look on. The Shellalees,
meanwhile, row swiftly and steadily. Already the river
seems to be running faster than usual; already the current feels stronger under our keel. And now, suddenly,
there is sparkle and foam on the surface yonder—there
are rocks ahead; rocks to right and left; eddies everywhere. The Sheykh lays down his pipe, kicks off his
shoes, and goes himself to the prow. His second in
command is stationed at the top of the stairs leading
to the upper deck. Six men take the tiller. The
rowers are reinforced, and sit two to each oar.

In the midst of these preparations, when everybody
looks grave, and even the Arabs are silent, we all at
once find ourselves at the mouth of a long and narrow
strait—a kind of ravine between two walls of rock—
through which, at a steep incline, there rushes a roaring mass of waters. The whole Nile, in fact, seems
to be thundering in wild waves down that terrible
channel.

It seems, at first sight, impossible that any Dahabeeyah should venture that way and not be dashed to
pieces. Neither does there seem room for boat and
oars to pass. The Sheykh, however, gives the word—
his second echoes it—the men at the helm obey.
They put the Dahabeeyah straight at that monster
mill-race. For one breathless second we seem to
tremble on the edge of the fall. Then the Philæ
plunges in headlong!

We see the whole boat slope down bodily under
our feet. We feel the leap—the dead fall—the staggering rush forward. Instantly the waves are foaming
and boiling up on all sides, flooding the lower deck,
and covering the upper deck with spray. The men

ship their oars, leaving all to helm and current; and, despite the hoarse tumult, we distinctly hear those oars scrape the rocks on either side.

Now the Sheykh, looking for the moment quite majestic, stands motionless with uplifted arm; for at the end of the pass there is a sharp turn to the right—as sharp as a street corner in a narrow London thorough-fare. Can the Philæ, measuring 100 feet from stem to stern, ever round that angle in safety? Suddenly, the uplifted arm is waved—the Sheykh thunders "Daffet!" (helm)—the men, steady and prompt, put the helm about—the boat, answering splendidly to the word of command, begins to turn before we are out of the rocks; then, shooting round the corner at exactly the right moment, comes out safe and sound, with only an oar broken!

Great is the rejoicing. Reïs Hassan, in the joy of his heart, runs to shake hands all round; the Arabs burst into a chorus of "Taibs" and "Salames;" and Talhamy, coming up all smiles, is set upon by half-a-dozen playful Shellalees, who snatch his kefiah from his head, and carry it off as a trophy. The only one unmoved is the Sheykh of the Cataract. His momentary flash of energy over, he slouches back with the old stolid face; slips on his shoes; drops on his heels; lights his pipe; and looks more like an owl than ever.

We had fancied till now that the Cataract Arabs for their own profit, and travellers for their own glory, had grossly exaggerated the dangers of the Big Bab. But such is not the case. The Big Bab is in truth a serious undertaking; so serious that I doubt whether any English boatmen would venture to take such a

boat down such a rapid, and between such rocks, as
the Shellalee Arabs took the Philæ that day.

All Dahabeeyahs, however, are not so lucky. Of
thirty-four that shot the fall this season, several had
been slightly damaged, and one was so disabled that
she had to lie up at Assouan for a fortnight to be
mended. Of actual shipwreck, or injury to life and
limb, I do not suppose there is any real danger. The
Shellalees are wonderfully cool and skilful, and have
abundant practice. Our Painter, it is true, preferred
rolling up his canvases and carrying them round on
dry land by way of the desert; but this was a precaution that neither he nor any of us would have
dreamed of taking on account of our own personal
safety. There is, in fact, little, if anything, to fear;
and the traveller who foregoes the descent of the
Cataract, foregoes a very curious sight, and a very exciting adventure.

At Assouan we bade farewell to Nubia and the
blameless Ethiopians, and found ourselves once more
traversing the Nile of Egypt. If instead of five miles
of Cataract we had crossed five hundred miles of sea
or desert, the change could not have been more complete. We left behind us a dreamy river, a silent shore,
an ever-present desert. Returning, we plunged back at
once into the midst of a fertile and populous region.
All day long, now, we see boats on the river; villages
on the banks; birds on the wing; husbandmen on the
land; men and women, horses, camels and asses, passing perpetually to and fro on the towing-path. There
is always something moving, something doing. The
Nile is running low, and the shadoofs—three deep, now
—are in full swing from morning till night. Again the

smoke goes up from clusters of unseen huts at close of day. Again we hear the dogs barking from hamlet to hamlet in the still hours of the night. Again, towards sunset, we see troops of girls coming down to the river-side with their water-jars on their heads. Those Arab maidens, when they stand with garments tightly tucked up and just their feet in the water, dipping the goollah at arm's length in the fresher gush of the current, almost tempt one's pencil into the forbidden paths of caricature.

Kom Ombo is a magnificent torso. It was as large once as Denderah—perhaps larger; for, being on the same grand scale, it was a double Temple and dedicated to two Gods, Horus and Sevek;* the Hawk and the Crocodile. Now there remain only a few giant columns buried to within eight or ten feet of their gorgeous capitals; a superb fragment of archi-trave; one broken wave of sculptured cornice and some fallen blocks graven with the names of Ptolemies and Cleopatras.

A great double doorway, a hall of columns, and a double sanctuary, are said to be yet perfect; though no longer accessible. The roofing blocks of three halls, one behind the other, and a few capitals, are yet visible behind the portico. What more may lie buried below the surface, none can tell. We only know that an ancient city and a mediæval hamlet have been slowly engulfed; and that an early Temple, contemporary with the Temple of Amada, once stood within the sacred enclosure. The sand here has been accumulating for

* "Sebek est un dieu solaire. Dans un papyrus de Boulak, il est appelé fils d'Isis, et il combat les ennemis d'Osiris; c'est une assimilation complète à Horus, et c'est à ce titre qu'il était adoré à Ombos."—*Dict. Arch.* P. PIERRET. Paris, 1875.

2000 years. It lies forty feet deep, and has never been excavated. It will never be excavated now; for the Nile is gradually sapping the bank, and carrying away piecemeal from below what the desert has buried from above. Half of one noble pylon—a cataract of sculptured blocks—strews the steep slope from top to bottom. The other half hangs suspended on the brink of the precipice. It cannot hang so much longer. A day must soon come when it will collapse with a crash, and thunder down like its fellow.

Between Kom Ombo and Silsilis, we lost our Painter. Not that he either strayed or was stolen; but that, having accomplished the main object of his journey, he was glad to seize the first opportunity of getting back quickly to Cairo. That opportunity—represented by a noble Duke honeymooning with a steam-tug—happened half-way between Kom Ombo and Silsilis. Painter and Duke being acquaintances of old, the matter was soon settled. In less than a quarter of an hour, the big picture and all the paraphernalia of the studio were transported from the stern-cabin of the Philæ to the stern-cabin of the steam-tug; and our Painter—fitted out with an extempore canteen, a cook-boy, a waiter, and his fair share of the necessaries of life—was soon disappearing gaily in the distance at the rate of twenty miles an hour. If the Happy Couple, so weary of head-winds, so satiated with Temples, followed that vanishing steam-tug with eyes of melancholy longing, the Writer at least asked nothing better than to drift on with the Philæ.

Still, the Nile is long, and life is short; and the tale told by our logbook was certainly not encouraging. When we reached Silsilis on the morning of the

17th of March, the north wind had been blowing with only one day's intermission since the 1st of February.

At Silsilis, one looks in vain for traces of that great barrier which once blocked the Nile at this point. The stream is narrow here, and the sandstone cliffs come down on both sides to the water's edge. In some places there is space for a footpath; in others, none. There are also some sunken rocks in the bed of the river—upon one of which, by the way, a Cook's steamer had struck two days before. But of such a mass as could have dammed the Nile, and, by its disruption not only have caused the river to desert its bed at Philæ,* but have changed the whole physical and climatic conditions of Lower Nubia, there is no sign whatever.

The Arabs here show a rock fantastically quarried in the shape of a gigantic umbrella, to which they pretend some king of old attached one end of a chain with which he barred the Nile. It may be that in this apocryphal legend there survives some memory of the ancient barrier.

The cliffs of the western bank are rich in memorial niches, votive shrines, tombs, historical stelæ, and inscriptions. These last date from the VIth to the XXIId Dynasties. Some of the tombs and alcoves are very curious. Ranged side by side in a long row close above the river, and revealing glimpses of seated figures and gaudy decorations within, they look like private boxes with their occupants. In most of these we found mutilated triads of Gods,** sculptured and painted; and

* See Chap. XI. p. 259 of vol. 1.
** "Le point de départ de la mythologie égyptienne est une *Triade*." CHAMPOLLION, *Lettres d'Égypte*, etc., XIe Lettre. Paris 1868. These Triads are best studied at Gerf Hossayn and Kalabsheh.

in one larger than the rest were three niches, each
containing three deities.

The great Speos of Horus, the last Pharaoh of the
XVIIIth Dynasty, lies farthest north, and the memorial
shrines of the Rameses family lie farthest south of the
series. The first is a long gallery, like a cloister supported on four square columns; and is excavated parallel
with the river. The walls inside and out are covered
with delicately executed sculptures in low relief, some
of which yet retain traces of colour. The triumph of
Horus on his return from conquest in the land of Cush,
and the famous subject on the south wall described by
M. Mariette * as one of the few really lovely things in
Egyptian art, have been too often engraved to need
description. The votive shrines of the Rameses family
are grouped all together in a picturesque nook green
with bushes to the water's edge. There are three; the
work of Seti I., Rameses II., and Menephthah—lofty
alcoves, each like a little proscenium, with painted
cornices and side pillars, and groups of Kings and
Gods still bright with colour. In most of the votive
sculptures of Silsilis there figure two deities but rarely
seen elsewhere; namely Sevek, the Crocodile God of
the province, and Hapi, the lotus-crowned God of the
Nile. This last was, in fact, the tutelary deity of
the spot, and was worshipped at Silsilis with special
rites. Hymns in his honour are found carved here and

---

* "L'un (paroi du sud) représente une déesse nourrissant de son lait divin
le roi Horus, encore enfant. L'Égypte n'a jamais, comme la Grèce, atteint
l'idéal du beau . . . mais en tant qu'art Égyptien, le bas-relief du Spéos de
Gebel-Silsileh est une des plus belles œuvres que l'on puisse voir. Nulle part,
en effect, la ligne n'est plus pure, et il règne dans ce tableau une certaine
douceur tranquille qui charme et étonne à la fois."—*Itinéraire de la Haute
Égypte.* A. MARIETTE: 1872, p. 246.

there upon the rocks.* Most curious of all, however, is a Goddess named Ta-ur-t,** represented in one of the side subjects of the shrine of Rameses II. This charming person, who has the body of a hippopotamus and the face of a woman, wears a tie-wig and a robe of state with five capes, and looks like a cross between a Lord Chancellor and a Coachman. Behind her stand Thoth and Nut; all three receiving the homage of Queen Nofreari, who advances with an offering of two sistrums. As a hippopotamus crowned with the disk and horns we had met with this Goddess before. She is not uncommon as a terra-cotta amulet; and we had already met with her at Philæ, where she occupies a prominent place in the façade of the Mammisi. But the grotesque elegance of her attire at Silsilis is, I imagine, quite unique.

The interest of the western bank centres in its sculptures and inscriptions; the interest of the eastern bank, in its quarries. We rowed over to a point nearly opposite the shrines of the Ramessides, and, climbing a steep verge of débris, came to the mouth of a narrow cutting between walls of solid rock, from forty to fifty feet in height. These walls are smooth, clean-cut, and faultlessly perpendicular. The colour of the sand-

---

* See *Sallier Papyrus, No. 2.* HYMN TO THE NILE—translation by G. MASPERO. Paris, 1868.

** *Ta-ur-t,* or *Apet the Great.* "Cette Déesse à corps d'hippopotame debout et à mamelles pendantes, paraît être une sorte de déesse nourrice. Elle semble, dans le bas temps, je ne dirai pas se substituer à Maut, mais compléter le rôle de cette déesse. Elle est nommée la grande nourrice; et présidait aux chambres où étaient représentées les naissances des jeunes divinités."—*Dict. Arch.* P. PIERRET. Paris, 1875.

"In the heavens, this Goddess personified the constellation Ursa Major, or the Great Bear."—*Guide to the First and Second Egyptian Rooms.* S. BIRCH. London, 1874.

Ta-ur-t was the wife of Typhon.

stone is rich amber. The passage is about ten feet in
width and perhaps four hundred in length. Seen at a
little after mid-day, with one side in shadow, the
other in sunlight, and a narrow ribbon of blue sky
overhead, it is like nothing else in the world; unless,
perhaps, the entrance to Petra.

Following this passage, we came presently to an
immense area, at least as large as Belgrave Square;
beyond which, separated by a thin partition of rock,
opened a second and somewhat smaller area. On the
walls of these huge amphitheatres, the chisel-marks and
wedge-holes were as fresh as if the last blocks had
been taken hence but yesterday; yet it is some 2000
years since the place last rang to the blows of the
mallet, and echoed back the voices of the workmen.
From the days of the Theban Pharaohs to the days of
the Ptolemies and Cæsars, those echoes can never have
been silent. The Temples of Karnak and Luxor, of
Goornah, of Medinet Haboo, of Esneh and Edfoo and
Hermonthis, all came from here, and from the quarries
on the opposite side of the river.

Returning, we climbed long hills of chips; looked
down into valleys of débris; and came back at last to
the river-side by way of an ancient inclined plane, along
which the blocks were wont to be slid down to the transport boats below. But the most wonderful thing about
Silsilis is the way in which the quarrying has been
done. In all these halls and passages and amphitheatres, the sandstone has been sliced out smooth
and straight, like hay from a hayrick. Everywhere the
blocks have been taken out square; and everywhere
the best of the stone has been extracted, and the worst
left. Where it was fine in grain and even in colour, it

has been cut with the nicest economy. Where it was whitish, or brownish, or traversed by veins of violet, it has been left standing. Here and there, we saw places where the lower part had been removed, and the upper part left projecting; like the overhanging storeys of our old mediæval timber houses. Compared with this puissant and perfect quarrying, our rough-and-ready blasting looks like the work of savages.

Struggling hard against the wind, we left Silsilis that same afternoon. The wrecked steamer was now more than half under water. She had broken her back and begun filling immediately, with all Cook's party on board. Being rowed ashore with what necessaries they could gather together, these unfortunates had been obliged to encamp in tents borrowed from the Moodeer of the district. Luckily for them, a couple of homeward-bound Dahabeeyahs came by next morning, and took off as many as they could accommodate. The Duke's steam-tug received the rest. The tents were still there; and a gang of natives, under the superintendence of the Moodeer, were busy getting off all that could be saved from the wreck.

As evening drew on, our head-wind became a hurricane; and that hurricane lasted, day and night, for thirty-six hours. All this time the Nile was driving up against the current in great rollers, like rollers on the Cornish coast when tide and wind set together from the west. To hear them roaring past in the darkness of the night—to feel the Philæ rocking, shivering, straining at her mooring-ropes, and bumping perpetually against the bank, was far from pleasant. By day, the scene was extraordinary. There were no clouds; but the air was thick with sand, through which the sun glimmered feebly. Some palms, looking gray and ghost-like on the bank above, bent as if they must break before the blast. The Nile was yeasty, and flecked with brown foam, large lumps of which came swirling every now and then against our cabin windows. The opposite bank was simply nowhere. Judging only by what was visible from the deck, one would have vowed that the Dahabeeyah was moored against an open coast, with an angry sea coming in.

The wind fell about five A.M. the second day; when the men at once took to their oars, and by breakfast-time brought us to Edfoo. Nothing now could be more delicious than the weather. It was a cool, silvery, misty morning—such a morning as one never knows in Nubia, where the sun is no sooner up than one is plunged at once into the full blaze and stress of day. There were donkeys waiting for us on the bank, and our way lay for about a mile through barley flats and cotton plantations. The country looked rich; the people smiling and well-conditioned. We met a troop of them going down to the Dahabeeyah with sheep, pigeons, poultry, and a young ox for sale. Crossing a back-water bridged by a few rickety palm-trunks, we now approached the village, which is perched, as usual, on the mounds of the ancient city. Meanwhile the great pylons—seeming to grow larger every moment— rose, creamy in light, against a soft blue sky.

Riding through lanes of huts, we came presently to an open space and a long flight of roughly-built steps in front of the Temple. At the top of these steps we were standing on the level of the modern village. At the bottom we saw the massive pavement that marked the level of the ancient city. From that level rose the

pylons which even from afar off had looked so large.
We now found that those stupendous towers not only
soared to a height of about seventy-five feet above our
heads, but plunged down to a depth of at least forty
more beneath our feet.

Ten years ago nothing was visible of the great
Temple of Edfoo save the tops of these pylons. The
rest of the building was as much lost to sight as if the
earth had opened and swallowed it. Its courtyards
were choked with foul débris. Its sculptured chambers
were buried under forty feet of soil. Its terraced roof
was a maze of closely-packed huts, swarming with
human beings, poultry, dogs, kine, asses, and vermin.
Thanks to the enlightened liberality of the present
ruler of Egypt, M. Mariette has been enabled to cleanse
these Augæan stables. Writing himself of this tremendous task, he says:—"I caused to be demolished the
sixty-four houses which encumbered the roof, as well
as twenty-eight more which approached too near the
outer wall of the Temple. When the whole shall be
isolated from its present surroundings by a massive
wall, the work of restoration at Edfoo will be accomplished." *

That wall has not yet been built; but the encroach-
ing mound has been cut clean away all round the
building, now standing free in a deep open space, the
sides of which are in some places as perpendicular as
the quarried cliffs of Silsilis. In the midst of this pit,
like a risen God issuing from the grave, the huge
building stands before us in the sunshine, erect and
perfect. The effect at first sight is overwhelming.

* Letter of M. Mariette to Vᵗᵉ E. DE ROUGÉ; *Révue Archéologique*,
vol. II. p. 33, 1860.

Through the great doorway, fifty feet in height, we catch glimpses of a grand courtyard, and of a vista of doorways, one behind another. Going slowly down, we see farther into those dark and distant halls at every step. At the same time the pylons, covered with gigantic sculptures, tower higher and higher, and seem to shut out the sky. The custode—a pigmy of six foot two, in semi-European dress—looks up grinning, expectant of backsheesh. For there is actually a custode here, and, which is more to the purpose, a good strong gate, through which neither pilfering visitors nor pilfering Arabs can pass unnoticed.

Who enters that gate crosses the threshold of the past, and leaves two thousand years behind him. In these vast courts and storied halls all is unchanged. Every pavement, every column, every stair, is in its place. The roof, but for a few roofing-stones missing just over the sanctuary, is not only uninjured, but in good repair. The hieroglyphic inscriptions are as sharp and legible as the day they were cut. If here and there a capital, or the face of a human-headed deity, has been mutilated, these are blemishes which at first one scarcely observes, and which in no wise mar the wonderful effect of the whole. We cross that great courtyard in the full blaze of the morning sunlight. In the colonnades on either side there is shade, and in the pillared portico beyond, a darkness as of night; save where a patch of deep blue sky burns through a square opening in the roof, and is matched by a corresponding patch of blinding light on the pavement below. Hence we pass on through a hall of columns, two transverse corridors, a side chapel, a series of pitch-dark side chambers, and a sanctuary. Outside all these, surrounding the actual Temple on three sides, runs an external corridor open to the sky, and bounded by a superb wall full forty feet in height. When I have said that the entrance-front, with its twin pylons and central doorway, measures 250 feet in width by 125 feet in height; that the first courtyard measures more than 160 feet in length by 140 in width; that the entire length of the building is 450 feet, and that it covers an area of 80,000 square feet, I have stated facts of a kind which convey no more than a general idea of largeness to the ordinary reader. Of the harmony of the proportions, of the amazing size and strength of the individual parts, of the perfect workmanship, of the fine grain and creamy amber of the stone, no description can do more than vaguely suggest an indefinite notion.

Edfoo and Denderah may almost be called twin Temples. They belong to the same period. They are built very nearly after the same plan.* They are even allied in a religious sense; for the myths of Horus** and Hathor*** are interdependent; the one being strictly the complement of the other. Thus in the inscriptions of Edfoo we find perpetual allusion to the cultus of Denderah, and vice versa. Both Edfoo and Denderah are rich in inscriptions; but as the extent of wall-space

* Edfoo is the elder Temple; Denderah the copy. Where the architect of Denderah has departed from his model, it has invariably been for the worse.
** Horus:—"Dieu adoré dans plusieurs nomes de la basse Egypte. Le personnage d'Horus se rattache sous des noms différents, à deux générations divines. Sous le nom de Haroëris il est né de Seb et Nout, et par conséquent frère d'Osiris, dont il est le fils sons un autre nom. . . . Horus, armé d'un dard avec lequel il transperce les ennemis d'Osiris, est appelé Horus le Justicier."— Dict. Arch. P. P. PIERRET, article "Horus."
*** Hathor:—"Elle est, comme Neith, Maut, et Nout, la personnification de l'espace dans lequel se meut le soleil, dont Horus symbolise le lever: aussi son nom, Hat-hor, signifie-t-il littéralement, l'habitation d'Horus."—Ibid., article "Hathor."

is greater at Edfoo, so is the literary wealth of this
Temple greater than the literary wealth of Denderah.
It also seemed to me that the surface was more closely
filled in at Edfoo than at Denderah. Every wall, every
ceiling, every pillar, every architrave, every passage and
side-chamber however dark, every staircase, every doorway, the outer wall, of the Temple the inner side of
the great wall of circuit, the huge pylons from top to
bottom, are not only covered, but crowded, with figures
and hieroglyphs.   Among these we find no enormous
battle-subjects as at Aboo Simbel—no heroic recitals,
like the poem of Pentaour.   Those went out with the
Pharaohs, and were succeeded by tableaux of religious
rites and dialogues of gods and kings.   Such are the
stock subjects of Ptolemaic edifices.   They abound at
Denderah and Esneh, as well as at Edfoo. But at Edfoo there are more inscriptions of a miscellaneous character than in any Temple of Egypt; and it is precisely
this secular information that is to us so priceless. Here
are geographical lists of Nubian and Egyptian nomes,
with their principal cities, their products, and their
tutelary gods; lists of tributary provinces and princes;
lists of temples, and of the lands pertaining thereunto;
lists of canals, of ports, of lakes; kalendars of feasts
and fasts; astronomical tables; genealogies and chro-
nicles of the gods; lists of the priests and priestesses
of both Edfoo and Denderah, with their names; lists
also of singers and assistant functionaries; lists of offerings; hymns; invocations; and such a profusion of religious legends as make of the walls of Edfoo alone a
complete text-book of Egyptian mythology.*

---

* *Rapport sur une Mission en Egypte.* VICOMTE E. DE ROUGÉ. See
Révue Arch., Nouvelle Série, vol. x. p. 63.

No great collection of these inscriptions, like the
"Denderah" of M. Mariette, has yet been published;
but every now and then some young and enterprising
Egyptologist, such as M. Naville or M. Jacques de
Rougé, plunges for awhile into the depths of the Edfoo
mine and brings back as much precious ore as he can
carry.* Some most singular and interesting details have
thus been brought to light. One inscription, for instance, records exactly in what month, and on what
day and at what hour, Isis gave birth to Horus. Another tells all about the sacred boats. We know now
that Edfoo possessed at least two; and that one was
called Hor-Hat, or The First Horus, and the other
Āa-Māfek, or Great of Turquoise. These boats, it
would appear, were not merely for carrying in procession, but for actual use upon the water. Another text
—one of the most curious—informs us that Hathor of
Denderah paid an annual visit to Horus (or Hor-Hat)
of Edfoo, and spent some days with him in his
Temple. The whole ceremonial of this fantastic trip
is given in detail. The Goddess travelled in her boat
called Neb-Mer-t, or Lady of the Lake. Horus, like a
polite host, went out in his boat Hor-Hat, to meet her.
The two deities with their attendants then formed one
procession, and so came to Edfoo, where the Goddess
was entertained with a succession of festivals.**

One would like to know whether Horus duly returned all these visits; and if the Gods, like modern
Emperors, had a gay time among themselves.

* I am informed by Professor G. Maspero that one of his pupils, M. de
Rochemonteix, has been in Egypt since November 1875 with the express ob-
ject of copying these Edfo inscriptions, by commission of the French govern-
ment.
** *Textes Géographiques du Temple d'Edfou*, par M. J. DE ROUGÉ. *Révue
Arch.*, vol. XII. p. 209.

Other questions inevitably suggest themselves, sometimes painfully, sometimes ludicrously, as one paces chamber after chamber, corridor after corridor, sculptured all over with strange forms and stranger legends. What about these Gods whose genealogies are so intricate; whose mutual relations are so complicated; who wedded and became parents; who exchanged visits, and who even travelled* at times to distant countries? What about those who served them in the Temples; who robed and unrobed them; who celebrated their birthdays, and paraded them in stately processions, and consumed the lives of millions in erecting these mountains of masonry and sculpture to their honour? We know now with what elaborate rites the Gods were adored; what jewels they wore; what hymns were sung in their praise. We know from what a subtle and philosophical core of solar myths their curious personal adventures were evolved. We may also be quite sure that the hidden meaning of these legends was almost wholly lost sight of in the later days of the religion,** and that the Gods were accepted for what they seemed to be, and not for what they symbolised. What, then, of their worshippers? Did they really believe all these things, or were any among them tormented with doubts of the Gods? Were there sceptics in those days who wondered how two hierogrammates could look each other in the face without laughing?

The custode told us that there were 242 steps to the top of each tower of the propylon. We counted

---

* See "The Possessed Princess" (Tablet of Rameses XII.) Translated by S. BIRCH, ESQ., LL.D., etc. *Records of the Past*, vol. IV.
** See APPENDIX III., *Religious Belief of the Ancient Egyptians.*

224, and dispensed willingly with the remainder. It
was a long pull: but had the steps been four times as
many, the sight from the top would have been worth
the climb. The chambers in the pylons are on a
grand scale, with wide bevelled windows like the
mouths of monster letter-boxes, placed at regular intervals all the way up. Through these windows the great
flagstaffs and pennons were regulated from within.
The two pylons communicate by a terrace over the
central doorway. The parapet of this terrace and the
parapets of the pylons above, are plentifully scrawled
with names, many of which were left there by the
French soldiers of 1799.

The cornices of these two magnificent towers are
unfortunately gone; but the total height without them
is 125 feet. From the top, as from the minaret of the
great mosque at Damascus, one looks down into the
heart of the town. Hundreds of mud-huts thatched
with palm-leaves, hundreds of little courtyards, lie
mapped out beneath one's feet; and as the Fellah lives
in his yard by day, using his hut merely as a sleeping
place at night, one looks down, like the Diable Boiteux,
upon the domestic doings of a roofless world. We see
people moving to and fro, unconscious of strange eyes
watching them from above—men lounging, smoking,
sleeping in shady corners—children playing—infants
crawling on all fours—women cooking at clay ovens
in the open air—cows and sheep feeding—poultry
scratching and pecking—dogs basking in the sun. The
huts look more like the lairs of prairie-dogs than the
dwellings of human beings. The little mosque with
its one dome and stunted minaret, so small, so far
below, looks like a clay toy. Beyond the village, which

reaches far and wide, lie barley fields, and cotton patches, and palm-groves, bounded on one side by the river, and on the other by the desert. A wide road, dotted over with moving specks of men and cattle, cleaves its way straight through the cultivated land and out across the sandy plain beyond. We can trace its course for miles where it is only a trodden track in the desert. It goes, they tell us, direct to Cairo. On the opposite bank glares a hideous white sugar-factory; and, bowered in greenery, a country villa of the Khedive. The broad Nile flows between. The sweet Theban hills gleam through a pearly haze on the horizon.

All at once, a fitful breeze springs up, blowing in little gusts and swirling the dust in circles round our feet. At the same moment, like a beautiful spectre, there rises from the desert close by an undulating semi-transparent stalk of yellow sand, which grows higher every moment, and begins moving northward across the plain. Almost at the same instant, another appears a long way off towards the south, and a third comes gliding mysteriously along the opposite bank. While we are watching the third, the first begins throwing off a wonderful kind of plume, which follows it, waving and melting in the air. And now the stranger from the south comes up at smooth, tremendous pace, towering at least 500 feet above the desert; till, meeting some cross-current, it is snapped suddenly in twain. The lower half instantly collapses; the upper, after hanging suspended for a moment, spreads and floats slowly, like a cloud. In the meanwhile, other and smaller columns form here and there—stalk a little way—waver—disperse—form again—and again drop away in dust. Then the breeze falls, and puts an abrupt end to this extraordinary spectacle. In less than two minutes there is not a sand-column left. As they came, they vanish—suddenly.

Such is the landscape that frames the Temple; and the Temple, after all, is the sight that one comes up here to see. There it lies far below our feet, the court-yard with its almost perfect pavement; the flat roof compact of gigantic monoliths; the wall of circuit with its panoramic sculptures; the portico, with its screen and pillars distinct in brilliant light against inner depths of dark; each pillar a shaft of ivory, each square of dark a block of ebony. So perfect, so solid, so splendid is the whole structure; so simple in unity of plan; so complex in ornament; so majestic in completeness, that one feels as if it solved the whole problem of religious architecture.

Take it for what it is—a Ptolemaic structure preserved in all its integrity of strength and finish—it is certainly the finest extant Temple in Egypt. It brings before us, with even more completeness than Denderah, the purposes of its various parts, and the kind of ceremonial for which it was designed. Every corridor and chamber tells its own story. Even the names of the different chambers are graven upon them in such wise that nothing, says M. Mariette,* would be easier than

---

* "Not only the names of the chambers, but their dimensions in cubits and sub-divisions of cubits are given. The name of the architect, Imhotep-Ur-Se-Phthah (Imhotep-The-Great-Son-of-Phthah), is also recorded." See *Itinéraire de la Haute Égypte.* A. Mariette-Bey, 1872, p. 241. Professor G. Maspero informs me, however, that this is not the name of the human architect, but of the *divine* designer of the Temple. "Ce n'est pas le nom de l'architecte *humain* qui a bâti le temple, mais celui de l'architecte *divin*. Imhotep le grand fils de Ptah, est le Dieu Imhotep de la triade Memphite à qui on attribue les plans du Temple." *Letter of Professor G. Maspero to the Author, April* 1878.

to reconstruct the ground-plan of the whole building in
hieroglyphic nomenclature. That neither the Ptolemaic
building nor the Ptolemaic mythus can be accepted as
strictly representative of either pure Egyptian art or
pure Egyptian thought, must of course be conceded.
Both are modified by Greek influences, and have so far
departed from the Pharaonic model. But then we have
no equally perfect specimen of the Pharaonic model.
The Ramesseum is but a grand fragment. Karnak
and Medinet Haboo are aggregates of many Temples
and many styles. Abydos is still half-buried. Amid
so much that is fragmentary, amid so much that is
ruined, the one absolutely perfect structure—Ptolemaic
though it be—is of incalculable interest, and equally
incalculable value.

While we are dreaming over these things, trying to
fancy how it all looked when the sacred flotilla came
sweeping up the river yonder and the procession of
Hor-Hat issued forth to meet the Goddess-guest—while
we are half-expecting to see the whole brilliant con-
course pour out, priests in their robes of panther-skin,
priestesses with the tinkling sistrum, singers and har-
pists, and bearers of gifts and emblems, and high
functionaries rearing aloft the sacred boat of the God
—in this moment a turbaned Muëddin comes out upon
the rickety wooden gallery of the little minaret below,
and intones the call to mid-day prayer. That plaintive
cry has hardly died away before we see men here and
there among the huts turning towards the east, and
assuming the first postures of devotion. The women
go on cooking and nursing their babies. I have seen
Moslem women at prayer in the mosques of Constan-
tinople, but never in Egypt.

Meanwhile, some children catch sight of us, and, notwithstanding that we are one hundred and twenty-five feet above their heads, burst into a frantic chorus of "Backsheesh!"

And now, with a last long look at the Temple and the wide landscape beyond, we come down again; and go to see a dismal little Mammesi three-parts buried among a wilderness of mounds close by. These mounds, which consist almost entirely of crude-brick débris with imbedded fragments of stone and pottery, are built up like coral-reefs, and represent the dwellings of some sixty generations. When they are cut straight through, as here round about the great Temple, the substance of them looks like rich plum-cake.

CHAPTER XXI.

Thebes.

WE had so long been the sport of destiny, that we
hardly knew what to make of our good fortune when
two days of sweet south wind carried us from Edfoo to
Luxor. We came back to find the old mooring-place
alive with Dahabeeyahs, and gay with English and
American colours. These two flags well-nigh divide the
river. In every twenty-five boats, one may fairly cal-
culate upon an average of twelve English, nine American, two German, one Belgian, and one French. Of all
these, our American cousins, ever helpful, ever cordial,
are pleasantest to meet. Their flag stands to me for a
host of brave and generous and kindly associations. It
brings back memories of many lands and many faces.
It calls up echoes of friendly voices, some far distant;
some, alas! silent. Wherefore—be it on the Nile, or
the Thames, or the high seas, or among Syrian camp-
ing-grounds, or drooping listlessly from the balconies
of gloomy diplomatic haunts in continental cities—
my heart warms to the stars and stripes whenever I
see them.

Our arrival brought all the dealers of Luxor to the
surface. They waylaid and followed us wherever we
went; while some of the better sort—grave men in
long black robes and ample turbans—installed themselves on our lower deck, and lived there for a fortnight. Go upstairs when we would, whether before

breakfast in the morning, or after dinner in the evening, there we always found them; patient; imperturbable; ready to rise up, and salaam, and produce from some hidden pocket a purseful of scarabs or a bundle of votive statuettes. Some of these gentlemen were Arabs, some Copts—all polite, plausible, and mendacious.

Where Copt and Arab drive the same doubtful trade, it is not easy to define the shades of difference in their dealings. As workmen, the Copts are perhaps the most artistic. As salesmen, the Arabs are perhaps the less dishonest. Both sell more forgeries than genuine antiquities. Be the demand what it may, they are prepared to meet it. Thothmes is not too heavy, nor Cleopatra too light, for them. Their carvings in old sycamore wood, their porcelain statuettes, their hieroglyphed limestone tablets, are executed with a skill that almost defies detection. As for genuine scarabs of the highest antiquity, they are turned out by the gross every season. Engraved, glazed, and administered to the turkeys in the form of boluses, they acquire by the simple process of digestion a degree of venerableness that is really charming.

Side by side with the work of production goes on the work of excavation. The professed diggers colonise the western bank. They live rent-free among the tombs; drive donkeys or work shadoofs by day, and spend their nights searching for treasure. Some hundreds of families live in this grim way, spoiling the dead and gone Egyptians for a livelihood.

Forgers, diggers, and dealers play, meanwhile, into one another's hands, and drive a roaring trade. Your Dahabeeyah, as I have just shown, is beset from the

moment you moor till the moment you pole off again
from shore. The boy who drives your donkey, the
guide who pilots you among the tombs, the half-naked
Fellah who flings down his hoe as you pass, and runs
beside you for a mile across the plain, have one and
all an "antichi" to dispose of. The turbaned official
who comes, attended by his secretary and pipe-bearer,
to pay you a visit of ceremony, warns you against im-
position and hints at genuine treasures, to which he
alone possesses the key. The gentlemanly native who
sits next to you at dinner has a wonderful scarab in
his pocket. In short, every man, woman, and child
about the place is bent on selling a bargain; and the
bargain, in ninety-nine cases out of a hundred, is
valuable in so far as it represents the industry of
Luxor—but no farther. A good thing, of course, is to
be had occasionally; but the good thing never comes
to the surface as long as a market can be found for
the bad. It is only when the dealer finds he has to
do with an experienced customer, that he produces
the best he has. I should not, for my own part, like
to buy anything at Luxor without first taking the
opinion of the English Consul. His experience is great,
and his courtesy inexhaustible. The Prussian Consul
has also a fine judgment in antiquities.

Flourishing as it is, the trade of Luxor labours,
however, under some uncomfortable restrictions. Private excavation being absolutely prohibited, the digger
lives in dread of being found out by the Governor. The forger, who has nothing to fear from the
Governor, lives in dread of being found out by the
tourist. As for the dealer, whether he sells an antique
or an imitation, he is equally liable to punishment.

In the one case he commits an offence against the state; and in the other, he obtains money under false pretences. Meanwhile, the Governor, who is a man of strict probity, deals out such even-handed justice as he can, and does his best to enforce the law on both sides of the river.

By a curious accident, L. and the Writer once actually penetrated into a forger's workshop. Not knowing that it had been abolished, we went to a certain house in which a certain Consulate had once upon a time been located, and there knocked for admission. An old deaf Fellaha opened the door, and after some hesitation showed us into a large unfurnished room with three windows. In each window there stood a workman's bench strewn with scarabs, amulets, and votive gods in every stage of progress. We examined these specimens with no little curiosity. Some were of wood; some were of limestone; some were partly coloured. The colours and brushes were there; to say nothing of files, gravers, and little pointed tools like gimlets. A magnifying glass of the kind used by engravers lay in one of the window-recesses. We also observed a small grindstone screwed to one of the benches and worked by a treadle; while a massive fragment of mummy-case in a corner behind the door showed whence came the old sycamore wood for the wooden statuettes. That three skilled workmen furnished with European tools had been busy in this room shortly before we were shown into it, was perfectly clear. We concluded that they had just gone away to breakfast.

Meanwhile we waited, expecting to be ushered into the presence of the Consul. In about ten minutes,

however, breathless with hurrying, arrived a well-
dressed Arab whom we had never seen before. Dis-
tracted between his Oriental politeness and his desire
to get rid of us, he bowed us out precipitately, explain-
ing that the house had changed owners, and that the
Power in question had ceased to be represented at
Luxor. We heard him rating the old woman savagely,
as soon as the door had closed behind us. I met that
well-dressed Arab a day or two after, near the Governor's house; and he immediately vanished round the
nearest corner.

Mariette Bey keeps a small gang of trained excavators always at work in the Necropolis of Thebes.
These men are superintended by the Governor, and
every mummy-case discovered is forwarded to Boulak
unopened. Thanks to the courtesy of the Governor,
we had the good fortune to be present one morning at
the opening of a tomb. He sent to summon us, just
as we were going to breakfast. With what alacrity we
manned the felucca, and how we ate our bread and
butter half in the boat and half on donkey-back, may
easily be imagined. How well I remember that early
morning ride across the Western plain of Thebes—the
young barley rippling for miles in the sun; the little
water-channel running beside the path; the white but-
terflies circling in couples; the wayside grave with its
tiny dome and prayer-mat, its well and broken goollah,
inviting the passer-by to drink and pray; the wild vine
that trailed along the wall; the vivid violet of the vetches
that blossomed unbidden in the barley. We had the
mounds and pylons of Medinet Haboo to the left—the
ruins of the Ramesseum to the right—the Colossi of
the Plain and the rosy western mountains before us all

the way. How the great statues glistened in the morning light! How they towered up against the soft blue sky! Battered and featureless, they sat in the old patient attitude, looking as if they mourned the vanished springs.

We found the new tomb a few hundred yards in the rear of the Ramesseum. The diggers were in the pit; the Governor and a few Arabs were looking on. The vault was lined with brickwork above, and cut square in the living rock below. We were just in time; for already, through the sand and rubble with which the grave had been filled in, there appeared an outline of something buried. The men, throwing spades and picks aside, now began scraping up the dust with their hands, and a mummy-case came gradually to light. It was shaped to represent a body lying at length with the hands crossed upon the breast. Both hands and face were carved in high relief. The ground-colour of the sarcophagus was white;* the surface covered with hieroglyphed legends and somewhat coarsely painted figures of the four lesser Gods of the Dead. The face, like the hands, was coloured a brownish yellow and highly varnished. But for a little dimness of the gaudy hues, and a little flaking off of the surface here and there, the thing was as perfect as when it was placed in the ground. A small wooden box roughly put together lay at the feet of the mummy. This was taken

---

* This was, no doubt, an interment of the period of the XXIIId or XXIVth Dynasty, the style of which is thus described by M. Mariette:—
"Succèdent les caisses à fond blanc. Autour de celles-ci court une légende en hiéroglyphes de toutes couleurs. Le devant du couvercle est divisé horizontalement en tableaux où alternent les représentations et les textes tracés en hiéroglyphes verdâtres. La momie elle-même est hermétiquement enfermée dans un cartonnage cousu par derrière et peint de couleurs tranchantes."— *Notice des Monuments à Boulak*, p. 46. Paris, 1872.

out first, and handed to the Governor, who put it aside
without opening it. The mummy-case was then raised
upright, hoisted to the brink of the pit, and laid upon
the ground.

It gave one a kind of shock to see it first of all
lying just as it had been left by the mourners; then
hauled out by rude hands, to be searched, unrolled,
perhaps broken up as unworthy to occupy a corner in
the Boulak collection. Once they are lodged and catalogued in a museum, one comes to look upon these
things as "specimens," and forgets that they once were
living beings like ourselves. But this poor mummy
looked startlingly human and pathetic lying at the
bottom of its grave in the morning sunlight.

After the sarcophagus had been lifted out, a small
blue porcelain cup, a ball of the same material, and
another little object shaped like a cherry, were found
in the débris. The last was hollow, and contained
something that rattled when shaken. The mummy,
the wooden box, and these porcelain toys, were then
removed to a stable close by; and the excavators, having laid bare what looked like the mouth of a bricked-
up tunnel in the side of the tomb, fell to work again
immediately. A second vault—perhaps a chain of
vaults—it was thought would now be discovered.

We went away, meanwhile, for a few hours, and
saw some of the famous painted tombs in that part of
the mountain-side just above which goes by the name
of Sheykh Abd-el-Koorneh.

It was a hot climb; the sun blazing over head; the
cliffs reflecting light and heat; the white débris glaring
under-foot. Some of the tombs up here are excavated
in terraces, and look from a distance like rows of pi-

geon holes; others are perched in solitary ledges of
rock; many are difficult of access; all are intolerably
hot and oppressive. They were numbered half a century ago by the late Sir Gardner Wilkinson, and the
numbers are there still. We went that morning into
14, 16, 17, and 35.

As a child, "*The Manners and Customs of the Ancient Egyptians*" had shared my affections with "*The
Arabian Nights.*" I had read every line of the old
six-volume edition over and over again. I knew every
one of the six hundred illustrations by heart. Now I
suddenly found myself in the midst of old and half-
forgotten friends. Every subject on these wonderful
walls was already familiar to me. Only the framework,
only the colouring, only the sand under-foot, only the
mountain slope outside, were new and strange. It
seemed to me that I had met all these kindly brown
people years and years ago—perhaps in some previous
stage of existence; that I had walked with them in
their gardens; listened to the music of their lutes and
tambourines; pledged them at their feasts. Here is
the funeral procession that I know so well; and the
trial scene after death, where the mummy stands upright in the presence of Osiris, and sees his heart
weighed in the balance. Here is that well-remembered
old fowler crouching in the rushes with his basket of
decoys. One withered hand is lifted to his mouth; his
lips frame the call; his thin hair blows in the breeze.
I see now that he has placed himself to the leeward of
the game; but that subtlety escaped me in the reading
days of my youth. Yonder I recognise a sculptor's
studio into which I frequently peeped at that time.
His men are at work as actively as ever; but I marvel

that they have not yet finished polishing the surface of
that red-granite colossus. This patient angler, still
waiting for a bite, is another old acquaintance; and
yonder, I declare, is that evening party at which I was
so often an imaginary guest! Is the feast not yet over?
Has that late comer whom we saw hurrying along just
now in a neighbouring corridor not yet arrived? Will
the musicians never play to the end of their concerto?
Are those ladies still so deeply interested in the patterns of one another's ear-rings? It seems to me that
the world has been standing still in here for these last
five-and-thirty years.

Did I say five-and-thirty? Ah me! I think we must
multiply it by ten, and then by ten again, ere we come
to the right figure. These people lived in the time of
the Thothmes and the Amenhoteps—a time upon which
Rameses the Great looked back as we look back to
the days of the Tudors and the Stuarts.

From the tombs above, we went back to the excavations below. The bricked-up opening had led, as
the diggers expected, into a second vault; and another
mummy-case, half-crushed by a fall of débris, had just
been taken out. A third was found later in the afternoon. Curiously enough, they were all three mummies of women.

The Governor was taking his luncheon with the
first mummy in the recesses of the stable, which had
been a fine tomb once, but reeked now with manure.
He sat on a rug, cross-legged, with a bowl of sour
milk before him and a tray of most uninviting little
cakes. He invited me to a seat on his rug, handed
me his own spoon, and did the honours of the stable
as pleasantly as if it had been a palace.

I asked him why the excavators, instead of working among these second-class graves, were not set to search for the tombs of the Kings of the XVIIIth Dynasty, supposed by M. Mariette to be waiting discovery in a certain valley called the Valley of the West. He shook his head. The way to the Valley of the West, he said, was long and difficult. Men working there must encamp upon the spot; and merely to supply them with water would be no easy matter. He was allowed, in fact, only a sum sufficient for the wages of fifty excavators; and to attack the Valley of the West with less than two hundred would be useless.

We had luncheon that morning, I remember, with the M. B.'s in the second hall of the Ramesseum. It was but one occasion among many; for the Writer was constantly at work on that side of the river, and we had luncheon in one or other of the western Temples every day. Yet that particular meeting stands out in my memory apart from the rest. I see the joyous party gathered together in the shade of the great columns—the Persian rugs spread on the uneven ground —the dragoman in his picturesque dress going to and fro—the brown and tattered Arabs, squatting a little way off, silent and hungry-eyed, each with his string of forged scarabs, his imitation gods, or his bits of mummy-case and painted cartonnage for sale—the glowing peeps of landscape framed in here and there through vistas of columns—the emblazoned architraves laid along from capital to capital overhead, each block sculptured with enormous cartouches yet brilliant with vermilion and ultramarine—the patient donkeys munching all together at a little heap of vetches in one corner—the intense depths of cloudless blue above. Of

all Theban ruins, the Ramesseum is the most cheerful.
Drenched in sunshine, the warm limestone of which it
is built seems to have mellowed and turned golden
with time. No walls enclose it. No towering pylons
overshadow it. It stands high, and the air circulates
freely among those simple and beautiful columns.
There are not many Egyptian ruins in which one can
talk and be merry; but in the Ramesseum one may
thoroughly enjoy the passing hour.

Whether Rameses the Great was ever actually buried
in this place is a mystery which future discoveries
may possibly solve; but that the Ramesseum and the
tomb of Osymandias were one and the same building
is a point upon which I never entertained a moment's
doubt. Spending day after day among these ruins;
sketching now here, now there; going over the ground
bit by bit, and comparing every detail, I came at last
to wonder how an identity so obvious could ever have
been doubted. Diodorus was of course inaccurate; but
then one as little looks for accuracy in Diodorus as in
Homer. Compared with some of his topographical
descriptions, the account he gives of the Ramesseum
is a marvel of exactness. He describes * a building
approached by two vast courtyards; a hall of pillars
opening by way of three entrances from the second
courtyard; a succession of chambers, including a sacred
library; ceilings of azure "bespangled with stars;" walls
covered with sculptures representing the deeds and
triumphs of the king whom he calls Osymandias,**

---

* Diodorus, *Biblioth. Hist.*, Bk. I. chap. IV. The fault of inaccuracy
ought, however, to be charged to Hecatæus, who was the authority followed
here by Diodorus.

** Possibly the Smendes of Manetho, and the Ba-en-Ded whose cartouche
is found by Brugsch on a sarcophagus in the museum at Vienna; see *Hist.*

amongst which are particularly noticed the assault of a fortress "environed by a river," a procession of captives without hands, and a series of all the Gods of Egypt, to whom the King was represented in the act of making offerings; finally, against the entrance to the second courtyard, three statues of the King, one of which, being of Syenite granite and made "in a sitting posture," is stated to be not only "the greatest in all Egypt," but admirable above all others "for its workmanship, and the excellence of the stone."

Bearing in mind that what is left of the Ramesseum is, as it were, only the backbone of the entire structure, one can still walk from end to end of the building, and still recognise every feature of this description. We turn our backs on the wrecked towers of the first propylon; crossing what was once the first courtyard, we leave to the left the fallen colossus; we enter the second courtyard, and see before us the three entrances to the hall of pillars, and the remains of two other statues; we walk up the central avenue of the great hall, and see above our heads architraves studded with yellow stars upon a ground colour so luminously blue that it almost matches the sky; thence, passing through a chamber lined with sculptures, we come to the library, upon the door-jambs of which Champollion found the figures of Thoth and Saf, the Lord of Letters and the Lady of the Sacred Books;* finally, among such fragments of sculptured decoration as yet remain, we find the King making offerings to a hieroglyphed list of Gods as well as to

d'Égypte, chap. x. p. 213, ed. 1859. Another claimant to this identification is found in a King named Se-Mentu, whose cartouches have been found by M. Mariette on some small gold tablets at Tanis.
    * Letter XIV. p. 235. _Lettres d'Égypte;_ Paris, 1868. See also Chap. XVIII. of the present volume; p. 130.

his deified ancestors; we see the train of captives, and
the piles of severed hands;* and we discover an immense battle-piece, which is in fact a replica of the
famous battle-piece at Aboo Simbel. This subject, like
its Nubian prototype, yet preserves some of its colour.
The enemy are shown to be fair-skinned and light-
haired, and wear the same Syrian robes; and the river,
more green than that at Aboo Simbel, is painted in
zigzags in the same manner. The King, alone in his
chariot, sends arrow after arrow against the flying foe.
They leap into the river, and swim for their lives.
Some are drowned; some cross in safety, and are helped
out by their friends on the opposite bank. A red-haired
chief, thus rescued, is suspended head-downwards by
his soldiers, in order to let the water that he has
swallowed run out of his mouth. The river is once
more the Orontes; the city is once more Kades; the
king is once more Rameses II.; and the incidents are
again the incidents of the poem of Pentaour.

The one wholly unmistakable point in the narrative
is, however, the colossal statue of Syenite, "the largest
in Egypt." The siege and the river, the troops of captives are to be found elsewhere; but nowhere, save
here, a colossus that answers to that description. This
statue was larger than even the twin Colossi of the Plain.
They measure eighteen feet and three inches across
the shoulders; this measures twenty-two feet and four
inches. They sit about fifty feet high, without their
pedestals; this one must have lifted his head some ten
feet higher still. "The measure of his foot," says Diodorus, "exceeded seven cubits;" the Greek cubit being
a little over eighteen inches in length. The foot of

* See Champollion, Letter XIV., as above, p. 238.

the fallen Rameses measures nearly eleven feet in length by four feet ten inches in breadth. This, also, is the only very large colossus sculptured in the red Syenite of Assouan.*

Ruined almost beyond recognition as it is, one never doubts for a moment that this statue was indeed the final wonder of Egyptian workmanship. It most probably repeated in every detail the colossi of Aboo Simbel; but it surpassed them as much in finish of carving as in perfection of material. The stone is even more beautiful in colour than that of the famous obelisks of Karnak; and is so close and hard in grain, that the scarab-cutters of Luxor are said to use splinters of it as our engravers use diamonds, for the points of their graving tools. The solid contents of the whole, when entire, are calculated at 887 tons; so that, regarded merely as quantity and quality, it must have been the grandest block of granite in the world. How this as-tounding mass was transported from Assouan, how it was raised, how it was overthrown, are problems upon which a great deal of ingenious conjecture has been wasted. One traveller affirms that the wedge-marks of the destroyer are distinctly visible. Another, having carefully examined the fractured edges, declares that the keenest eye can detect neither wedge-marks nor any other evidences of violence. We looked for none of these signs and tokens. We never asked ourselves how or when the ruin had been done. It was enough that the mighty had fallen.

Inasmuch as one can clamber upon and measure

---

* The Syenite colossus of which the British Museum possesses the head, and which is popularly known as the Young Memnon, measured twenty-four feet in height before it was broken up by the French.

14*

these stupendous fragments, the fallen colossus is more astonishing, perhaps, as a wreck than it would have been as a whole. Here, snapped across at the waist and flung helplessly back, lie a huge head and shoulders, to climb which is like climbing a rock. Yonder, amid piles of unintelligible débris, we see a great foot, and nearer the head, part of an enormous trunk, together with the upper halves of two huge thighs clothed in the usual shenti or striped tunic. The klaft or headdress is also striped, and these stripes, in both instances, retain the delicate yellow colour with which they were originally filled in. To judge from the way in which this colour was applied, one would say that the statue was tinted rather than painted. The surface-work, wherever it remains, is as smooth and highly finished as the cutting of the finest gem. Even the ground of the superb cartouche on the upper half of the arm is elaborately polished. Finally, in the pit which it ploughed out in falling, lies the great pedestal, hieroglyphed with the usual pompous titles of Rameses Mer-Amen. Diodorus, knowing nothing of Rameses or his style, interprets the inscription after his own fanciful fashion:—"I am Osymandias, King of Kings. If any would know how great I am, and where I lie, let him excel me in any of my works."

The fragments of wall and shattered pylon that yet remain standing at the Ramesseum face N.W. and S.W. Hence it follows that some of the most interesting of the surface sculpture (being cut in very low relief) is so placed with regard to the light as to be actually invisible after midday. It was not till the occasion of my last visit, when I came early in the morning to make a certain sketch by a certain light, that I succeeded in

distinguishing a single figure of that celebrated tableau*
on the S. wall of the Great Hall, in which the Egyptians
are seen to be making use of the testudo and scaling
ladder to assault a Syrian fortress. The wall sculptures
of the second hall are on a bolder scale, and can be
seen at any hour. Here Thoth writes the name of
Rameses on the egg-shaped fruit of the persea tree,
and processions of shaven priests carry on their shoulders
the sacred boats of various Gods. In the centre of
each boat is a shrine supported by winged genii or
cherubim. The veils over these shrines, the rings
through which the bearing-poles were passed, and all
the appointments and ornaments of the *bari*, are distinctly shown. One seems here, indeed, to be admitted to a glimpse of those original shrines upon which
Moses—learned in the sacred lore of the Egyptians—
modelled, with but little alteration, his Ark of the
Covenant.

Next in importance to Karnak, and second in interest to none of the Theban ruins, is the vast group
of buildings known by the collective name of Medinet
Haboo. To attempt to describe these would be to
undertake a task as hopeless as the description of
Karnak. Such an attempt lies, at all events, beyond the
compass of these pages, so many of which have already
been given to similar subjects. For it is of Temples as
of mountains—no two are alike, yet all sound so much
alike when described that it is scarcely possible to
write about them without becoming monotonous. In
the present instance, therefore, I will note only a few
points of special interest, referring those who wish for

* See woodcut No. 340 in Sir G. Wilkinson's *Manners and Customs of the
Ancient Egyptians*, vol. i. edition, 1871.

fuller particulars to the elaborate account of Medinet
Haboo in Murray's *Handbook of Egypt*.

In the second name of Medinet Haboo—Medinet
being the common Arabic for city, and Haboo, Haboot,
Aboo, or Taboo being variously spelled—there survives
almost beyond doubt the ancient name of that famous
city which the Greeks called Thebes. It is a name for
which many derivations* have been suggested, but
upon which the learned are not yet agreed.

The ruins at Medinet Haboo consist of a smaller
Temple founded by Queen Hatasou of the XVIIIth
Dynasty, a large and magnificent Temple entirely built
by Rameses III. of the XXth Dynasty, and an extremely
curious and interesting building, part palace, part fortress, which is popularly known as the Pavilion.

The walls of this pavilion, the walls of the great
forecourt leading to the smaller Temple, and a corner
of the original wall of circuit, are crowned in the Egyptian style with shield-shaped battlements, precisely as
the Khetan and Amorite fortresses are battlemented in
the sculptured tableaux at Aboo Simbel and elsewhere.
From whichever side one approaches Medinet Haboo,
these stone shields strike the eye as a new and interesting feature. They are, moreover, as far as I know,
the only specimens of Egyptian battlementing that have
survived destruction. Those of the wall of circuit are
of the time of Rameses V.; those of the pavilion of the
time of Rameses III.; and the latest, which are those of
the forecourt, are of the period of Roman occupation.

As biographical material, the Temple and Pavilion

---

* Among these are *Abot* or abode; meaning the abode of Ammon; *Ta-
Uaboo*, the mound; *Ta-Api*, the head or capital, etc. etc. See *Recherches sur
le nom Égyptien de Thèbes*, CHABAS: 1863; *Textes Géographiques d'Edfoo*,
J. DE ROUGÉ: *Revue Arch.*, Nouvelle Sèrie, vol. XII. 1865; etc. etc.

at Medinet Haboo and the great Harris papyrus,* are to the life of Rameses III. precisely what Aboo Simbel, the Ramesseum, and the poem of Pentaour, are to the life of Rameses II. Great wars, great victories, magnificent praises of the prowess of the King, pompous lists of enemies slain and captured, inventories of booty and of precious gifts offered by the victor to the Gods of Egypt, in both instances cover the sculptured walls and fill the written pages. A comparison of the two masses of evidence — due allowance being made both ways for Oriental fervour of diction — shows that in Rameses III. we have to do with a king as brilliant, as valorous, and as successful as Rameses II.**

* The *Great Harris Papyrus* is described by Dr. Birch as "one of the finest, best written, and best preserved, that have been discovered in Egypt. It measures 133 feet long, by 16¾ inches broad, and was found with several others in a tomb behind Medinet Haboo. Purchased soon after by the late A. C. Harris of Alexandria, it was subsequently unrolled and divided into seventy-nine leaves, and laid down on card-board. With the exception of some small portions which are wanting in the first, the rest of the text is complete throughout. The object of the papyrus is the address after death of the King, Rameses III., recounting the benefits he had conferred upon Egypt by his administration, and by the delivery of the country from foreign subjection, and also the immense gifts which he had conferred on the Temples of Egypt, of Ammon at Thebes, Tum at Heliopolis, and Phthah at Memphis, etc. The last part is addressed to the officers of the army, consisting partly of Sardinian and Libyan mercenaries, and to the people of Egypt, in the thirty-second year of his reign, and is a kind of posthumous panegyrical discourse, or political will, like that of Augustus discovered at Ancyra. The papyrus itself consists of the following divisions, three of which are preceded by large coloured plates or vignettes:—Introduction: donations to the Theban deities; donations to the gods of Heliopolis; donations to the gods of Memphis; donations to the gods of the north and south; summary of donations; historical speech and conclusion. Throughout the monarch speaks in the first person, the list excepted." Introduction to *Annals of Rameses III.*; S. BIRCH: *Records of the Past*, vol. VI. p. 21; 1876.
** "Rameses III. was one of the most remarkable monarchs in the annals of Egypt. A period of political confusion and foreign conquest of the country preceded his advent to the throne. His father, Setnecht, had indeed succeeded in driving out the foreign invaders, and re-establishing the native dynasty of the Theban kings, the twentieth of the list of Manetho. But Rameses had a great task before him, called to the throne at a youthful age. . . . The first task of Rameses was to restore the civil government and military discipline. In his fifth year, he defeated the Maxyes and Libyans with great slaughter when they invaded Egypt, led by five chiefs; and in the same year he had

It may be that before the time of this Pharaoh certain Temples were used also as royal residences. It is
possible to believe this of Temples such as Goornah
and Abydos, the plan of which includes, besides the
usual halls, side-chambers, and sanctuary, a number of
other apartments, the uses of which are unknown. It
may also be that former kings dwelt in houses of brick
and carved woodwork, such as we see represented in
the wall-paintings of various tombs.

It is at all events a fact that the only two royal
palaces of which any vestiges have come down to the
present day were erected by Rameses III. To one (not
long since discovered in the mounds of Tel el Yahoodeh)
reference has been made in a former chapter.* The
other, or what remains of the other, is this little pavilion at Medinet Haboo.

also to repulse the Satu, or eastern foreigners, who had attacked Egypt. The
maritime nations of the west, it appears, had invaded Palestine and the Syrian
coast in his eighth year, and after taking Carchemish, a confederation of the
Palusata, supposed by some to be the Pelasgi, *Tekkaru* or Teucri, *Sakalusa*
or Siculi, *Tanau* or Daunians, if not Danai, and Uasasa or Osci, marched to
the conquest of Egypt. It is possible that they reached the mouth of the
eastern branch of the Nile. But Rameses concentrated an army at Taka, in
Northern Palestine, and marched back to defend the Nile. Assisted by his
mercenary forces, he inflicted a severe defeat on the confederated west, and
returned with his prisoners to Thebes. In his eleventh year the Mashuasha
or Maxyes, assisted by the Tahennu or Libyans, again invaded Egypt, to
suffer a fresh defeat, and the country seems from this period to have remained
in a state of tranquillity. . . . The vast Temple at Medinet Haboo, his palaces
and treasury, still remain to attest his magnificence and grandeur; and if his
domestic life was that of an ordinary Egyptian monarch, he was as distinguished in the battlefield as the palace. Treason, no doubt, disturbed his
latter days, and it is not known how he died; but he expired after a reign of
thirty-one years and some months, and left the throne to his son, it is supposed,
about B.C. 1200." See *Remarks upon the Cover of the Granite Sarcophagus
of Rameses III.:* S. BIRCH, I.L.D., Cambridge, 1876. Opinion, it should be
said, is divided on the subject of these Western nationalities. The late Vte
E. de Rougé, M. Chabas, and others, identify the Sakalusa, or Shakalash, with
the Siculi, the Uasasa with the Osci, &c. &c. Professor G. Maspero, on the
contrary, sees in all these nations only various tribes of Asia Minor, and in
Shakalash, or Shagalash, a striking resemblance to the name of the ancient city
of Sagalassos in Pisidia.

* Chap. XV., p. 402.

It may not have been a palace. It may have been only a fortified gate; but though the chambers are small, they are well lighted, and the plan of the whole is certainly domestic in character. It consists, as we now see it, of two lodges connected by zigzag wings with a central tower. The lodges and tower stand to each other as the three points of an acute angle. These structures enclose an oblong courtyard leading by a passage under the central tower to the sacred enclosure beyond. So far as its present condition enables us to judge, this building contained only eight rooms; namely three, one above the other, in each of the lodges, and two over the gateway.* These three towers communicate by means of devious passages in the connecting wings. Two of the windows in the wings are adorned with balconies supported on brackets; each bracket representing the head and shoulders of a crouching captive, in the attitude of a gargoyle. The heads and dresses of these captives — conceived as they are in a vein of Gothic barbarism—are still bright with colour.

The central, or gateway-tower, is substantially perfect. The Writer, with help, got as high as the first chamber; the ceiling of which is painted in a rich and intricate pattern, as in imitation of mosaic. The top room is difficult of access; but can be reached by a good climber. Our friend F. W. S., who made his way up there a year or two before, found upon the

---

* "There is reason to believe that this is only a fragment of the building, and foundations exist which render it probable that the whole was originally a square of the width of the front, and had other chambers, probably in wood or brick, besides those we now find. This would hardly detract from the playful character of the design, and when coloured, as it originally was, and with its battlements or ornaments complete, it must have formed a composition as pleasing as it is unlike our usual conceptions of Egyptian art."—*Hist. of Architecture*, by J. FERGUSSON, bk. i., ch. IV., p. 118. Lond. 1865.

walls some interesting sculptures of cups and vases,
apparently part of an illustrated inventory of domestic
utensils. The lid of one of these vases was represented
as opening by means of a lever spooned out for the
thumb to rest in, just like the lid of a German beer-
mug of the present day.

The external decorations of the two lodges are of
especial interest. The lower subjects are historical.
Those upon the upper storeys are domestic or symbolical, and are among the most celebrated of Egyptian
bas-reliefs. They have long been supposed to represent Rameses III. in his hareem, entertained and waited
upon by female slaves. In one group the king, distinguished always by his cartouches, sits at ease in a
kind of folding chair, his helmet on his head, his san-
dalled feet upon a footstool, as one returned and resting after battle. In his left hand he holds a round
object like a fruit. With the right he chucks under
the chin an ear-ringed and necklaced damsel who presents a lotus blossom at his nose. In another much
mutilated subject, they are represented playing a game
at draughts. This famous subject—which can only be
seen when the light strikes sidewise—would scarcely
be intelligible save for the help to be derived from the
cuts in Wilkinson and the plates in Rosellini. It is
not that the sculptures are effaced, but that the great
blocks which bore them are gone from their places,
having probably been hurled down bodily upon the
heads of the enemy during a certain siege of which
the ruins bear evident traces.*   Of the lady, there

* Medinet Haboo continued up to the period of the Arab invasion to be
inhabited by the Coptic descendants of its ancient builders. They fled, however, before Amr and his army, since which time the place has been deserted.
It is not known whether the siege took place at the time of the Arab invasion,

remains little beside one arm and the hand that holds
the pawn. The table has disappeared. The king has
lost his legs. It happens, however, though the table
is missing, that the block next above it contained the
pawns, which can still be discerned from below by the
help of a glass. Rosellini mentions three or four more
subjects of a similar character, including a second
group of draught-players, all visible in his time. The
Writer, however, looked for them in vain.

These tableaux are popularly supposed to illustrate
the home-life of Rameses III., and to confirm the
domestic character of the pavilion. Even the scarab-
selling Arabs that haunt the ruins, even the donkey-
boys of Luxor, call it the Hareem of the Sultan. Modern science, however, threatens to dispel one at least
of these pleasant fancies.

The king, it seems, under the name of Rhampsini-
tus, is the hero of a very ancient legend related by
Herodotus. While he yet lived, runs the story, he
descended into Hades, and there played a game at
draughts with the Goddess Demeter, from whom he
won a golden napkin; in memory of which adventure,
and of his return to earth, "the Egyptians," says Herodotus, "instituted a festival which they certainly celebrated in my day." * In another version as told by
Plutarch, Isis is substituted for Demeter. Viewing
these tales by the light of a certain passage of the
Ritual, in which the happy dead is promised "power
to transform himself at will, to play at draughts, to

or during the raid of Cambyses; but whenever it was, the place was evidently
forced by the besiegers. The author of Murray's Handbook draws attention
to the fact that the granite jambs of the doorway leading to the smaller Temple
are cut through exactly at the place where the bar was placed across the door.

* Herodotus, bk. II. chap. 122.

repose in a pavilion," Dr. Birch has suggested that the whole of this scene may be of a memorial character, and represent an incident in the Land of Shades.*

Below these "hareem" groups come colossal bas-reliefs of a religious and military character. The King, as usual, smites his prisoners in presence of the Gods. A slender and spirited figure in act to slay, the fiery hero strides across the wall "like Baal** descended from the heights of heaven. His limbs are endued with the force of victory. With his right hand he seizes the multitudes; his left reaches like an arrow after those who fly before him. His sword is sharp as that of his father Mentu." ***

Below these great groups run friezes sculptured with kneeling figures of vanquished chiefs, among whom are Libyan, Sicilian, Sardinian, and Etruscan leaders. Every head in these friezes is a portrait. The Libyan is beardless; his lips are thin; his nose is hooked; his forehead retreats; he wears a close-fitting cap with a

---

* "A Medinet Habou, dans son palais, il s'est fait représenter jouant aux dames avec des femmes qui, d'après certaines copies, semblent porter sur la tête les fleurs symbolique de l'Égypte supérieure et inférieure, comme les déesses du monde supérieur et inférieur, ou du ciel et de la terre. Cette dualité des déesses, qui est indiquée dans les scènes religieuses et les textes sacrés par la réunion de Satis et Anoucis, Pasht et Bast, Isis et Nephthys, etc., me fait penser que les tableaux de Medinet Habou peuvent avoir été considérés dans les légendes populaires comme offrant aux yeux l'allégorie de la scène du jeu de dames entre le roi et la déesse Isis, dont Hérodote a fait la Déméter égyptienne, comme il a fait d'Osiris le Dionysus du même peuple."— *Le Roi Rhampsinite et le Jeu des Dames*, par S. BIRCH. *Revue Arch., Nouvelle Série*, vol. XII. p. 58. Paris: 1865.

** BAAL, written sometimes Bar, was, like Sutech, a God borrowed from the Phœnician mythology. The worship of Baal seems to have been introduced into Egypt during the XIXth dynasty. The other God here mentioned, Mentu or Month, was a solar deity adored in the Thebaid, and especially worshipped at Hermonthis, now Erment; a modern town of some importance, the name of which is still almost identical with the Per-Mentu of ancient days. Mentu was the Egyptian, and Baal the Phœnician god of war.

*** From one of the inscriptions at Medinet Haboo, quoted by Chabas, See *Antiquité Historique*, ch. IV. p. 238. Ed. 1873.

pendant hanging in front of the ear. The features of
the Sardinian chief* are no less Asiatic. He wears
the usual Sardinian helmet surmounted by a ball and
two spikes. The profile of the Sicilian closely resembles
that of the Sardinian. He wears a head-dress like the
modern Persian cap. As ethnological types, these heads
are extremely valuable. Colonists not long since departed from the western coasts of Asia Minor, these
early European settlers are seen with the Asiatic stamp
of features; a stamp which has now entirely disappeared.

Other European nations are depicted elsewhere in
these Medinet Haboo sculptures. Pelasgians from the
Greek isles, Oscans perhaps from Pompeii, Daunians
from the districts between Tarentum and Brundusium,
figure here, each in their national costume. Of these,
the Pelasgian alone resembles the modern European.
On the left wall of the pavilion gateway, going up
towards the Temple, there is a large bas-relief of
Rameses III. leading a string of captives into the presence of Ammon Ra. Among these, the sculptures
being in a high state of preservation, there are a number of Pelasgians, some of whom have features of the
classical Greek type, and are strikingly handsome.
The Pelasgic head-dress resembles our old infantry
shako; and some of the men wear disc-shaped amulets
pierced with a hole in the centre, through which is
passed the chain that suspends it round the neck.

* It is a noteworthy fact (and one which has not, so far as I know, been
previously noticed) that while the Asiatic and African chiefs represented in
these friezes are insolently described in the accompanying hieroglyphic inscriptions as "the vile Libyan," "the vile Cushite," "the vile Mashuasha," and so
forth, the European leaders, though likewise prostrate and bound, are more
respectfully designated as "the Great (◇⟺) of Sardinia," "the Great of
Sicily," "the Great of Etruria," etc. etc. May this be taken as an indication
that their strength as military powers was already more formidable than that of
the Egyptians' nearer neighbours?

Leaving to the left a fine sitting statue of Khons
in green basalt, and to the right his prostrate fellow,
we pass under the gateway, cross a space of desolate
crude-brick mounds, and see before us the ruins of
the first pylon of the Great Temple of Khem. Once
past the threshold of this pylon, we enter upon a succession of magnificent courtyards. The hieroglyphs
here are on a colossal scale, and are cut deeper than
any others in Egypt. They are also coloured with a
more subtle eye to effect. Struck by the unusual
splendour of some of the blues, and by a peculiar
look of scintillation which they assumed in certain
lights, I examined them particularly, and found that
the effect had been produced by very subtle shades of
gradation in what appeared at first sight to be simple
flat tints. In some of the reeds, for instance, the
ground-colour begins at the top of the leaf in pure
cobalt, and passes imperceptibly down to a tint that
is almost emerald green at the bottom.*

The inner walls of this great courtyard, and the
outer face of the N.E. wall, are covered with sculptures
outlined, so to say, in intaglio, and relieved in the
hollow, so that the forms, though rounded, remain
level with the general surface. In these tableaux the
old world lives again. Rameses III., his sons and
nobles, his armies, his foes, play once more the brief
drama of life and death. Great battles are fought;
great victories are won; the slain are counted; the
captured drag their chains behind the victor's chariot;

---

* The grand blue of the ceiling of the colonnade of the Great Hypæthral
Court is also very remarkable for brilliancy and purity of tone; while to those
interested in decoration the capital and abacus of the second column to the
right on entering this courtyard, offer an interesting specimen of polychrome
ornamentation on a gold-coloured ground.

the king triumphs, is crowned, and sacrifices to the gods. Elsewhere more wars; more slaughter. There is revolt in Libya; there are raids on the Asiatic border; there are invaders coming in ships from the islands of the Great Sea. The royal standard is raised; troops assemble; arms are distributed. Again the king goes forth in his might, followed by the flower of Egyptian chivalry. "His horsemen are heroes; his foot soldiers are as lions that roar in the mountains." The king himself flames "like Mentu in his hour of wrath." He falls upon the foe "with the swiftness of a meteor." Here, crowded in rude bullock-trucks, the vanquished seek safety in flight. Yonder their galleys are sunk; their warriors are slain, drowned, captured, scathed, as it were, in a devouring fire. "Never again will they sow seed or reap harvest on the fair face of the earth."

"Behold!" says the Pharaoh, "Behold, I have taken their frontiers for my frontiers! I have devastated their towns, burned their crops, trampled their people under foot. Rejoice, O Egypt! Exalt thy voice to the heavens; for behold! I reign over all the lands of the barbarians! I King of Upper and Lower Egypt, Rameses III.! *

Such, linked each to each by a running commentary of text, are the illustrations; the story is written elsewhere. Elaborately hieroglyphed in upwards of seventy closely-packed columns, it covers the whole eastern face of the great north tower of the second propylon. This propylon divides the Osiride and Hypæthral courts, so that the inscription faces those entering the Temple and precedes the tableaux.

---

* Inscriptions at Medinet Haboo. See Chabas' *Antiquité Historique*, chap. IV. Paris: 1876.

Not even the poem of Pentaour is more picturesque,
not even the Psalms of David are more fervid, than
the style of this great Chronicle.*

M. Mariette is of opinion that the Temple of
Medinet Haboo, erected as it is on the side of the
great Theban necropolis, is, like the Ramesseum, a
funereal monument erected by Rameses III. in his
own lifetime to his own memory. The caryatid colossi
represent the king in the character of Osiris, and are
in fact on a huge scale precisely what the ordinary
funereal statuettes are upon a small scale. They
would be out of place in any but a monumental
edifice; and they alone suffice to determine the character of the building.

And such, no doubt, was the character of the
Amenophium; of the little Temple called Dayr el
Medinet; of the Temple of Queen Hatasu, known as
Dayr el Bahree; of the Temple of Goornah; of every
important structure, in short, erected upon this side of
the river. Of the Amenophium there remain only a
few sculptured blocks, a few confused foundations,
and—last representatives of an avenue of statues of
various sizes—the famous Colossi of the Plain.** The

* The whole of this chronicle is translated by M. Chabas in *L'Antiquité
Historique*, chap. IV. p. 246, *et seq.* It is also engraved in full in Rosellini
(*Monumenti Storici*); and has been admirably photographed by both M.
Hammerschmidt and Signor Beata.
** These two statues—the best-known, probably, of all Egyptian monuments—have been too often described, painted, engraved, and photographed,
to need more than a passing allusion. Their featureless faces, their attitude,
their surroundings, are familiar as the Pyramids, even to those who know not
Egypt. We all know that they represent Amenhotep, or Amunoph, III.; and that
the northernmost was shattered to the waist by the earthquake of B.C. 27. Being
heard to give out a musical sound during the first hour of the day, the statue
was supposed by the ancients to be endowed with a miraculous voice. The
Greeks, believing it to represent the fabled son of Tithonus and Aurora, gave
it the name of Memnon; notwithstanding that the Egyptians themselves
claimed the statues as portraits of Amenhotep III. Prefects, Consuls, Emperors,

Temple of Dayr el Bahree—built in terraces up the
mountain side, and approached once upon a time by
a magnificent avenue of sphinxes, the course of which
is yet visible—would probably be, if less ruined, the
most interesting temple on the western side of the
river. The monumental intention of this building is
perhaps shown by its dedication to Hathor, the Lady
of Amenti.

As for the Temple of Goornah, it is, at least in
part, as distinctly a memorial edifice as the Medici
Chapel at Florence or the Superga at Turin. It was
begun by Seti I. in memory of his father Rameses I.,
the founder of the XIXth Dynasty. Seti, however,
died before the work was completed. Hereupon
Rameses II., his son and successor, extended the
general plan, finished the part dedicated to his grand-
father, and added sculptures to the memory of Seti I.
Later still, Menepthah, the son and successor of
Rameses II., left his cartouches upon one of the doorways. The whole building, in short, is a family
monument, and contains a family portrait gallery.
Here all the personages whose names figure in the
shrines of the Ramessides at Silsilis are depicted in
their proper persons. In one tableau, Rameses I.,

and Empresses, came "to hear Memnon," as the phrase then ran. Among
the famous visitors who travelled thither on this errand, we find Strabo, Ger-
manicus, Hadrian, and the Empress Sabina. Opinion is divided as to the
cause of this sound. There is undoubtedly a hollow space inside the throne of
this statue, as may be seen by all who examine it from behind; and Sir G.
Wilkinson, in expressing his conviction that the musical sound was a piece of
priestly jugglery, represents the opinion of the majority. The author of a carefully considered article in the *Quarterly Review*, No. 276, April 1875, after
bringing together and sifting the evidence on both sides, comes to the contrary
conclusion, and attributes the sound to natural causes. The statue, which,
like its companion, was originally one solid monolith of gritstone, was repaired
with sandstone during the reign of Septimius Severus.

A Thousand Miles up the Nile. II.   15

defunct, deified,* swathed, enshrined, and crowned
like Osiris, is worshipped by Seti I. Behind Seti
stands his Queen Tuaa, the mother of Rameses II.
Elsewhere Seti I., being now dead, is deified and worshipped by Rameses II., who pours a libation to his
father's statue.   Through all these handsome heads
there runs a striking family likeness.   All more or less
partake of that Dantesque type which characterises the
portraits of Rameses II. in his youth.   The features of
Rameses I. and Seti I. are somewhat pinched and
stern, like the Dante of elder days.   The delicate
profile of Queen Tuaa, which is curiously like some
portraits of Queen Elizabeth, is perhaps too angular
to be altogether pleasing.   But in the well-known face
of Rameses II. these harsher details vanish, and the
beauty of the race culminates. The artists of Egyptian
Renaissance, always great in profile-portraiture, are
nowhere seen to better advantage than in this interesting series.
  Adjoining what may be called the monumental
part of the building, we find a number of halls and
chambers, the uses of which are unknown.   Most
writers assume that they were the private apartments
of the King.   Some go so far as to give the name of
Temple-Palaces to all these great funereal structures.
M. Mariette has, however, suggested a much likelier

  * This deification of the dead was not deification in the Roman sense;
neither was it canonisation in the modern sense.   The Egyptians believed the
justified dead to be assimilated, or rather identified, in the spirit with Osiris,
the beneficent Judge and Deity of the lower world.   Thus, in their worship of
ancestry, they adored not mortals immortalised, but the dead in Osiris, and
Osiris in the dead.
  It is worth noting, by the way, that notwithstanding the subsequent
deification of Seti I., Rameses I. remained, so to say, the tutelary saint of the
Temple.   He alone is represented with the curious pointed and upturned
beard, like a chamois horn reversed, which is the peculiar attribute of deity.

solution of the problem. He conceives that these Western Temples were erected in connection, though not in direct communication, with the royal tombs in the adjacent valley of Bab-el-Molook.

Now every Egyptian tomb of importance has its outer chamber or votive oratory, the walls of which are covered with paintings descriptive, in some instances, of the occupations of the deceased upon earth, and in others of the adventures of his soul after death. Here at stated seasons the survivors repaired with offerings. No priest, it would seem, of necessity officiated at these little services. A whole family would come, bringing the first fruits of their garden, the best of their poultry, cakes of home-made bread, bouquets of lotus blossoms. With their own hands they piled the altar, burned the incense, poured the libations. It is a scene constantly reproduced upon monuments* of every epoch. These votive oratories, however, are wholly absent in the valley of Bab-el-Molook. The royal tombs consist of only tunnelled passages and sepulchral vaults, the entrances to which were closed for ever as soon as the sarcophagus was occupied. Hence M. Mariette concludes that each memorial temple played to the tomb of its tutelary saint and sovereign that part which is played by the

---

* There is among the funereal tablets of the Boulak collection a small bas-relief sculpture representing the arrival of a family of mourners at the tomb of a deceased ancestor. The statue of the defunct sits at the upper end. The mourners are laden with offerings. One little child carries a lamb; another a goose. A scribe stands by, waiting to register the gifts. The tablet commemorates one Psamtiknefer-Sam, a hierogrammate under some king of the XXIVth Dynasty. The natural grace and simple pathos with which this little frieze is treated, lift it far above the level of ordinary Egyptian art; and it may fairly be said to bear comparison with the class of monuments lately discovered on the Eleusinian road at Athens.

external oratory attached to the tomb of a private individual.

An oratory on so grand a scale would imply an
elaborate ceremonial. A dead and deified king would
doubtless have his train of priests, his daily liturgies,
processions, and sacrifices. All this again implies additional accommodation, and accounts, I venture to
think, for any number of extra halls and chambers.
Such sculptures as yet remain on the walls of these
ruined apartments are, in fact, wholly funereal and
sacrificial in character. It is also to be remembered
that we have here a temple dedicated to two kings,
and served most likely by a twofold college of
priests.*

The wall-sculptures at Goornah are extremely
beautiful, especially in those parts erected by Seti I.
Where it has been accidentally preserved, the surface
is as smooth, the execution as brilliant, as the finest
mediæval ivory carving. Behind a broken column,
for instance, that leans against the S.W. wall of the
sanctuary,** one may see, by peeping this way and
that, the ram's-head prow of a sacred boat, quite unharmed, and of surpassing delicacy. The modelling
of the ram's head is simply faultless. It would indeed
be scarcely too much to say that this one fragment, if
all the rest had perished, would alone place the de-

* As early as the time of the Pyramid Kings, there were special priests
and votive chapels attached to each pyramid. "Une dignité tout à fait particulier est celle que les inscriptions hiéroglyphiques désignent par le titre
'prophète de la pyramide, de tel pharaon.' Il paraît qu'après sa mort chaque
roi était vénéré par un culte spécial." *Histoire d'Égypte:* BRUGSCH. 2d. ed.,
chap. v. p. 35. Leipzig: 1875.
** There is a very curious window at the end of this sanctuary, with
grooves for the shutter, and holes in which to slip and drop the bar by which it
was fastened.

corative sculpture of ancient Egypt in a rank second
only to that of Greece.

The Temple of Goornah — northernmost of the
Theban group—stands at the mouth of that famous
valley called by the Arabs Bab-el-Molook, and by
travellers, the Valley of the Tombs of the Kings.
This valley may be described as a bifurcated ravine,
ending in two *culs de sac*, and hemmed in on all
sides by lime-stone precipices. It winds round behind
the cliffs which face Luxor and Karnak, and runs
almost parallel with the Nile. This range of cliffs is
perforated on both sides with tombs. The priests and
nobles of many dynasties were buried terrace above
terrace on the side next the river. Back to back with
them, in the silent and secret valley beyond, slept the
kings in their everlasting sepulchres.

Most travellers moor for a day or two at Karnak,
and thence make their excursion to Bab-el-Molook. By
so doing they lose one of the most interesting rides
in the neighbourhood of Thebes. L. and the Writer
started from Luxor one morning about an hour after
day-break, crossing the river at the usual point and
thence riding northwards along the bank, with the
Nile on the one hand, and the corn-lands on the other.
In the course of such rides, one discovers the almost
incredible fertility of the Thebaid. Every inch of
arable ground is turned to account. All that grows,
grows lustily. The barley ripples in one uninterrupted
sweep from Medinet Haboo to a point half-way between the Ramesseum and Goornah. Next come plantations of tobacco, cotton, hemp, linseed, maize and
lentils, so closely set, so rich in promise, that the country
looks as if it were laid out in allotment ground for

miles together. Where the rice crop has been gathered,
clusters of temporary huts have sprung up in the clearings; for the fellaheen come out from their crowded
villages in "the sweet o' the year," and live in the
midst of the crops which now they guard, and which
presently they will reap. The walls of these summer
huts are mere wattled fences of Indian corn straw, with
bundles of the same laid lightly across the top by way
of roofing. This pastoral world is everywhere up and
doing. Here are men plying the shadoof by the river's
brink; women spinning in the sun; children playing;
dogs barking; larks soaring and singing overhead.
Against the foot of the cliffs yonder, where the vegetation ends and the tombs begin, there flows a calm
river edged with palms. A few months ago, we should
have been deceived by that fairy water. We know
now that it is the mirage.

Striking off by and by towards the left, we make
for a point where the mountains recede and run low,
and a wedge-like "spit" of sandy desert encroaches
upon the plain. On the verge of this spit stands a
clump of sycamores and palms. A row of old yellow
columns supporting a sculptured architrave gleams
through the boughs; a little village nestles close by;
and on the desert slope beyond, in the midst of a
desolate Arab burial-ground, we see a tiny mosque
with one small cupola, dazzling white in the sunshine.
This is Goornah. There is a spring here, and some
girls are drawing water from the well near the Temple.
Our donkeys slake their thirst from the cattle-trough—
a broken sarcophagus that may once have held the
mummy of a king. A creaking sakkieh is at work
yonder, turned by a couple of red cows with mild

Hathor-like faces. The old man who drives them sits in the middle of the cog-wheel, and goes slowly round as if he was being roasted.

We now leave behind us the well, and the trees, and the old Greek-looking Temple, and turn our faces westward, bound for an opening yonder among cliffs pitted with the mouths of empty tombs. It is plain to see that we are now entering upon what was once a torrent-bed. Rushing down from the hills, the pent-up waters have here spread fan-like over the slope of the desert, strewing the ground with boulders, and plough-ing it into hundreds of tortuous channels. Up that torrent-bed lies our road to-day.

The weird rocks stand like sentinels to right and left as one enters the mouth of the valley, and take strange shapes as of obelisks and sphinxes. Some, worn at the base, and towering like ruined pyramids above, remind us of tombs on the Appian Way. As the ravine narrows, the limestome walls rise higher. The chalky track glares underfoot. Piles of shivered chips sparkle and scintillate at the foot of the rocks. The cliffs burn at a white heat. The atmosphere palpi-tates like gaseous vapour. The sun blazes overhead. Not a breath stirs; neither is there a finger's breadth of shade on either side. It is like riding into the mouth of a furnace. Meanwhile one looks in vain for any sign of life. No blade of green has grown here since the world began. No breathing creature makes these rocks its home. All is desolation—such desolation as one dreams of in a world scathed by fire from heaven.

When we have gone a long way, always tracking up the bed of the torrent, we come to a place where our donkeys turn off from the main course and make

for what is evidently a forced passage cut clean through
a wall of solid limestone. The place was once a mere
recess in the cliffs, but on the farther side, masked by
a natural barrier of rock, there lay another valley leading to a secluded amphitheatre among the mountains.
The first Pharaoh who chose his place of burial among
those hidden ways, must have been he who cut the
pass and levelled the road by which we now travel.
This cutting is Bab-el-Molook—the Gate of the Sultan;
a name which doubtless perpetuates that by which the
place was known to the old Egyptians. Once through
the Gate, a grand mountain rises into view. Egypt is
the land of strange mountains; and here is one that
reproduces on a giant scale every feature of the pyramid
of Ouenephes at Sakkarah. It is square; it rises stage
above stage in ranges of columnar cliffs with slopes of
débris between; and it terminates in a blunt four-sided
peak nearly 2000 feet above the level of the plain.

Keeping this mountain always before us, we now
follow the windings of the second valley, which is even
more narrow, parched, and glaring than the first. Perhaps the intense heat makes the road appear longer
than it really is; but it seems to us like several miles.
At length the uniformity of the way is broken. Two
small ravines branch off, one to the right, one to the
left; and in both, at the foot of the rocks, there are
here and there to be seen square openings, like cellar-
doors, half sunk below the surface, and seeming to
shoot downwards into the bowels of the earth. In another moment or so, our road ends suddenly in a wild
tumbled waste, like an exhausted quarry, shut in all
round by impending precipices, at the base of which
more rock-cut portals peep out at different points.

From the moment when it first came into sight, I had made certain that in that pyramidal mountain we should find the Tombs of the Kings—so certain, that I can scarcely believe our guide when he assures us that these cellars are the places we have come to see, and that the mountain contains not a single tomb. We alight, however; climb a steep slope; and find ourselves on the threshold of No. 17.

"Belzoni-tomb," says our guide; and Belzoni's tomb, as we know, is the tomb of Seti the First.

I am almost ashamed to remember now that we took our luncheon in the shade of that solemn vestibule, and rested and made merry, before going down into the great gloomy sepulchre whose staircases and corridors plunged away into the darkness below, as if they led straight to the land of Amenti.

The tombs in the Valley of Bab-el-Molook are as unlike the tombs in the cliffs opposite Luxor as if the Theban kings and the Theban nobles were of different races and creeds. Those sacred scribes and dignitaries, with their wives and families and their numerous friends and dependents, were a joyous set. They loved the things of this life, and would fain have carried their pursuits and pleasures with them into the land beyond the grave. So they decorated the walls of their tombs with pictures of the way in which their lives were spent, and hoped perhaps that the mummy, dreaming away its long term of solitary waiting, might take comfort in those shadowy reminiscences. The kings, on the contrary, covered every foot of their last palaces with scenes from the life to come. The wanderings of the soul after its separation from the body, the terrors

and dangers that beset it during its journey through
Hades, the demons it must fight, the accusers to whom
it must answer, the transformations it must undergo,
afforded subjects for endless illustration. Of the fishing
and fowling and feasting and junketting that we saw
the other day in those terraces behind the Ramesseum,
we discover no trace in the tombs of Bab-el-Molook.
In place of singing and lute-playing, we find here
prayers and invocations; for the pleasant Nile-boat, and
the water-parties, and the chase of the gazelle and the
ibex, we now have the bark of Charon, and the basin
of purgatorial fire, and the strife with the infernal
deities. The contrast is sharp and strange. It is as
if an Epicurean aristocracy had been ruled by a line
of Puritan kings. The tombs of the subjects are
Anacreontics. The tombs of their sovereigns are
penitential psalms.

To go down into one of these great sepulchres is
to descend one's-self into the Lower World, and to
tread the path of the shades. Crossing the threshold,
we look up half-expecting to read those terrible words
in which all who enter are warned to leave hope be·
hind. The passage slopes before our feet; the daylight
fades behind us. At the end of the passage comes a
flight of steps, and from the bottom of that flight of
steps we see another corridor slanting down into depths
of utter darkness. The walls on both sides are covered
with close-cut columns of hieroglyphic text, interspersed
with ominous shapes, half-deity, half-demon. Huge
serpents writhe beside us along the walls. Guardian
spirits of threatening aspect advance, brandishing
swords of flame. A strange heaven opens overhead—
a heaven where the stars travel in boats across the seas

of space; and the Sun, escorted by the hours, the
months, and the signs of the zodiac, issues from the
East, sets in the West, and traverses the hemisphere of
Everlasting Night. We go on, and the last gleam of
daylight vanishes in the distance. Another flight of
steps leads now to a succession of passages and halls,
some smaller, some larger, some vaulted, some supported on pillars. Here yawns a great pit half full of
débris. Yonder opens a suite of unfinished chambers
abandoned by the workmen. The farther we go, the
more weird become our surroundings. The walls swarm
with ugly and evil things. Serpents, and bats, and
crocodiles, some with human heads and legs, some
vomiting fire, some armed with spears and darts, pursue
and torture the wicked. These unfortunates have their
hearts torn out; are boiled in cauldrons; are suspended
head downwards over seas of flame; are speared, de-
capitated, and driven in headless gangs to scenes of
further torment. Beheld by the dim and shifting light
of a few candles, these painted horrors assume an
aspect of ghastly reality. They start into life as we
pass, then drop behind us into darkness. That darkness alone is awful. The atmosphere is suffocating.
The place is ghostly and peopled with nightmares.

Elsewhere we come upon scenes less painful. The
Sun emerges from the lower hemisphere. The justified
dead sow and reap in the Elysian fields, gather celestial
fruits, and bathe in the waters of truth. The royal
mummy reposes in its shrine. Funereal statues of the
king are worshipped with incense, and offerings of
meat, and libations of wine.* Finally the king arrives,

* These funereal statues are represented each on a stand or platform,
erect, with one foot advanced, as if walking, the right hand holding the Tau,

purified and justified, at the last stage of his spiritual journey. He is welcomed by the Gods, ushered into the presence of Osiris, and received into the Abode of the Blest. *

Coming out for a few moments into blinding daylight, we drink a long draught of pure air, cross a few yards of uneven ground, arrive at the mouth of another excavation, and plunge again into underground darkness. A third and a fourth time we repeat this strange experience. It is like a feverish sleep, troubled by gruesome dreams, and broken by momentary wakings.

These tombs in a general way are very much alike. Some are longer than others; ** some loftier. In some the descent is gradual; in others it is steep and sudden.

or symbol of life, the left hand grasping a staff. The attitude is that of the wooden statue at Boulak; and it is worth remark that the figures stand detached, with no support at the back, which was never the case with those carved in stone or granite. There can be no doubt that this curious series of funereal statues represents those which were actually placed in the tomb; and that the ceremonies here represented were actually performed before them, previous to closing the mouth of the sepulchre. One of these very wooden statues, from this very tomb, was brought to England by Belzoni, and is now in the British Museum (No. 854, Central Saloon). The wood is much decayed, and the statue ought undoubtedly to be placed under glass. The tableaux representing the above ceremonies are well copied in Rosellini, *Mon. del Culto*, plates 60-63.

 * A remarkable inscription in this tomb, relating the wrath of Ra and the destruction of mankind, is translated by M. Naville in vol. IV. pt. i., of the *Transactions of the Biblical Arch. Society*. In this singular myth, which bears a family resemblance to the Chaldæan record of the Flood, the deluge is a deluge of human blood. The inscription covers the walls of a small chamber known as the Chamber of the Cow.

 * The longest tomb in the valley, which is that of Seti I., measures 470 feet in length to the point where it is closed by the falling in of the rock; and the total depth of its descent is about 180 feet. The tomb of Rameses III. (No. 11) measures in length 405 feet, and descends only 31 feet. The rest average from about 350 to 150 feet in length, and the shortest is excavated to a distance of only 65 feet.

We visited, however, one tomb in the Assaseef, which in extent far exceeds any of the tombs of the kings. This astonishing excavation, which consists of a bewildering labyrinth of halls, passages, staircases, pits, and chambers, is calculated at 23,809 square feet. The name of the occupant was Petamunap, a priest of uncertain date.

Certain leading features are common to all. The great serpent,* the scarab,** the bat*** and the crocodile,† are always conspicuous on the walls. The judgment-scene, and the well-known typical picture of the four races of mankind, are continually reproduced. Some tombs,†† however, vary both in plan and decoration. That of Rameses III., though not nearly so beautiful as the tomb of Seti I., is perhaps the most curious of all. The paintings here are for the most part designed on an unsculptured surface coated with white stucco. The drawing is often indifferent, and the colouring is uniformly coarse and gaudy. Yellow abounds; and crude reds and blues remind us of the coloured picture-books of our childhood. It is difficult to understand, indeed, how the builder of Medinet Haboo, with the best Egyptian art of the day at his command, should have been content with such wall-paintings as these.

Still Rameses III. seems to have had a grand idea of going in state to the next world, with his retainers around him. In a series of small antechambers opening off from the first corridor, the great officers of the Royal Household—the High Steward, the Treasurer, the Chief Baker, the Superintendents of the Boats, the

* *Apophis,* in Egyptian *Apap;* the great serpent of darkness, over whom Ra must triumph after he sets in the west, and before he again rises in the east.
** Kheper, the scarab deity. See Chap. VI. p. 135 of vol. I.
*** Symbolical of darkness.
† The crocodile represents Sebek. In one of the Boulak papyri, this God is called the son of Isis, and combats the enemies of Osiris. Here he combats Apophis in behalf of Ra.
†† The tomb numbered 3 in the first small ravine to the left as one rides up the valley, bears the cartouches of Rameses II. The Writer crawled in as far as the choked condition of the tomb permitted, but the passage becomes quite impassable after the first thirty or forty yards. See chap. XV. p. 49 of this vol.

Armoury, and the Palace-furniture—are supposed to
have been buried. Under the floor of each chamber
is a pit, now filled up; and the walls are decorated
with subjects believed to be descriptive of the office of
each functionary. In one, the cooks and bakers are
seen preparing the royal dinner. In the others are
depicted magnificent thrones; gilded galleys with parti-
coloured sails; gold and silver vases; rich store of arms
and armour; piles of precious woods, of panther skins,
of fruits, and birds, and curious baskets, and all such
articles of personal luxury as a palace-building Pharaoh
might delight in. Here also are the two famous harpers; cruelly defaced, but still sweeping the strings
with the old powerful touch that erewhile soothed the
King in hours of melancholy. These two spirited
figures—which are undoubtedly portraits *—almost re-
deem the poverty of the rest of the paintings.

In many tombs, the empty sarcophagus yet occupies its ancient place. ** We saw one in No. 2
(Rameses IV.), and another in No. 9 (Rameses VI.);
the first, a grand monolith of dark granite overturned
and but little injured; the second, shattered by early
treasure-seekers.

---

* When first seen by Sir G. Wilkinson these harpers were still in such
good preservation, that he reported of one at least, if not both, as obviously
blind. The harps are magnificent, richly inlaid and gilded, and adorned with
busts of the king. One has eleven strings, the other fourteen.

** The sarcophagus of Seti I., which was brought to England by Belzoni,
is in Sir J. Soane's Museum. It is carved from a single block of the finest
alabaster, and is covered with incised hieroglyphic texts and several hundred
figures, descriptive of the passage of the sun through the hours of the night.
See *Le Sarcophage de Seti I.* P. PIERRET. *Révue Arch.*, vol. XXI. p. 285:
1870.

The sarcophagus of Rameses III. is in the Fitz-William Museum, Cambridge, and the lid thereof is in the Egyptian collection of the Louvre. See
Remarks on the Sarcophagus of Rameses III. S, BIRCH, LL.D.; Cambridge,
1876. Also *Notice Sommaire des Monuments Égyptiens du Louvre.* E. DE
ROUGÉ, p. 51: Paris, 1873.

Most of the tombs at Bab-el-Molook were open in Ptolemaic times. Being then, as now, among the stock sights and wonders of Thebes, they were visited by crowds of early travellers, who have as usual left their neatly-scribbled graffiti on the walls. When and by whom the sepulchres were originally violated is of course unknown. Some, doubtless, were sacked by the Persians; others were plundered by the Egyptians themselves, long enough before Cambyses. Not even in the days of the Ramessides, though a special service of guards was told off for duty in "the Great Valley," were the kings safe in their tombs. During the reign of Rameses IX.—whose own tomb is here, and known as No. 6—there seems to have been an organised band, not only of robbers, but of receivers, who lived by depredations of the kind. A contemporary papyrus * tells how in one instance the royal mummies were found lying in the dust, their gold and silver orna- ments, and the treasures of their tombs, all stolen. In another instance, a king and his queen were carried

* Abbott Papyrus, British Museum. This papyrus, which has been trans- lated by M. Chabas (*Mélanges Égyptologiques*, 3ième Série: Paris and Chalon, 1870), gives a list of royal tombs inspected by an Egyptian Commission in the month of Athyr (year unknown), during the reign of Rameses IX. Among the tombs visited on this occasion mention is especially made of "the funeral monument of the king En-Aa, which is at the north of the Amenophium of the terrace. The monument is broken into from the back, at the place where the stela is placed before the monument, and having the statue of the king upon the front of the stela, with his hound, named Bahuka, between his legs. Verified this day, and found intact." Such was the report of the writer of this papyrus of 3000 years ago. Now comes one of the wonders of modern discovery. In 1860, or 1861, M. Mariette, excavating in that part of the Necropolis called the Assaseef, which lies to the north of the ruins of the Amenophium, discovered the remains of the tomb of this very king, and the broken stela bearing upon its face a full-length bas-relief of King En-Aa (or Entef-Aa), with three dogs before him and one between his legs; the dog Bahuka having his name engraved over his back in hieroglyphic characters.— See *Tablet of Antefaa II.* S. BIRCH, LL.D. *Transactions of the Bib. Arch. Society*, vol. IV. part I. p. 172.

away bodily, to be unrolled and rifled at leisure. This curious information is all recorded in the form of a report, drawn up by the Commandant of Western Thebes, who, with certain other officers and magistrates, officially inspected the tombs of the "Royal Ancestors" during the reign of Rameses IX.

No royal tomb has, I believe, been found absolutely intact in the valley of Bab-el-Molook. Even that of Seti the First had been secretly entered ages before ever Belzoni discovered it. He found in it statues of wood and porcelain, and the mummy of a bull; but nothing of value save the sarcophagus, which was empty. There can be no doubt that the priesthood were largely implicated in these contemporary sacrileges. Of thirty-nine persons accused by name in the papyrus just quoted, seven are priests, and eight are sacred scribes.

To rob the dead was always a lucrative trade at Thebes. The mummy of Queen Aah-Hotep,* discovered a few years since in an unpretending sepulchre at Drah Aboo-l-Neggah, was found loaded with jewels, and weapons, and precious toys in gold and silver. Yet Aah-Hotep was only a queen-consort, and lived in the less ostentatious days of the XVIIth Dynasty. The splendid Pharaohs of 400 years later, we may be certain, went to their dark palaces still more magnificently equipped for the life to come.** When, indeed, one

---

* These invaluable relics are exhibited in the Salle des Bijoux of the Boulak Museum.

** There is in one of the Papyri of the Louvre a very curious illustration, representing—1st, the funeral procession of one Neb-Set, deceased; 2d, the interior of the sepulchre, with the mummy, the offerings, and the furniture of the tomb, elaborately drawn and coloured. Among the objects here shown are two torches, three vases, a coffer, a mirror, a Kohl bottle, a pair of sandals, a staff, a vase for ointment, a perfume bottle, and an ablution jar. "These ob-

thinks of the jewels, furniture, vases, ointments, clothing, arms, and precious documents which were as certainly buried in those tombs as the royal mummies for whom they were excavated, it seems far more wonderful that one queen and her parure should have remained undiscovered, than that all the rest of these dead and gone royalties should have fallen among thieves.

Of all tombs in the Valley of Bab-el-Molook, one would rather, I think, have discovered that of Rameses III. As he was one of the richest of the Pharaohs * and an undoubted virtuoso in his tastes, so we may be sure that his tomb was furnished with all kinds of beautiful and precious things. What would we not give now to find some of those elaborate gold and silver vases, those cushioned thrones and sofas, those bows and quivers and shirts of mail so carefully catalogued on the walls of the side chambers in the first corridor! I do not doubt that specimens of all these things were buried with the king and left ready for his use. He died, believing that his soul would come back after long cycles of probation, and make its home once more in the mummied body. He thought

jects, all belonging to the toilette (for the coffer would have contained clothing), were placed in the tomb for that day of waking which the popular belief promised to the dead. The tomb was therefore furnished like the abodes of the living."—Translated from T. DEVÉRIA, *Catalogue des Manuscrits Égyptiens du Louvre:* Paris, 1875, p. 80. The plan of the sepulchre of Neb-Set is also drawn upon this papyrus; and the soul of the deceased, represented as a human-headed bird, is shown flying down towards the mummy. A fine sarcophagus in the Boulak museum (No. 84) is decorated in like manner, with a representation of the mummy on its bier being visited, or finally rejoined, by the soul. I have also in my own collection a funeral papyrus vignetted on one side with this same subject; and bearing on the reverse side an architectural elevation of the monument erected over the sepulchre of the deceased.

    * "King Rhampsinitus (Rameses III.) was possessed, they said, of great riches in silver, indeed, to such an amount that none of the princes, his successors, surpassed or even equalled his wealth."—HERODOTUS, book II, chap. 121.

he should rise as from sleep; cast off his bandages;
eat and be refreshed, and put on sandals and scented
vestments, and take his staff in his hand, and go forth
again into the light of everlasting day. Poor ghost,
wandering bodiless through space! where now are thy
funeral-baked meats, thy changes of raiment, thy per-
fumes and precious ointments? Where is that body
for which thou wert once so solicitous, and without
which resurrection * is impossible? One fancies thee
sighing forlorn through these desolate halls when all
is silent and the moon shines down the valley.

Life at Thebes is made up of incongruities. A
morning among temples is followed by an afternoon of
antiquity-hunting; and a day of meditation among
tombs winds up with a dinner-party on board some
friend's Dahabeeyah, or a fantasia at the British Consulate. L. and the Writer did their fair share of
antiquity-hunting both at Luxor and elsewhere; but
chiefly at Luxor. I may say, indeed, that our life
here was one long pursuit of the pleasures of the
chase. The game, it is true, was prohibited; but we
enjoyed it none the less because it was illegal. Perhaps we enjoyed it the more.

There were whispers about this time of a tomb
that had been discovered on the Western side—a wonderful tomb, rich in all kinds of treasures. No one, of

---

* Impossible from the Egyptian point of view. "That the body should
not waste or decay was an object of anxious solicitude; and for this purpose
various bandlets and amulets, prepared with certain magical preparations, and
sanctified with certain spells or prayers, or even offerings and small sacrifices,
were distributed over various parts of the mummy. In some mysterious manner
the immortality of the body was deemed as important as the passage of the
soul; and at a later period the growth or natural reparation of the body was
invoked as earnestly as the life or passage of the soul to the upper regions."—
See *Introduction to the Funereal Ritual*, S. BIRCH, LL.D., in vol. v. of
BUNSEN'S *Egypt*: Lond., 1867.

course, had seen these things. No one knew who had
found them. No one knew where they were hidden.
But there was a solemn secrecy about certain of the
Arabs, and a conscious look about some of the visitors,
and an air of awakened vigilance about the government officials, which savoured of mystery. These
rumours by and by assumed more definite proportions.
Dark hints were dropped of a possible papyrus; the
M.B.'s babbled of mummies; and an American Dahabeeyah, lying innocently off Karnak, was reported to
have a mummy on board. Now, neither L. nor the
Writer desired to become the happy proprietor of an
ancient Egyptian; but the papyrus was a thing to be
thought of. In a fatal hour we expressed a wish to
see it. From that moment every mummy-snatcher in
the place regarded us as his lawful prey. Beguiled
into one den after another, we were shown all the
stolen goods in Thebes. Some of the things were
very curious and interesting. In one house we were offered two bronze vases, each with a band of delicately-
engraved hieroglyphs running round the lip; also a
square stand of basket-work in two colours, precisely
like that engraved in Sir G. Wilkinson's first volume, *
after the original in the Berlin Museum. Pieces of
mummy-case and wall-sculpture and sepulchral tablets
abounded; and on one occasion we were introduced
into the presence of—a mummy!

All these houses were tombs, and in this one the
mummy was stowed away in a kind of recess at the
end of a long rock-cut passage; probably the very
place once occupied by the original tenant. It was a

* *The Ancient Egyptians*, Sir G. Wilkinson; vol. I. chap. II., woodcut
No. 92. Lond., 1871.

mummy of the same period as that which we saw dis-
entombed under the auspices of the Governor, and
was enclosed in the same kind of cartonnage, patterned in many colours on a white ground. I shall
never forget that curious scene—the dark and dusty
vault; the Arabs with their lanterns; the mummy in
its gaudy cerements lying on an old mat at our feet.

Meanwhile we tried in vain to get sight of the
coveted papyrus. A grave Arab dropped in once or
twice after nightfall, and talked it over vaguely with the
dragoman; but never came to the point. He offered it
first, with a mummy, for £100. Finding, however, that
we would neither buy his papyrus unseen nor his
mummy at any price, he haggled and hesitated for a
day or two, evidently trying to play us off against
some rival or rivals unknown, and finally disappeared.
These rivals, we afterwards found, were the M.B.'s.
They bought both mummy and papyrus at an enormous
price; and then, unable to endure the perfume of their
ancient Egyptian, drowned the dear departed at the
end of a week.

Other purchasers are possibly less sensitive. We
heard, at all events, of fifteen mummies successfully
insinuated through the Alexandrian Custom-house by
a single agent that winter. There is, in fact, a growing passion for mummies among Nile travellers. Unfortunately, the prices rise with the demand; and although the mine is practically inexhaustible, a mummy
now-a-days becomes not only a prohibited, but a costly
luxury.

At Luxor, the British, American, and French Consuls are Arabs. The Prussian Consul is a Copt. The
Austrian Consul is, or was, an American. The French

Consul showed us over the old tumble-down building called "The French House," which, though but a rude structure of palm-timbers and sun-dried clay, built partly against and partly over the Temple of Luxor, has its place in history. For here, in 1829, Champollion and Rosellini lived and worked together, during part of their long sojourn at Thebes. Rosellini tells how they used to sit up at night, dividing the fruits of the day's labour; Champollion copying whatever might be useful for his Egyptian grammar, and Rosellini, the new words that furnished material for his dictionary. Here, too, lodged the naval officers sent out by the French in 1831, to remove the obelisk which now stands in the Place de la Concorde. And here, writing those charming letters that delight the world, Lady Duff Gordon lingered through the last few winters of her life. The rooms in which she lived first, and the balcony in which she took such pleasure, are no longer accessible, owing to the ruinous state of one of the staircases; but we saw the rooms she last inhabited. Her couch, her rug, her folding chair are there still. The walls are furnished with a few cheap prints and a pair of tin sconces. All is very bare and comfortless.

We asked if it was just like this when the Sittèh lived here. The Arab Consul replied that she had "a table, and some books." He looked himself in the last stage of consumption, and spoke and moved like one that had done with life.

We were shocked at the dreariness of the place— till we went to the window. That window, which commands the Nile and the Western plain of Thebes furnished the room and made its poverty splendid.

The sun was near setting. We could distinguish
the mounds and pylons of Medinet Haboo and the site
of the Ramesseum. The terraced cliffs, overtopped by
the pyramidal mountain of Bab-el-Molook, burned crimson against a sky of stainless blue. The footpath
leading to the Valley of the Tombs of the Kings
showed like a hot white scar winding along the face of
the rocks. The river gave back the sapphire tones of
the sky. I thought I could be well content to spend
many a winter in no matter how comfortless a lodging,
if only I had that wonderful view, with its infinite
beauty of light and colour and space, and its history,
and its mystery, always before my windows.

Mehemet Ali gave this house to the French, and to
the French it still belongs. It disfigures and encum-
bers the Temple, and it is going fast to ruin; yet one
cannot wish it away.

Another historical house is that built by Sir G.
Wilkinson, among the tombs of Sheykh-Abd-el-Koorneh.
Here he lived while amassing the materials for his
Manners and Customs of the Ancient Egyptians; and
here Lepsius and his company of artists put up while
at work on the Western bank. Science makes little
impression on the native mind. No one now remem-
bers Champollion, or Rosellini, or Sir G. Wilkinson;
but every Arab in Luxor cherishes the memory of
Lady Duff Gordon in his heart of hearts, and speaks
of her with blessings.

The French House lies at the southern end of the
Temple. At the northern end, built up between the
enormous sandstone columns of the Great Colonnade,
is the house of Mustapha Aga, most hospitable and
kindly of British Consuls. Mustapha Aga has travelled

in Europe, and speaks fluent Italian, English, and French. His eldest son is Governor of Luxor; his younger—the "little Ahmed" whom Lady Duff Gordon delighted to educate—having spent two years in England as the guest of Lord D., is an accomplished Englishman. We used to see him of a morning looking like a beautiful young Prince just stepped out of the *Arabian Nights*, turbaned and slippered, and robed in a magnificent cream-coloured beneesh of Damascene embroidery. After dinner, he would pay us a visit in faultless evening dress, coming in, hat in hand, with the *élancé* step and the drawing-room smile of the gilded youth of Belgravia.

In the round of gaiety that goes on at Luxor the British Consulate plays the leading part. Mustapha Aga entertains all the English Dahabeeyahs, and all the English Dahabeeyahs entertain Mustapha Aga. We were invited to several Fantasias at the Consulate, and dined with Mustapha Aga at his suburban house the evening before we left Luxor.

The appointed hour was 8.30 P. M. We arrived amid much barking of dogs, and were received by our host in a large empty hall surrounded by a divan. Here we remained till dinner was announced. We were next ushered through an anteroom where two turbaned and barefooted servants were in waiting; the one with a brass basin and ewer, the other with an armful of Turkish towels. We then, each in turn, held our hands over the basin; had water poured on them; and received a towel apiece. These towels we were told to keep; and they served for dinner-napkins. The anteroom opened into a brilliantly-lighted dining-room of moderate size, having in the centre a round brass table with an upright fluted rim, like a big tray. For each person were placed a chair, a huge block of bread, a wooden spoon, two tumblers, and a bouquet. Plates, knives, forks, there were none.

The party consisted of the Happy Couple, the Director of the Luxor Telegraph Office, L., the Writer, young Ahmed, and our host.

"To-night we are all Arabs," said Mustapha Aga, as he showed us where to sit. "We drink Nile water, and we eat with our fingers."

So we drank Nile water; and for the first time in our lives we ate with our fingers. In fact, we found them exceedingly useful.

The dinner was excellent. Without disrespect to our own accomplished chef, or to the accomplished chefs of our various friends upon the river, I am bound to say that it was the very best dinner I ever ate out of Europe. Everything was hot, quickly served, admirably dressed and the best of its kind. Here is the *menu:*—

MENU.   MARCH 31, 1874.

White soup :—(Turkey).

FISH.
Fried Kishr. *

ENTRÉES.
Stewed pigeons.   Spinach and rice.

ROAST.
Dall. **

---

* *Kishr ;* one of the few good fish of the Nile,
** *Dall;* roast shoulder of lamb,

ENTRÉES.

Kebobs* of mutton.   Kebobs of lamb's kidneys.
Tomatoes with rice.   Kuftah.**

ROAST.
Turkey, with cucumber sauce.

ENTRÉE.
Pilaff*** of rice.

SECOND COURSE.

Mish-mish. †   Rus Blebban. †††
Kunáfah. ††   Totleh. §

These dishes were placed one at a time in the
middle of the table, and rapidly changed. Each dipped
his own spoon in the soup, dived into the stew, and
pulled off pieces of fish or lamb with his fingers. Having no plates, we made plates of our bread. Meanwhile Mustapha Aga, like an attentive host, tore off an
especially choice morsel now and then, and handed it
to one or other of his guests.

To eat gracefully with one's fingers is a fine art; to
carve with them skilfully is a science. None of us, I
think, will soon forget the wonderful way in which our
host attacked and vanquished the turkey — a solid
colossus weighing twenty lbs., and roasted to perfection. Half-rising, he turned back his cuff, poised his
wrist, and, driving his forefinger and thumb deep into
the breast, brought out a long, stringy, smoking fragment, which he deposited on the plate of the Writer.

* *Kebobs:* small lumps of meat grilled on skewers.
** *Kuftah:* broiled mutton.
*** *Pilaff:* boiled rice, mixed with a little butter, and seasoned with salt
and pepper.
† *Mish-mish:* apricots (preserved).
†† *Kunáfah:* A rich pudding made of rice, almonds, cream, cinnamon,
etc. etc.
††† *Rus Blebban:* rice cream.
§ *Totleh:* sweet jelly, encrusted with blanched almonds.

Thus begun, the turkey went round the table amid
peals of laughter, and was punished by each in turn.
The pilaff which followed is always the last dish served
at an Egyptian or Turkish dinner.   After this, our
spoons were changed and the sweets were put upon
the table.   The drinks throughout were plain water,
rice-water, and lemonade.   Some native musicians
played in the anteroom during dinner; and when we
rose from table, we washed our hands as before.

We now returned to the large hall, and not being
accomplished in the art and mystery of sitting cross-
legged, curled ourselves up on the divans as best we
could.   The Writer was conducted by Mustapha Aga
to the corner seat at the upper end of the room, where
he said the Princess of Wales had sat when their Royal
Highnesses dined with him the year before.   We were
then served with pipes and coffee.   The gentlemen
smoked chibouques and cigarettes, while for us there
were gorgeous rose-water narghilehs with long flexible
tubes and amber mouthpieces.   L. had the Princess's
pipe, and smoked it very cleverly all the evening.

By and by came the Governor, the Kadee of Luxor,
the Prussian Consul and his son, and some three or
four grave-looking merchants in rich silk robes and
ample turbans.   Meanwhile the band—two fiddles, a
tambourine and a darrabooka—played at intervals at
the lower end of the hall; pipes, coffee, and lemonade
went continually round; and the entertainment wound
up, as native entertainments always do wind up at
Luxor, with a performance of Ghawazee.

We had already seen these dancers at two previous
Fantasias, and we admired them no more the third
time than the first.   They wore baggy Turkish trowsers,

loose gowns of gaudy pattern, and a profusion of jewellery. The *première danseuse* was a fine woman and rather handsome; but in the "belle" of the company, a thick-lipped Nubian, we could discover no charm whatever. The performances of the Ghawazee —which are very ungraceful and almost wholly pantomimic—have been too often described to need description here. Only once, indeed, did we see them perform an actual dance; and then they swam lightly to and fro, clattering their castanets, crossing and recrossing, and bounding every now and then down the whole length of the room. This dance, we were told, was of unknown antiquity. They sang occasionally; but their voices were harsh and their melodies inharmonious.

There was present, however, one native performer whom we had already heard many times, and of whose skill we never tired. This was the leader of the little band—an old man who played the Kemengeh,* or cocoa-nut fiddle. A more unpromising instrument than the Kemengeh it would be difficult to conceive; yet our old Arab contrived to make it discourse most eloquent music. His solos consisted of plaintive airs and extemporised variations, embroidered with difficult, and sometimes extravagant, cadenzas. He always began sedately, but warmed to his work as he went on; seeming at last to forget everything but his own delight in his own music. At such times one could see that he was weaving some romance in his thoughts, and translating it into sounds. As the strings throbbed under his fingers, the whole man became in-

* The kemengeh is a kind of small two-stringed fiddle, the body of which is made of half a cocoa-nut shell. It has a very long neck, and a long foot that rests upon the ground, like the foot of a violoncello; and it is played with a bow about a yard in length. The strings are of twisted horsehair.

spired: and more than once when, in shower after
shower of keen despairing notes, he had described the
wildest anguish of passion, I have observed his colour
change and his hand tremble.

Although we heard him repeatedly, and engaged
him more than once when we had friends to dinner,
I am sorry to say that I forget the name of this really
great artist.   He is, however, celebrated throughout
the Thebaid, and is constantly summoned to Erment,
Esneh, Keneh, Girgeh and other large towns, to perform at private entertainments.

While at Luxor, we went one Sunday morning to
the Coptic Church—a large building at the northern
extremity of the village.   Church, schools and Bishop's
house, are here grouped under one roof and enclosed
in a courtyard.   For Luxor is the centre of one of the
twelve sees into which Coptic Egypt is divided.

The church, which has been rebuilt of late years,
is constructed of sun-dried brick, having a small apse
towards the East, and at the lower or Western end a
screened atrium for the women.   The centre aisle is
perhaps thirty feet in width; the side-aisles, if aisles
they can be called, being thickly planted with stone
pillars supporting round arches.   These pillars came
from Karnak, and were the gift of the Khedive.   They
have lotus-bud capitals, and measure about fifteen feet
high in the shaft.   At the upper end of the nave,
some eighteen or twenty feet in advance of the apse,
there stands a very beautiful screen inlaid in the old
Coptic style with cedar, ebony, rosewood, ivory, and
mother-of-pearl.   This screen is the pride of the church.
Through the opening in the centre, one looks straight
into the little waggon-roofed apse, which contains a

small table and a suspended lamp, and is as dark as the sanctuary of an Egyptian Temple. The reading-desk, like a rickety office stool, faces the congregation; and just inside the screen stands the Bishop's chair. Upon this plan, which closely resembles the plan of the first cathedral of St. Peter at Rome, most Coptic churches are built. They vary chiefly in the number of apses, some having as many as five. The atrium generally contains a large tank, called the Epiphany tank, into which, in memory of the baptism of our Lord, the men plunge at their festival of El Gheetàs.

Young Todroos, the son of the Prussian Consul, conducted us to the church. We went in at about eleven o'clock and witnessed the end of the service, which had then been going on since daybreak. The atrium was crowded with women and children, and the side-aisles with men of the poorer sort. A few groups of better dressed Copts were gathered near the screen listening to a black-robed deacon, who stood reading at the reading desk with a lighted taper in his left hand. A priest in a white vestment embroidered on the breast and hood with a red Maltese cross, was squatting on his heels at the entrance to the adytum. The Bishop, all in black with a black turban, sat with his back to the congregation.

Every face was turned upon us when we came in. The reader paused. The white-robed priest got up. Even the Bishop looked round. Presently a couple of acolytes, each carrying two cane-bottomed chairs, came bustling down the nave; and, unceremoniously driving away all who were standing near, placed us in a row across the middle of the church. This interruption over, the reading was resumed.

We now observed with some surprise that every
word of the lessons as they were read in Coptic was
translated, *viva voce*, into Arabic by a youth in a sur-
plice, who stood against the screen facing the congregation. He had no book, but went on fluently enough,
following close upon the voice of the reader. This, we
were told, was done only during the reading of the
lessons, the Gospel, and the Lord's Prayer. The rest
of the service is performed without translation;* and,
the Coptic being a dead language, is consequently unintelligible to the people.

When the reading of the Gospel was over, the
deacon retired. The priest then came forward and
made a sign to the school children, who ran up noisily
from all parts of the church, and joined with the
choristers in a wild kind of chant. It seemed to us
that this chant concluded the first part of the service.

The second part closely resembled the celebration
of mass. The priest came to the door of the screen;
looked at the congregation; folded his hands palm to
palm; went up to the threshold of the apse, and began
reciting what sounded like a litany. He then uncovered the sacred vessels, which till now had been
concealed under two blue cotton handkerchiefs, and,
turning, shook the handkerchiefs towards the people.
He then consecrated the wine and wafer; elevated the
host; and himself partook of the Eucharist in both
elements. A little bell was rung during the consecra-

* The very same thing was done on the introduction of Christianity into
Egypt. The mass of the Egyptian people then knew no Greek; and, the services of the new church being performed in Greek, it became necessary to
explain and translate the Scriptures into the Coptic vernacular, (or "recent
Egyptian" as it was then called) just as they are now translated into the
vernacular Arabic.

tion and again at the elevation. The people, meanwhile, stood very reverently, with their heads bent; but no one knelt during any part of the service. After this, the officiating priest washed his hands in a brass basin; and the deacon—who was also the schoolmaster—came round the church holding up his scarf, which was heaped full of little cakes of unleavened bread. These he distributed to all present. An acolyte followed with a plate, and collected the offerings of the congregation.

We now thought the service was over; but there remained four wee, crumpled, brown mites of babies to be christened. These small Copts were carried up the church by four acolytes, followed by four anxious fathers. The priest then muttered a short prayer; crossed the babies with water from the basin in which he had washed his hands; drank the water; wiped the basin out with a piece of bread; ate the bread; and dismissed the little newly-made Christians with a hasty blessing.

Finally, the Bishop—who had taken no part in the service, nor even partaken of the Eucharist—came down from his chair, and stood before the altar to bless the congregation. Hereupon all the men and boys ranged themselves in single file and trooped through between the screen and the apse, crowding in at one side and out at the other; each being touched by the Bishop on his cheek, as he went by. If they lagged, the Bishop clapped his hands impatiently, and the schoolmaster drove them through faster. When there were no more to come (the women and little girls, be it observed, coming in for no share of this benediction), the priest took off his vestments and laid them

in a heap on the altar; the deacon distributed a basketful
of blessed cakes among the poor of the congregation;
and the Bishop walked down the nave, eating a cake
and giving a bit here and there to the best dressed
Copts as he went along. So ended this interesting and
curious service, which I have described thus minutely
for the reason that it represents, with probably but
little change, the earliest ceremonial of Christian worship in Egypt. *

Before leaving, we asked permission to look at the
books from which the service had been read. They
were all very old and dilapidated. The New Testa-
ment, however, was in better condition than the rest,
and was beautifully written upon vellum, in red and
black ink. The Coptic, of course, looks like Greek to
the eyes of the uninitiated; but some of the illuminated
capitals struck us as bearing a marked resemblance
to certain of the more familiar hieroglyphic characters.

While we were examining the books, the Bishop
sent his servant to invite us to pay him a visit. We
accordingly followed the man up an outer flight of
wooden steps at one corner of the courtyard, and were
shown into a large room built partly over the church.
Here we found the Bishop—handsome, plump, dignified, with soft brown eyes, and a slightly grizzled beard
—seated cross-legged on a divan, and smoking his

* "The Copts are Christians of the sect called Jacobites, Eutychians,
Monophysites, and Monothelites, whose creed was condemned by the Council
of Chalcedon in the reign of the Emperor Marcian. They received the
appellation of 'Jacobites,' by which they are generally known, from Jacobus
Baradæus, a Syrian, who was a chief propagator of the Eutychian doctrines.
. . . The religious orders of the Coptic Church consist of a patriarch, a metro-
politan of the Abyssinians, bishops, arch-priests, priests, deacons, and monks.
In Abyssinia, Jacobite Christianity is still the prevailing religion." See *The
Modern Egyptians*; by E. W. LANE. Supplement 1, p. 531. London; 1860.

chibouque. On a table in the middle of the room
stood two or three blue and white bottles of Oriental
porcelain. The windows, which were sashless and very
large, looked over to Karnak. The sparrows flew in
and out as they listed.

The Bishop received us very amiably, and the proceedings opened as usual with pipes and coffee. The
conversation that followed consisted chiefly of questions
on our part, and of answers on his. We asked the
extent of his diocese, and learned that it reached
from Assouan on the south to Keneh on the north.
The revenue of the see, he said, was wholly derived
from endowments in land. He estimated the number
of Copts in Luxor at 2000, being two-thirds of the
entire population. The church was built and decorated
in the time of his predecessor. He had himself been
Bishop here for rather more than four years. We then
spoke of the service we had just witnessed, and of the
books we had seen. I showed him my prayer-book,
which he examined with much curiosity. I explained
the differences indicated by the black and the rubricated
matter, and pointed out the parts that were sung. He
was, however, more interested in the outside than in
the contents, and tapped the binding once or twice, to
see if it was leather or wood. As for the gilt corners
and clasp, he undoubtedly took them for solid gold.

The conversation next turned upon Coptic; the Idle
Man asking him if he believed it to be the tongue
actually spoken by the ancient Egyptians.

To this he replied: —

"Yes, undoubtedly. What else should it be?"

The Idle Man hereupon suggested that it seemed
to him, from what he had just seen of the church

books, as if it might be a corrupt form of Byzantine
Greek.

The Bishop shook his head.

"The Coptic is a distinct language," he said.
"Eight Greek letters were added to the Coptic alphabet
upon the introduction of Christianity into Egypt; and
since that time many Greek words have been imported
into the Coptic vocabulary; but the main body of the
tongue is Coptic, purely; and it has no radical affinity
whatever with the Greek." *

This was the longest speech we heard him make,
and he delivered it with some emphasis.

I then asked him if the Coptic was in all respects
a dead language; to which he replied that many Coptic
words, such as the names of the months and of certain

---

* The Bishop was for the most part right. The Coptic *is* the ancient
Egyptian language (that is to say, it is late and somewhat corrupt Egyptian)
written in Greek characters instead of in hieroglyphs. For the abolition of
the ancient writing was, next to the abolition of the images of the Gods, one of
the first great objects of the early Church in Egypt. Unable to uproot and
destroy the language of a great nation, the Christian Fathers took care so to
reclothe it that every trace of the old symbolism should disappear and be forgotten. Already, in the time of Clement of Alexandria (A.D. 211), the hieroglyphic style had become obsolete. The secret of reading the hieroglyphs, however, was not lost till the time of the fall of the Eastern Empire.
How the lost key was recovered by Champollion after more than 800 years is
told in a quotation from Mariette Bey, in the footnote to vol. I. p. 268, Chap. XII.
of this book. Of the relation of Coptic to Egyptian, Champollion says, "La
langue égyptienne antique ni différait en rien de la langue appelée vulgaire-
ment Copte ou Cophte. . . . Les mots égyptiens écrits en caractères hiero-
glyphiques sur les monuments les plus anciens de Thèbes, et en caractères
Grecs dans les livres Coptes, ne different en général que par l'absence de certaines voyelles médiales omises, selon la méthode orientale, dans l'orthographe
primitive."—*Grammaire Égyptienne*, p. 18.

The Bishop, though perfectly right in stating that Coptic and Egyptian
were one, and that the Coptic was a distinct language having no affinity with
the Greek, was, however, entirely wrong in that part of his explanation which
related to the alphabet. So far from eight Greek letters having been added to
the Coptic alphabet upon the introduction of Christianity into Egypt, there was
no such thing as a Coptic alphabet previous to that time. The Coptic alphabet
is the Greek alphabet as imposed upon Egypt by the Fathers of the early Greek
Church; and that alphabet being found insufficient to convey all the sounds of
the Egyptian tongue, eight new characters were borrowed from the demotic to
supplement the deficiency.

festivals, were still in daily use. This, however, was not quite what I meant; so I put the question in another form, and asked if he thought any fragments of the tongue yet survived among the peasantry.

He pondered a moment before replying.

"That," he said, "is a question to which it is difficult to give a precise answer, but I think you might yet find, in some of the remoter villages, an old man here and there who would understand it a little."

I thought this a very interesting reply to a very interesting question.

After sitting about half-an-hour we rose and took leave. The Bishop shook hands with us all round, and, but that we protested against it, would have accompanied us to the head of the stairs.

This interview was altogether very pleasant. The Copts are said to be sullen in manner, and so bigoted that even a Moslem is less an object of dislike to them than a Christian of any other denomination. However this may be, we saw nothing of it. We experienced, on the contrary, many acts of civility from the Copts with whom we were brought into communication. No traveller in Egypt should, I think, omit being present at a service in a Coptic church. For a Coptic church is now the only place in which one may hear the last utterances of that far-off race with whose pursuits and pleasures the tomb-paintings make us so familiar. We know that great changes have come over the language since it was spoken by Rameses the Great and written by Pentaour. We know that the Coptic of to-day bears to the Egyptian of the Pharaohs some such resemblance, perhaps, as the English of Macaulay bears to the English of Chaucer. Yet it is at bottom the tongue of old

17*

Egypt, and it is something to hear the last lingering echoes of that ancient speech read by the undoubted descendants of the Egyptian people. In another fifty years or so, the Coptic will in all probability be super-seded by the Arabic in the services of this Church; and then the very tradition of its pronunciation will be lost. The Copts themselves, it is said, are fast going over to the dominant faith. Perhaps by the time our own descendants are counting the two thousandth an-niversary of the Christian Era, both Copts and Coptic will be extinct in Egypt.

A day or two after this we dropped down to Karnak, where we remained till the end of the week; and on the following Sunday we resumed our down-ward voyage.

If the universe of literature was unconditioned, and the present book was independent of time and space, I would write another chapter here about Karnak. But Karnak, to be fairly dealt by, would ask, not a chapter, but a volume. So, having already told something of the impression first made upon us by that wilderness of wonders, I will say no more.

CHAPTER XXII.

Abydus and Cairo.

OUR last weeks on the Nile went by like one long, lazy, summer's day. Events now were few. We had out-stayed all our fellow-travellers. Even the faithful Bagstones had long since vanished northwards; and the Philæ was the last Dahabeeyah of the year. Of the great sights of the river, we had only Abydus and Beni Hassan left to see; while for minor excursions, daily walks, and explorations by the way, we had little energy left. For the thermometer was rising higher and the Nile was falling lower every day; and we should have been more than mortal, if we had not felt the languid influences of the glowing Egyptian Spring.

The natives call it spring; but to our northern fancy it is spring, summer, and autumn in one. Of the splendour of the skies, of the lavish bounty of the soil at this season, only those who have lingered late in the land can form any conception. There is a breadth of repose now about the landscape that it has never worn before. The winter green of the palms is fading fast. The harvests are ripening; the pigeons are pairing; the time of the singing of birds is come. There is just enough south wind most days to keep the boat straight, and the sail from flapping. The heat is great; yet it is a heat which, up a certain point, one

can enjoy. The men ply their oars by night; and
sleep under their benches, or croon old songs and tell
stories among themselves, by day. But for the thin
canopy of smoke that hangs over the villages, one
would fancy now that those clusters of mud-huts were
all deserted. Not a human being is to be seen on the
banks when the sun is high. The buffaloes stand up
to their necks in the shallows. The donkeys huddle
together wherever there is shade. The very dogs have
given up barking, and lie asleep under the walls.

The whole face of the country, and even of the
Nile, is wonderfully changed since we first passed this
way. The land, then newly squared off like a gigantic
chess-board and intersected by thousands of little
channels, is now one sea of yellowing grain. The
river is become a labyrinth of sand-banks, some large,
some small; some just beginning to thrust their heads
above water; others so long that they divide the river
for a mile or more at a stretch. Reïs Hassan spends
half his life at the prow, poling for shallows; and when
we thread our way down one of these sandy straits, it
is for all the world like a bit of the Suez Canal. The
banks, too, are twice as steep as they were when we
went up. The lentil patches, which then blossomed on
the slope next the water's edge, now lie far back on
the top of a steep brown ridge, at the foot of which
stretches a moist flat planted with water-melons. Each
melon-plant is protected from the sun by a tiny gable-
roof of palm-thatch.

Meanwhile, the river being low and the banks high,
we unfortunates benefit scarcely at all by the faint
breezes that now and then ruffle the barley. Day by
day the thermometer (which hangs in the coolest

corner of the saloon) creeps up higher and higher,
working its way by degrees to above 99⁰; but never
succeeding in getting up quite to 100⁰. We, however,
living in semi-darkness, with closed jalousies, and wet
sails hung round the sides of the Dahabeeyah, and
wet towels hung up in our cabins, find 99⁰ quite warm
enough to be pleasant. The upper deck is of course
well deluged several times a day; but even so, it is
difficult to keep the timbers from starting. Meanwhile
L. and the Idle Man devote their leisure to killing
flies, keeping the towels wet, and sprinkling the floors.

Our progress all this time is of the slowest. The
men cannot row by day; and at night the sandbanks
so hedge us in with dangers, that the only possible
way by which we can make a few miles between sunset and sunrise is by sheer hard punting. Now and
then we come to a clear channel, and sometimes we
get an hour or two of sweet south breeze; but these
flashes of good luck are few and far between.

In such wise, and in such a temperature, we found
ourselves becalmed one morning within six miles of
Denderah. Not even L. could be induced to take a
six-mile donkey-ride that day in the sun. The Writer,
however, ordered out her sketching-tent and paid a
last visit to the Temple; which, seen amid the ripening splendour of miles of barley, looked gloomier, and
grander, and more solitary than ever.

Two or three days later, we came within reach of
Abydus. Our proper course would have been to push
on to Bellianeh, which is one of the recognised start-
ing-points for Abydus. But an unluckly sandbank
barred the way; so we moored instead at Samata, a
village about two miles nearer to the southward. Here

our dragoman requisitioned the inhabitants for donkeys. As it happened, the harvest had begun in the
neighbourhood and all the beasts of burden were at
work, so that it was near midday before we succeeded
in getting together the three or four wretched little
brutes with which we finally started. Not one of these
steeds had ever before carried a rider. We had a
frightful time with them. My donkey bolted about
every five minutes. L.'s snarled like a camel and
showed its teeth like a dog. The Idle Man's, bent on
flattening its rider, lay down and rolled at short intervals. In this exciting fashion, we somehow or another accomplished the seven miles that separate Samata from Abydus.

Skirting some palm-groves and crossing the dry
bed of a canal, we came out upon a vast plain, level
as a lake, islanded here and there with villages, and
presenting one undulating surface of bearded corn.
This plain—the plain of ancient Thinis—runs parallel
with the Nile, like the plain of Thebes, and is bounded
to the westward by a range of flat-topped mountains.
The distance between the river and the mountains,
however, is here much greater than at Thebes, being
full six miles; while to north and south the view ends
only with the horizon.

Our way lies at first by a bridle-track through the
thick of the barley; then falls into the Bellianeh road
—a raised causeway embanked some twenty feet above
the plain. Along this road, the country folk are coming and going. In the cleared spaces where the maize
has been cut, little encampments of straw huts have
sprung up. Yonder, steering their way by unseen
paths, go strings of camels; their gawky necks and

húmped backs undulating above the surface of the
corn, like galleys with fantastic prows upon a sea of
rippling green. The pigeons fly in great clouds from
village to village. The larks are singing and circling
madly in the clear depths overhead. The bee-eaters
flash like live emeralds across our path. The hoopoes
strut by the wayside. At rather more than half-way
across the plain, we come into the midst of the harvest.
Here the brown reapers, barelegged and naked to the
waist, are at work with their sickles, just as they are
pictured in the tomb of Ti. The women and children
follow, gleaning, at the heels of those who bind the
sheaves. The Sheykh in his black robe and scarlet
slippers rides to and fro upon his ass, like Boaz among
his people. As the sheaves are bound up, the camels
carry them homeward. A camel-load is fourteen
sheaves; seven to each side of the hump. A little
farther, and the oxen, yoked two and two, are plough-
ing up the stubble. In a day or two, the land will be
sown with millet, indigo, or cotton, to be gathered in
once more before the coming of the inundation.

Meanwhile, as the plain lengthens behind us and
the distance grows less between ourselves and the
mountains, we see a line of huge irregular mounds
reaching for apparently a couple of miles or more
along the foot of the cliffs. From afar off, the mounds
look as if crowned by majestic ruins; but as we draw
nearer, these outlines resolve themselves into the village
of Kharábat at Madfooneh, which stands upon part of
the mounds of Abydus. And now we come to the end
of the cultivated plain—that strange line of demarca-
tion where the inundation stops and the desert begins.
Of actual desert, however, there is here but a narrow

strip, forming a first step, as it were, above the alluvial plain. Next comes the artificial platform, about a quarter of a mile in depth, on which stands the modern village; and next again, towering up sheer and steep, the great wall of limestone precipice. The village is extensive, and the houses, built in a rustic Arabesque, tell of a well-to-do population. Arched gateways ornamented with black, white, and red bricks, windows of turned lattice-work, and pigeon-towers in courses of pots and bricks, give a singular picturesqueness to the place; while the slope down to the desert is covered with shrubberies and palms. Below these hanging gardens, on the edge of the desert, lies the cut corn in piles of sheaves. Here the camels are lying down to be unladen Yonder the oxen are already treading out the grain, or chopping the straw by means of a curious sledge-like machine set with revolving rows of circular knives.* Meanwhile, fluttering from heap to heap, settling on the sheaves, feeding unmolested in the very midst of the threshing floors, strutting all over the margin of the desert, trailing their wings, ruffling their plumes, cooing, curtseying, kissing, courting, filling the air with sweet sounds and setting the whole lovely idyll to a pastoral symphony of their own composing, are thousands and tens of thousands of pigeons.**

   * This machine is called the Nóreg.
   ** The number of pigeons kept by the Egyptian fellaheen is incredible. Mr. Zincke says on this subject that "the number of domestic pigeons in Egypt must be several times as great as the population," and suggests that if the people kept pigs, they would keep less pigeons. But it is not as food chiefly that the pigeons are encouraged. They are bred and let live in such ruinous numbers for the sake of the manure they deposit on the land. M. About has forcibly demonstrated the error of this calculation. He shows that the pigeons do thirty million francs' worth of damage to the crops in excess of any benefit they may confer upon the soil.

Now our path turns aside and we thread our way among the houses, noticing here a sculptured block built into a mud wall—yonder an alabaster sarcophagus broken beside a dried-up well—farther on, a granite column still erect in the midst of a palm-garden. And now, the village being left behind, we find ourselves at the foot of a great hill of newly excavated rubbish, from the top of which we presently look down into a kind of crater, and see the Great Temple of Abydus at our feet.

It was now nearly three o'clock; so, having seen what we could in the time, and having before us a long ride through a strange country, we left again at six. I will not presume to describe the Temples of Abydus—one of which is so ruined as to be almost unintelligible, and the other so singularly planned and so obscure in its general purport, as to be a standing puzzle to archæologists—after a short visit of three hours. Enough if I sketch briefly what I saw but cursorily.

Buried as it is, Abydus,* even under its mounds, is a place of profound historical interest. At a time so remote that it precedes all written record of Egyptian story, there existed a little way to the northward of this site a city called Teni.** We know not to what

* The Arabic name of the modern village, Kharábat at Madfooneh, means literally Arabat the Buried.
** *Teni*, or perhaps more probably Tini, called by the Greeks This or Thinis. It was the capital of the VIIIth Nome. "Quoique nous ayons très-peu de chose à rapporter sur l'histoire de la ville de Teni qui à la basse époque, sous la domination romaine, n'était connue que par ses teinturiers en pourpre, elle doit avoir joui d'une très grande renommée chez les anciens Egyptiens. Encore au temps du XIXeme dynastie les plus hauts fonctionnaires de sang royal étaient distingués par le titre de 'Princes de Teni.'"—*Hist. d'Egypte.* BRUGSCH, vol. I. chap. v. p. 29; Leipzig, 1874. "Des monuments trouvés il y a deux ans, me portent à croire que Thini était située assez loin à l'Est au village actuel de Aoulad-Yahia" *Letter of Professor G. Maspero to the Author,* April 1878.

aboriginal community of prehistoric Egypt this city belonged; but here, presumedly, the men of Kem* built
their first Temple, evolved their first notions of art, and
groped their way to an alphabet which in its origin
was probably a mere picture-writing, like the picture-
writing of Mexico. Here, too, was born a man named
Mena, whose cartouche from immemorial time has
stood first in the long list of Egyptian Pharaohs. Of
Mena,** a shadowy figure hovering on the border-land
of history and tradition, we know only that he was the
first primitive chieftain who took the title of King of
Upper and Lower Egypt, and that he went northward
and founded Memphis. Not, however, till after some
centuries was the seat of government removed to the
new city. Teni—the supposed burial-place of Osiris
—then lost its political importance; but continued to
be for long ages the Holy City of Egypt. I have already suggested in another part of this book,*** when
and for what reasons I believe it possible that the tra-
ditionary relics of the God may have been transferred
to Philæ.

In the meanwhile, Abydus had sprung up close to
Teni. Abydus, however, though an important city, was

---

* The ancient name of Egypt was *Kem*, or *Kam*, signifying Black, or the
Black Land; in allusion to the colour of the soil.
** "Mena, tel que nous le presente la tradition, est le type le plus complet
du monarque egyptien. Il est à la fois constructeur et législateur: il fonde le
grand temple de Phtah à Memphis et régle le culte des dieux. Il est guerrier,
et conduit les expéditions hors de ses frontières."—*Hist. Ancienne des Peuples
de l'Orient.* G. MASPERO. Chap. II. p. 55: Paris 1876.
   "N'oublions pas qu'avant Ménès l'Egypte était divisée en petits royaumes
indépendants que Ménès réunit le premier sous un sceptre unique. Il n'est pas
impossible que des monuments de cette antique période de l'histoire Egyptienne
subsistent encore."—*Itinéraire de la Haute Egypte.* A. MARIETTE-BEY.
Avant Propos, p. 40. Alexandrie, 1872.
*** Chap. XII., pp. 275-6 of vol. I.

never the capital of Egypt. The seat of power shifted strangely with different dynasties, being established now in the Delta, now at Thebes, now at Elephantine; but having once departed from the site which, by reason of its central position and the unbounded fertility of its neighbourhood, was above all others best fitted to play this great part in the history of the country, it never again returned to the point from which it had started. That point, however, was unquestionably the centre from which the great Egyptian people departed upon its wonderful career. Here was the nursery of its strength. Hence it derived its proud title to an unmixed autochthonous descent. For no greater proof of the native origin of the race can possibly be adduced than the position which their first city occupies upon the map of Egypt. That any tribe of colonists should have made straight for the heart of the country and there have established themselves in the midst of barbarous and probably hostile aborigines, is evidently out of the question. It is, on the other hand, equally clear that if Egypt had been colonised from Asia or Ethiopia, the strangers would in the one case have founded their earliest settlement in the neighbourhood of the Isthmus; or in the other, have halted first among the then well-watered plains of Nubia. * But the Egyptains started from the fertile heart of their own mother country, and began by being great at home.

* See Opening Address of Professor R. Owen. C.B., etc. etc. *Report of Proceedings of the Second International Congress of Orientalists, Ethnological Section:* London 1874. See also a paper on *The Ethnology of Egypt*, by the same, published in the Journal of the Anthropological Institute, vol. IV., No. 1, p. 246; Lond., 1874.

Abydus and Teni, planted on the same platform of desert, were probably united at one time by a straggling suburb inhabited by the embalmers and other trades-folk concerned in the business of death and burial. A chain of mounds, excavated only where the Temples are situated, now stands to us for the famous city of Abydus. An ancient crude-brick enclosure and an artificial tumulus mark the site of Teni. The Temples and the tumulus, divided by the now exhausted necro-polis, are about as distant from one another as Medinet Haboo and the Ramesseum.

There must have been many older Temples at Abydus than these which we now see, one of which was built by Seti I., and the other by Rameses II. Or possibly, as in so many instances, the more ancient buildings were pulled down and rebuilt. Be this as it may, the Temple of Seti, as regards its sculptured decorations, is one of the most beautiful of Egyptian ruins; and as regards its plan, is one of the most sin-gular. A row of square limestone piers, which must once have supported an architrave, are now all that remains of the façade. Immediately behind these comes a portico of twenty-four columns leading by seven entrances to a hall of thirty-six columns. This hall again opens into seven parallel sanctuaries, behind which lie another hall of columns and a number of small chambers. So much of the building seems to be homogeneous. Adjoining this block, however, and leading from it by doorways at the Southern end of the great hall, come several more halls and chambers connected by corridors, and conducting apparently to more chambers not yet excavated. All these piers, columns, halls, and passages, and all the seven sanctuaries,* are most delicately sculptured and brilliantly coloured.

There is so far a family resemblance between Temples of the same style and period, that after a little experience one can generally guess before crossing the threshold of a fresh building, what one is likely to see in the way of sculptures within. But almost every subject in the Temple of Seti at Abydus is new and strange. All the Gods of the Egyptian pantheon seem to have been worshipped here, and to have had each his separate shrine. The walls are covered with paintings of these shrines and their occupants; while before

---

* M. Mariette, in his great work on the excavations at Abydus, observes that these seven vaulted sanctuaries resemble sarcophagi of the form most commonly in use; namely oblong boxes with vaulted lids. Two sarcophagi of this shape are shown in cut 496 of Sir Gardner Wilkinson's second vol. (see figures 1 and 6) *A Popular account of the Ancient Egyptians.* Vol. II. chap. X. London, 1871. Of the uses and purport of the temple, M. Mariette also says—"What do we know of the *idée mère* that presided at its construction? What was done in it? Is it consecrated to a single divinity, who would be Osiris; or to seven Gods, who would be the Seven Gods of the Seven vaulted chambers; or to the nine divinities enumerated in the lists of deities dispersed in various parts of the temple? . . . . One leaves the temple in despair, not at being unable to make out its secret from the inscriptions, but on finding that its secret has been kept for itself alone, and not trusted to the inscriptions."—*Description des Fouilles d' Abydos.* MARIETTE-BEY. Paris: 1869.

"Les sept chambres voûtées du grand temple d'Abydos sont relatifs aux cérémonies que le roi devait y célébrer successivement. Le roi se présentait au côté droit de la porte, parcourait la salle dans tout son pourtour et sortait par le côté gauche. Des statues étaient disposées dans la chambre. Le roi ouvrait la porte ou naos où elles étaient enfermées. Dès que la statue apparaissait à ses yeux il lui offrait l'encens, il enlevait le vêtement qui la couvrait, il lui imposait les mains, il la parfumait, il la recouvrait de son vêtement," etc. etc.—MARIETTE-BEY. *Itinéraire de la Haute Egypt:* Avant Propos, p. 62. Alex., 1872.

There is at the upper end of each of these seven sanctuaries a singular kind of false door, or recess, conceived in a style of ornament more Indian than Egyptian, the cutting being curiously square, deep, and massive, the surface of the relief-work flattened, and the whole evidently intended to produce its effect by depths of shadow in the incised portions rather than by sculpturesque relief. These recesses, or imitation doors, may have been designed to serve as backgrounds to statues, but are not deep enough for niches. There is a precisely similar recess sculptured on one of the walls of the westernmost chamber in the Temple of Goornah.

each the King is represented performing some act of adoration. A huge blue frog, a greyhound, a double-headed goose, a human-bodied creature with a Nilo-meter for its head,* and many more than I can now remember, are thus depicted. The royal offerings, too, though incense and necklaces and pectoral ornaments abound, are for the most part of a kind that we have not seen before. In one place the King presents to Isis a column with four capitals, having on the top capital a globe and two asps surmounted by a pair of ostrich feathers.

The centre sanctuary of the seven is dedicated to Khem, who is here, as in the great Temple of Seti at Karnak, the presiding divinity. In this principal sanc-tuary, which is resplendent with colour and in mar-vellous preservation, we especially observed a portrait of Rameses II.,** in the act of opening the door of a shrine by means of a golden key formed like a human hand and arm. The lock seems to consist of a number of bolts of unequal length, each of which is pushed back in turn by means of the forefinger of the little hand. This, doubtless, gives a correct representation of the kind of locks in use at that time.

It was in a corridor opening out from the great

---

* These are all representations of minor Gods commonly figured in the funereal papyri, but very rarely seen in the Temple sculptures. The frog Goddess, for instance, is Hek, and symbolised eternity. She is a very ancient divinity, traces of her being found in monuments of the Vth Dynasty. The goose-headed God is Seb, another very old God. The object called the Nilo-meter was a religious emblem signifying stability, and probably stands in this connection as only a deified symbol.

** Rameses II. is here shown with the side-lock of youth. This Temple, founded by Seti I., was carried on through the time when Rameses the prince was associated with his father upon the throne. The building is strictly coeval in date and parallel in style with the Temple of Goornah and the Speos of Bayt-el-Wely.

hall in this Temple that M. Mariette discovered that precious sculpture known as the New Tablet of Abydus. In this tableau, Seti I. and Rameses II. are seen, the one offering incense, the other reciting a hymn of praises, to the manes of seventy-six Pharaohs,* beginning with Mena, and ending with Seti himself. To our great disappointment—though one cannot but acquiesce in the necessity for precaution—we found the entrance to this corridor closed and mounded up. A ragged old Arab who haunts the Temple in the character of custode, told us that the tablet could now only be seen by the special permission of Mariette Bey.

We seemed to have been here about half-an-hour, when the guide came to warn us of approaching evening. We had yet the site and the great Tumulus of Teni to see; the tumulus being distant about twenty minutes' ride. The guide shook his head; but we insisted on going. The afternoon had darkened over; and for the first time in many months a gathering canopy of cloud shut out the glory of sunset. We however mounted our donkeys and rode northwards. With better beasts we might perhaps have gained our end; as it was, seeing that it grew darker every mo-

---

* M. Mariette is of opinion that these seventy-six Pharaohs (represented by their cartouches) were either princes born of families originally from Abydus, or that they were sovereigns who had acquired a special title to veneration at this place on account of monuments or pious foundations presented by them to the holy city. A similar inscription framed apparently on the same principles though not comprising altogether the same kings, was sculptured by Thothmes III. on the wall of a side chamber of the Great Temple at Karnak, and is now in the Bibliothêque Nationale, Paris.

The great value of the present monument consists in its chronological arrangement. It is also said to be of most beautiful execution, and in perfect preservation. "Comme perfection de gravure, comme conservation, comme étendue, il est peu de monuments qui la dépassent." See *La Nouvelle Table d'Abydos*, par A. MARIETTE BEY: *Rêvue Arch.*, vol. VII., Nouvelle Série, p. 98. This volume of the Review also contains an engraving in outline of the Tablet.

ment, we presently gave in, and instead of trying to push on farther, contented ourselves with climbing a high mound that commanded the view towards Teni.

The clouds by this time were fast closing round, and waves of shadow were creeping over the plain. To our left rose the 'near mountain barrier, dusk and lowering; to our right stretched the misty corn-flats; at our feet, all hillocks and open graves, lay the desolate necropolis. Beyond the palms that fringed the edge of the desert—beyond a dark streak that marked the site of Thinis—rose, purple in shadow against the twilight, a steep and solitary hill. This hill, called by the natives Kom-es-Sultan, or the Mound of the King, was the tumulus we so desired to see. Viewed from a distance and by so uncertain a light, it looked exactly like a volcanic cone of perhaps a couple of hundred feet in height. It is however wholly artificial, and consists of a mass of graves heaped one above another in historic strata; each layer, as it were, the record of an era; the whole, a kind of human coral-reef built up from age to age with the ashes of generations.

For some years past, the Egyptian Government has been gradually excavating this extraordinary mound. The lower it is opened, the more ancient are its contents. So steadily retrogressive, indeed, are the interments, that the spade of the digger, it is hoped, must ere long strike tombs of the First Dynasty, and restore to light relics of men who lived in the age of Mena. "According to Plutarch," says M. Mariette,* "wealthy

* See *Itinéraire de la Haute Egypte:* A. MARIETTE BEY: p. 147. Alex. 1872. See also my Paper *On Recent Excavations in the Necropolis of Abydus,* Second Congress of Orientalists, Hamitic Section, Thursday, Sept. 17th, 1874.

Egyptians came from all parts of Egypt to be buried
at Abydus, in order that their bones might rest near
Osiris. Very probably the tombs of Kom-es-Sultan
belong to those personages mentioned by Plutarch. Nor
is this the only interest attaching to the mound of
Kom-es-Sultan. The famous tomb of Osiris cannot be
far distant; and certain indications lead us to think
that it is excavated in precisely that foundation of rock
which serves as the nucleus of this mound. Thus the
persons buried in Kom-es-Sultan lay as near as possible to the divine tomb. The works now in progress
at this point have therefore a twofold interest. They
may yield tombs yet more and more ancient—tombs
even of the First Dynasty; and some day or another
they may discover to us the hitherto unknown and
hidden entrance to the tomb of the God." *

I bitterly regretted at the time that I could not at
least ride to the foot of Kom-es-Sultan; but I think
now that I prefer to remember it as I saw it from afar
off, clothed with mystery, in the gloom of that dusky
evening.

There was a heavy silence in the air, and a melancholy as of the burden of ages. The tumbled hillocks
looked like a ghastly sea, and beyond the verge of the
desert it was already night. Presently, from among
the grave-pits there crept towards us a slowly-moving

* See *Itinéraire de la Haute Egypte*, by A. MARIETTE BEY, p. 148.
Alexandria, 1872. The hope here expressed by the learned Conservator of
Egyptian Antiquities may sound extravagant to those who have not seen the
treasures of the Boulak Museum; but there is in truth no limit to the con-
servative power of the Egyptian desert. "Where neither moth nor dust doth
corrupt," and where even the light of day is excluded, things put away in the
darkness of the tomb last literally for ever. The stelæ and the minor articles
found in tombs of the IVth Dynasty are as fresh in substance and as bright
where coloured, as those of the time of the latest Ptolemies.

18*

cloud. As it drew nearer—soft, filmy, shifting, unreal
—it proved to be the dust raised by an immense flock
of sheep. On they came, a brown compact mass,
their shepherd showing dimly now and then, through
openings in the cloud. The last pale gleam from
above caught them for a moment ere they melted,
ghost-like, into the murky plain. Then we went down
ourselves, and threaded the track between the mounds
and the valley. Palms and houses loomed vaguely out
of the dusk; and a caravan of camels, stalking by with
swift and noiseless footfall, looked like shadows pro-
jected on a background of mist. As the night deepened,
the air became stifling. There were no stars, and we
could scarcely see a yard before us. Crawling slowly
along the steep causeway, we felt, but could distinguish
nothing of, the plain stretching away on either side.
Meanwhile the frogs croaked furiously, and our donkeys
stumbled at every step. When at length we drew near
Samata, it was close upon ten o'clock, and Reïs Hassan
had just started with men and torches to meet us.

Next morning early we once again passed Girgeh,
with its ruined mosque and still unfallen column; and
about noonday moored at a place called Ayserat, where
we paid a visit to a native gentleman, one Ahmed
Aboo Ratab Aga, to whom we carried letters of introduction. Ratab Aga owns large estates in this province; is great in horse-flesh; and lives in patriarchal
fashion surrounded by a numerous clan of kinsfolk and
dependents. His residence at Ayserat consists of a
cluster of three or four large houses, a score or so of
pigeon-towers, an extensive garden, stabling, exercising-
ground, and a large courtyard; the whole enclosed by
a wall of circuit, and entered by a fine Arabesque

gateway. He received us in a loggia of lattice-work overlooking the courtyard, and had three of his finest horses — a gray, a bay, and a chestnut — brought out for us to admire. They were just such horses as Velasquez loved to paint—thick in the neck, small in the head, solid in the barrel, with wavy manes, and long silky tails set high and standing off straight in true Arab fashion. We doubted, however, that they were altogether *pur sang*. They looked wonderfully picturesque with their gold-embroidered saddlecloths, peaked saddles covered with crimson, green, and blue velvet, long shovel-stirrups and tasselled head-gear. The Aga's brother and nephews put them through their paces. They knelt to be mounted; lay down and died at the word of command; dashed from perfect immobility into a furious gallop; and when at fullest speed, stopped short, flung themselves back upon their haunches, and stood like horses of stone. We were told that our host had a hundred such standing in his stables. Pipes, coffee, and an endless succession of different kinds of sherbets went round all the time our visit lasted; and in the course of conversation, we learned that not only the wages of agricultural labourers, but even part of the taxes to the Khedive, are here paid in corn.

Before leaving, L., the Little Lady, and the Writer were conducted to the Hareem, and introduced to the ladies of the establishment. We found them in a separate building with a separate courtyard, living after the usual dreary way of Eastern women, with apparently no kind of occupation and not even a garden to walk in. The Aga's principal wife (I believe he had but two) was a beautiful woman, with auburn hair, soft brown eyes, and a lovely complexion. She received us on the threshold, led us into a saloon surrounded by a divan, and with some pride showed us her five children. The eldest was a graceful girl of thirteen; the youngest, a little fellow of four. Mother and daughter were dressed precisely alike in black robes embroidered with silver, pink velvet slippers on bare feet, silver bracelets and anklets, and full pink Turkish trowsers. They wore their hair cut straight across the brow, plaited in long tails behind, and dressed with coins and pendants; while from the back of the head there hung a veil of thin black gauze, also embroidered with silver. Another lady, whom we took for the second wife, and who was extremely plain, had still richer and more massive ornaments, but seemed to hold an inferior position in the Hareem. There were perhaps a dozen women and girls in all, two of whom were black.

One of the little boys had been ill all his short life, and looked as if he could not last many more months. The poor mother implored us to prescribe for him. It was vain to tell her that we knew nothing of the nature of his disease and had no skill to cure it. She still entreated, and would take no refusal; so in pity we sent her some harmless medicines.

We had little opportunity of observing domestic life in Egypt. L. visited some of the vice-regal Hareems at Cairo, and brought away on each occasion the same impression of dreariness. A little embroidery, a few musical toys of Geneva manufacture, a daily drive on the Shoobra road, pipes, cigarettes, sweetmeats, jewellery, and gossip, fill up the aimless days of most Egyptian ladies of rank. There are, however, some who

take an active interest in politics; and in Cairo and
Alexandria the opera-boxes of the Khedive and the
Great Pashas are nightly occupied by ladies. But it is
not by the daily life of the wives of princes and
nobles, but by the life of the lesser gentry and upper
middle class, that a domestic system should be judged.
These ladies of Ayserat had no London-built brougham,
no Shoobra road, no opera. They were absolutely
without mental resources; and they were even without
the means of taking air and exercise. One could see
that time hung heavy on their hands, and that they
took but a feeble interest in the things around them.
The Hareem stairs were dirty; the rooms were untidy;
the general aspect of the place was slatternly and
neglected. As for the inmates, though all good-nature
and gentleness, their faces bore the expression of
people who are habitually bored. At Luxor, L. and
the Writer paid a visit to the wife of an intelligent and
gentlemanly Arab, son of the late governor of that
place. This was a middle-class Hareem. The couple
were young, and not rich. They occupied a small
house which commanded no view and had no garden.
Their little courtyard was given up to the poultry;
their tiny terrace above was less than twelve feet
square; and they were surrounded on all sides by
houses. Yet in this stifling prison the young wife
lived, apparently contented, from year's end to year's
end. She literally never went out. As a child, she
had no doubt enjoyed some kind of liberty; but as a
marriageable girl, and as a bride, she was as much a
prisoner as a bird in a cage. Born and bred in Luxor,
she had never seen Karnak; yet Karnak is only two
miles distant. We asked her if she would like to go

there with us; but she laughed and shook her head. She was incapable even of curiosity.

It seemed to us that the wives of the Fellaheen were in truth the happiest women in Egypt. They work hard, and are bitterly poor; but they have the free use of their limbs, and they at least know the fresh air, the sunshine, and the open fields.

When we left Ayserat, there still lay 335 miles between us and Cairo. From this time, the navigation of the Nile became every day more difficult. The Dahabeeyah, too, got heated through and through, so that not even sluicing and swabbing availed to keep down the temperature. At night when we went to our sleeping cabins, the timbers alongside of our berths were as hot to the hand as a screen in front of a great fire. Our crew, though to the manner born, suffered even more than ourselves; and L. at this time had generally a case of sunstroke on her hands. One by one, we passed the places we had seen on our way up —Siout, Manfaloot, Gebel Aboo-Fayda, Roda, Minieh. After all, we did not see Beni Hassan. The day we reached that part of the river, a furious sandstorm was raging; such a storm that even the Writer was daunted. Three days later, we took the rail at Bibi and went on to Cairo, leaving the Philæ to follow as fast as wind and weather might permit.

We were so wedded by this time to Dahabeeyah-life, that we felt lost at first in the big rooms at Shepherd's Hotel, and altogether bewildered in the crowded streets. Yet here was Cairo, more picturesque, more beautiful than ever. Here were the same merchants squatting on the same carpets and smoking the same pipes, in the Tunis bazaar; here was the same

old cake-seller still ensconced in the same doorway in
the Moskee; here were the same jewellers selling
bracelets in the Siàgha; the same money-changers sitting behind their little tables at the corners of the
streets; the same veiled ladies riding on donkeys and
driving in carriages; the same hurrying funerals, and
noisy weddings; the same odd cries, and motley cos-
tumes, and unaccustomed trades. Nothing was changed.
We soon dropped back into the old life of sight-seeing
and shopping—buying rugs and silks, and silver ornaments, and old embroideries, and Turkish slippers,
and all sorts of antique and pretty trifles; going from
Mohammedan mosques to rare old Coptic churches;
dropping in for an hour or two most afternoons at the
Boulak Museum; and generally ending the day's work
with a drive on the Shoobra road, or a stroll round the
Esbekeeyah Gardens.

The Moolid-en-Nebee, or Festival of the Birth of
the Prophet, was being held at this time in a tract of
waste ground on the road to Old Cairo. Here, in
some twenty or thirty large open tents ranged in a
circle, there were readings of the Koran and meetings
of dervishes going on by day and night, without intermission, for nearly a fortnight. After dark, when the
tents were all ablaze with lighted chandeliers, and the
dervishes were howling and leaping, and fireworks were
being let off from an illuminated platform in the middle
of the area, the scene was extraordinary. All Cairo
used to be there, on foot or in carriages, between eight
o'clock and midnight every evening; the veiled ladies
of the Khedive's Hareem in their miniature broughams
being foremost among the spectators.

The Moolid-en-Nebee ends with the performance of

the Dóseh, when the Sheykh of the Saädeeyeh Dervishes
rides over a road of prostrate fanatics. L. and the Writer
witnessed this sight from the tent of the Governor of
Cairo.   Drunk with opium, fasting, and praying, rolling
their heads, and foaming at the mouth, some hundreds
of wretched creatures lay down in the road packed as
close as paving stones, and were walked and ridden
over before our eyes.   The standard-bearers came first;
then a priest reading the Koran aloud; then the Sheykh
on his white Arab, supported on either side by barefooted priests.   The beautiful horse trod with evident
reluctance, and as lightly and swiftly as possible, on
the human causeway under his hoofs.   The Moham-
medans aver that no one is injured, or even bruised,
on this holy occasion;* but I saw some men carried
away in convulsions, who looked as if they would never
walk again.
    It is difficult to say but a few inadequate words
of a place about which an instructive volume might be
written; yet to pass over the Boulak Museum in silence
is impossible.   This collection is entirely due to the
liberality of the Khedive and the devotion of M. Mariette.   With the exception of Mehemet Ali, who excavated the Temple of Denderah, no former Viceroy
of Egypt has ever interested himself in the archæology
of the country.   Those who cared for such rubbish as

---

* "It is said that these persons, as well as the Sheykh, make use of
certain words (that is, repeat prayers and invocations) on the day preceding
this performance, to enable them to endure without injury the tread of the
horse; and that some not thus prepared, having ventured to lie down to be
ridden over, have, on more than one occasion, been either killed or severely injured.   The performance is considered as a miracle vouchsafed through supernatural power, and which has been granted to every successive Sheykh of the
Saädeeyeh." See Lane's *Modern Egyptians*, chap. xxiv., p. 453. London,
1860.

encumbered the soil or lay hidden beneath the sands of the desert, were free to take it; and no favour was more frequently asked, or more readily granted, than permission to dig for "antichi." Hence the Egyptian wealth of our museums. Hence the numerous private collections dispersed throughout Europe. Ismail Pasha, however, has put an end to this wholesale pillage. Now, for the first time since ever "mummy was sold for balsam," or for bric-à-brac, it is illegal to export antiquities. Now, for the first time, Egypt has her own collection; while in M. Mariette—formerly an assistant-keeper in the Oriental department of the Louvre —the Khedive, with his accustomed tact, has found the best possible Director of the Service of Conservation of National Antiquities.

Traversing these rooms so rich in treasures, one can scarcely believe that the Boulak Museum had no existence thirteen years ago, or that nearly all these wonders have been discovered since that time. Yet such are the facts. Save a small collection purchased from a late Consul General of Austria, every object here exhibited is the result of recent excavations undertaken by M. Mariette at the cost of the Khedive.

Youngest of great museums, the Boulak collection is the richest in the world in portrait-statues of private individuals, in funereal tablets, in amulets, and in personal relics of the ancient inhabitants of the Nile Valley. It is necessarily wanting in such colossal statues as fill the great ground-floor galleries of the British Museum and the Louvre. These, being above ground and few in number, were seized upon long since and transported to Europe. The Boulak statues are the product of the tombs. The famous wooden "Sheykh"

about which so much has been written,* the magnificent
diorite statue of Shafra (Chephren), the builder of the
Second Pyramid, the two marvellous sitting statues of
Prince Ra-hotep and Princess Nefer-t, are all portraits;
and, like their tombs, were executed during the lifetime of the persons represented. Crossing the threshold of the Great Vestibule,** one is surrounded by a
host of these extraordinary figures, erect; coloured;
clothed; all but in motion. It is like entering the
crowded anteroom of a royal palace in the time of the
Ancient Empire.

The greater number of the Boulak portrait-statues
are sculptured in what is called the hieratic attitude;
that is, with the left arm down and pressed close to
the body, the left hand holding a roll of papyrus, the
right leg advanced, and the right hand raised, as
grasping the walking staff. It occurred to me that
there might be a deeper significance than at first sight
appears in this conventional attitude, and that it perhaps suggests the moment of resurrection, when the
deceased, holding fast by his copy of the Book of the
Dead, walks forth from his tomb into the light of life
eternal.

Of all the statues here—one may say, indeed, of all
known Egyptian statues—those of Prince Ra-hotep and
Princess Nefer-t are the most wonderful. They are the
oldest statues in the world.*** They come from a

* See *Egypt of the Pharaohs and the Khedive*, J. B. KINCKE, chap. IX.
p. 72. Lond. 1873. Also *La Sculpture Egyptienne*, par E. SOLDI, p. 57.
Paris: 1876. Also *The Ethnology of Egypt*, by PROFESSOR OWEN, C.B.,
Journal of Anthropological Institute, vol IV., 1784, p. 227. The name of this
personage was Ra-em-ka.
** It is in the Great Vestibule that we find the statue of Ti. See chap. IV.
p. 92 of vol. I.
*** There is no evidence to show that the statues of Sepa and Nesa in the
Louvre are older than the IVth Dynasty.

tomb of the Third Dynasty, and are contemporary
with Snefru, * a king who reigned before the time of
Cheops and Chephren. That is to say, these people
who sit before us side by side, coloured to the life,
fresh and glowing as the day when they gave the artist
his last sitting, lived at a time when the great pyramids of Gheezeh were not yet built, and at a date
which is variously calculated at from about 6300 to
4000 years before the present day. The Princess wears
her hair precisely at it is still worn in Nubia, and her
necklace of cabochon drops is of a pattern much fav-
oured by the modern Ghawazee. The eyes of both
statues are inserted. The eyeball, which is set in an
eyelid of bronze, is made of opaque white quartz, with
an iris of rock-crystal enclosing a pupil of some kind
of brilliant metal. This treatment—of which there are
one or two other instances extant—gives to the eyes a
look of intelligence that is almost appalling. There is
a play of light within the orb, and apparently a living
moisture upon the surface, which has never been approached by the most skilfully made glass eyes of
modern manufacture. **

* Snefru is believed to be the builder of the pyramid of Meydoom, which
has never yet been opened, and which probably contains his mummy.

** "Enfin nous signalerons l'importance des statues de Meydoum au point
de vue ethnographique. Si la race Egyptienne était à cette époque celle dont
les deux statues nous offrent le type, il faut convenir qu'elle ne ressemblait en
rien à la race qui habitait le nord de l'Egypte quelques années seulement
après Snefrou."—*Cat. du Musée de Boulaq.* A. MARIETTE-BEY. P. 277;
Paris, 1872.

Of the heads of these two statues Professor Owen remarks that " the brain-
case of the male is a full oval, the parietal bosses feebly indicated; in vertical
contour the fronto-parietal part is little elevated, rather flattened than convex;
the frontal sinuses are slightly indicated; the forehead is fairly developed but
not prominent. The lips are fuller than in the majority of Europeans; but the
mouth is not prognathic. . . . The features of the female conform in type to
those of the male, but show more delicacy and finish. . . . The statue of the
female is coloured of a lighter tint than that of the male, indicating the effects

Of the jewels of Queen Aah-hotep, of the superb series of engraved scarabæi, of the rings, amulets, and toilette ornaments, of the vases in bronze, silver, alabaster, and porcelain, of the libation-tables, the woven stuffs, the terra-cottas, the artists' models, the lamps, the silver boats, the weapons, the papyri, the thousand-and-one curious personal relics and articles of domestic use which are brought together within these walls, I have no space to tell. Except the collection of Pompeian relics in Naples, there is nothing elsewhere to compare with the collection at Boulak; and the villas of Pompeii have yielded no such gems and jewels as the tombs of ancient Egypt. It is not too much to say that if these dead and mummied people could come back to earth, the priest would here find all the Gods of his Pantheon; the king his sceptre; the queen her crown-jewels; the scribe his palette; the soldier his arms; the workman his tools; the barber his razors; the husbandman his hoe; the housewife her broom; the child his toys; the beauty her combs and kohl bottles and mirrors. The furniture of the house is here, as well as the furniture of the tomb. Here, too, is the broken sistrum buried with the dead in token of the grief of the living.

Waiting the construction of a suitable edifice, the present building gives temporary shelter to the collection. In the meanwhile, if there was nothing else to

of better clothing and less exposure to the sun. And here it may be remarked that the racial character of complexion is significantly manifested by such evidences of the degree of tint due to individual exposure. . . . The primitive race-tint of the Egyptians is perhaps more truly indicated by the colour of the princess in these painted portrait-statues than by that of her more scantily clad husband or male relative."—*The Ethnology of Egypt*, by PROFESSOR OWEN, C.B. *Journal of Anthropological Institute*, vol. IV., Lond., 1874; p. 225 *et seq.*

tempt the traveller to Cairo, the Boulak Museum would alone be worth the journey.

The first excursion one makes on returning to Cairo, the last one makes before leaving, is to Gheezeh. It is impossible to get tired of the Pyramids. Here L. and the Writer spent their last day with the Happy Couple.

We left Cairo early, and met all the market-folk coming in from the country—donkeys and carts laden with green stuff, and veiled women with towers of baskets on their heads. The Khedive's new palace was swarming already with masons, and files of camels were bringing limestone blocks for the builders. Next comes the open corn-plain, part yellow, part green— the long straight road bordered with acacias—beyond all, the desert-platform, and the Pyramids, half in light, half in greenish-gray shadow, against the horizon. I never could understand why it is that the Second Pyramid, though it is smaller and farther off, looks from this point of view bigger than the First. Farther on, the brown Fellaheen, knee-deep in purple blossom, are cutting the clover. The camels carry it away. The goats and buffaloes feed in the clearings. Then comes the half-way tomb nestled in greenery, where men and horses stay to drink; and soon we are skirting a great backwater that reflects the pyramids like a mirror. Villages, shadoofs, herds and flocks, tracts of palms, corn-flats, and spaces of rich, dark fallow, now succeed each other; and then once more comes the sandy slope, and the cavernous ridge of ancient yellow rock, and the Great Pyramid with its shadow-side towards us, darkening the light of day.

Neither L. nor the Writer ever went inside the

ed`

Great Pyramid. The Idle Man did so this day, and L.'s maid on another occasion; and both reported of the place as so stifling within, so foul underfoot, and so fatiguing, that, somehow, we each time put it off, and ended by missing it. The ascent is extremely easy. Rugged and huge as are the blocks, there is scarcely one upon which it is not possible to find a half-way rest for the toe of one's boot, so as to divide the distance. With the help of three Arabs, nothing can well be less fatiguing. As for the men, they are helpful and courteous, and as clever as possible; and coax one on from block to block in all the languages of Europe.

"Pazienza, Signora! Allez doucement—all serene! We half-way now—den halben Weg, Fräulein. Ne vous pressez-pas, Mademoiselle. Chi va sano, va lontano. Six step more, and ecco la cima!"

"You should add the other half of the proverb, amici," said I. "Chi va forte, va alla morte."

My Arabs had never heard this before, and were delighted with it. They repeated it again and again, and committed it to memory with great satisfaction. I asked them why they did not cut steps in the blocks, so as to make the ascent easier for ladies. The answer was ready and honest.

"No, no, Mademoiselle! Arab very stupid to do that. If Arab makes good steps, Howadji goes up alone. No more want Arab man to help him up, and Arab man earn no more dollars!"

They offered to sing "Yankee Doodle" when we reached the top; then, finding we were English, shouted "God save the Queen!" and told us that the Prince of Wales had given £40 to the Pyramid Arabs when he

came here with the Princess two years before; which,
however, we took the liberty to doubt.

The space on the top of the Great Pyramid is said
to be 30 feet square. It is not, as I had expected, a
level platform. Some blocks of the next tier remain,
and two or three of the tier next above that; so making
pleasant seats and shady corners. What struck us most
on reaching the top, was the startling nearness, to all
appearance, of the Second Pyramid. It seemed to rise
up beside us like a mountain; yet so close, that I fancied I could almost touch it by putting out my hand.
Every detail of the surface, every crack and parti-
coloured stain in the shining stucco that yet clings
about the apex, was distinctly visible.

The view from this place is immense. The country
is so flat, the atmosphere so clear, the standpoint so
isolated, that one really sees more and sees farther than
from many a mountain summit of ten or twelve thousand feet. The ground lies, as it were, immediately
under one; and the great Necropolis is seen as in a
ground-plan. The effect must, I imagine, be exactly
like the effect of a landscape seen from a balloon.
Without ascending the Pyramid, it is certainly not possible to form a clear notion of the way in which this
great burial-field is laid out. We see from here how
each royal pyramid is surrounded by its quadrangle of
lesser tombs, some in the form of small pyramids,
others partly rock-cut, partly built of massive slabs, like
the roofing-stones of the Temples. We see how Cheops
and Chephren and Mycerinus lay, each under his
mountain of stone, with his family and his nobles
around him. We see the great causeways which moved
Herodotus to such wonder, and along which the giant

stones were brought. Recognising how clearly the
place is a great cemetery, one marvels at the ingenious
theories that turn the pyramids into astronomical ob-
servatories, and abstruse standards of measurement.
They are the grandest graves* in all the world—and
they are nothing more.

A little way to the Southward, from the midst of
a sandy hollow, rises the head of the Sphinx. Older
than the Pyramids themselves, older perhaps than even
the Pyramid of Ouenephes at Sakkarah, the monster
lies couchant like a watchdog, looking ever to the
East, as if for some dawn that has not yet risen.**
A depression in the sand close by marks the site of
that strange monument miscalled the Temple of the
Sphinx.*** Farther away to the west, on the highest

---

* The word *pyramid*, for which so many derivations have been suggested,
is shown in the Geometrical Papyrus of the British Museum to be distinctly
Egyptian, and is written *Per-em-us.*

** "On sait par une stèle du musée de Boulaq, que le grand Sphinx est
antérieur au Roi Chéops de la IVᵉ Dynastie." *Dist. d'Arch. Egyptienne:*
Article *Sphinx.* P. PIERRET. Paris 1875.

  A long disputed question as to the meaning of the Sphinx has of late been
finally solved. The Sphinx is shown by M. J. de Rougé, according to an inscription at Edfoo, to represent a transformation of Horus, who in order to
vanquish Set (Typhon) took the shape of a human-headed lion. It was under
this form that Horus was adored in the Nome Leontopolites. In the above-
mentioned Stela of Boulak, known as the stone of Cheops, the Great Sphinx is
especially designated as the Sphinx of Hor-em-Khou, or Horus-of-the-Horizon.
This is evidently in reference to the orientation of the figure. It has often been
asked why the Sphinx is turned to the East. I presume the answer would be,
Because Horus, avenger of Osiris, looks to the East, awaiting the return of his
father from the lower world. As Horus was supposed to have reigned over
Egypt, every Pharaoh took the title of Living Horus, Golden Hawk, etc. etc.
Hence the features of the reigning King were always given to the Sphinx form
when architecturally employed, as at Karnak, Wady Sabooah, Tanis, etc. etc

*** It is certainly not a Temple. It may be a mastaba, or votive chapel.
It looks most like a tomb. It is entirely built of plain and highly-polished monoliths of alabaster and red granite, laid square and simply, like a sort of costly
and magnificent Stonehenge; and it consists of a forecourt, a hall of pillars,
three principal chambers, and a well. The chambers contain horizontal niches
which it is difficult to suppose could have been intended for anything but the
reception of mummies; and at the bottom of the well were found three statues
of King Shafra (Chephren); one of which is the famous diorite portrait-statue

ABYDUS AND CAIRO. 291

slope of this part of the desert platform, stands the Pyramid of Mycerinus. It has lost but five feet of its original height, and from this distance it looks quite perfect.

Such—set in a waste of desert—are the main objects, and the nearest objects, on which our eyes first rest. As a whole, the view is more long than wide, being bounded to the Westward by the Libyan range, and to the Eastward by the Mokattam hills. At the foot of those yellow hills, divided from us by the cultivated plain across which we have just driven, lies Cairo, all glittering domes half seen through a sunlit haze. Overlooking the fairy city stands the Mosque of the Citadel, its mast-like minarets piercing the clearer atmosphere. Far to the Northward, traversing reach after reach of shadowy palm-groves, the eye loses itself in the dim and fertile distances of the Delta. To the West and South, all is desert. It begins here at our feet—a rolling wilderness of valleys, and slopes, and rivers, and seas of sand, broken here and there by abrupt ridges of rock, and mounds of ruined masonry, and open graves. A silver line skirts the edge of this dead world, and vanishes Southward in the sun-mist that shimmers on the farthest horizon. To the left of that silver line we see the quarried cliffs of Toora, marble-white; opposite Toora, the plumy palms of Memphis; on the desert platform above, clear though faint, the Pyramids of Abooseer, and Sakkarah, and Dashoor. Every stage of the

of the Boulak Museum. In an interesting article contributed to the *Rêvue Arch*: (Vol. XXVI. Paris: 1873), M. du Barry-Merval has shown, as it seems, quite clearly, that the Temple of the Sphinx is in fact the votive chapel of Chephren, and a dependency of the Second Pyramid. It is possible that the niches may have been designed for his Queen and family.

Pyramid of Ouenephes, banded in light and shade, is plain to see. So is the dome-like summit of the great Pyramid of Dashoor. Even the brick ruin beside it, which we took for a black rock as we went up the river, and which looks like a black rock still, is perfectly visible. Farthest of them all, showing pale and sharp amid the palpitating blaze of noon, stands, like an unfinished tower of Babel, the Pyramid of Meydoom. It is in this direction that our eyes turn oftenest—to the measureless desert in its mystery of light and silence; to the Nile where it gleams out again and again, till it melts at last into that faint far distance beyond which lie Thebes, and Philæ, and Aboo Simbel.

APPENDIX No. I.

A. M'CALLUM, Esq., to the EDITOR of the 'TIMES.'*

SIR—It may interest your readers to learn that at the south side of the great Temple of Aboo Simbel, I found the entrance to a painted chamber, rock-cut, and measuring 21 ft. 2½ in., by 14 ft. 8 in., and 12 ft. high to the spring of the arch, elaborately sculptured and painted in the best style of the best period of Egyptian art, bearing the portraits of Rameses the Great and his cartouches, and in a state of the highest preservation. This chamber is preceded by the ruins of a vaulted atrium, in sun-dried brick-work, and adjoins the remains of what would appear to be a massive wall or pylon, which contains a staircase terminating in an arched doorway leading to the vaulted atrium before mentioned.

The doorway of the painted chamber, the staircase, and the arch, were all buried in sand and débris. The chamber appears to have been covered and lost sight of since a very early period, being wholly free from mutilation, and from the scribbling of travellers ancient and modern.

The staircase was not opened until the 18th, and the bones of a woman and child, with two small cinerary urns, were there discovered by a gentleman of our party, buried in the sand. This was doubtless a subsequent interment. Whether this painted chamber is the inner sanctuary of a small Temple, or part of a tomb, or only a speos, like the well-known grottoes at Ibrim, is a question for future excavators to determine.—I have the honour to be, Sir, yours, etc. etc.

ANDREW M'CALLUM.

KOROSKO, NUBIA, *Feb. 16th,* 1874.

* This letter appeared in the 'Times' of March 18th, 1874.

APPENDIX II.

THE EGYPTIAN PANTHEON.

"The deities of ancient Egypt consist of celestial, terrestrial, and infernal gods, and of many inferior personages, either representatives of the greater gods or else attendants upon them. Most of the gods were connected with the Sun, and represented that luminary in its passage through the upper hemisphere or Heaven and the lower hemisphere or Hades. To the deities of the Solar cycle belonged the great gods of Thebes and Heliopolis. In the local worship of Egypt the deities were arranged in local triads: thus, at Memphis, Ptah, his wife Merienptah, and their son Nefer Atum, formed a triad, to which was sometimes added the goddess Bast or Bubastis. At Abydos the local triad was Osiris, Isis, and Horus, with Nephthys; at Thebes, Amen Ra or Ammon, Mut, and Chons, with Neith, at Elephantine, Kneph, Anuka, Sati, and Hak. In most instances the names of the gods are Egyptian; thus, Ptah meant 'the opener;' Amen, 'the concealed;' Ra, 'the sun' or 'day;' Athor, 'the house of Horus;' but some few, especially of later times, were introduced from Semitic sources, as Bal or Baal, Astaruta or Astarte, Khen or Kiun, Respu or Reseph. Besides the principal gods, several inferior or parhedral gods, sometimes personifications of the faculties, senses, and other objects, are introduced into the religious system, and genii, spirits, or personified souls of deities formed part of the same. At a period subsequent to their first introduction the gods were divided into three orders. The first or highest comprised eight deities, who were different in the Memphian and Theban systems. They were supposed to have reigned over Egypt before the time of mortals. The eight gods of the first order at Memphis were—I. Ptah; 2. Shu; 3. Tefnu; 4. Seb; 5. Nut; 6. Osiris; 7. Isis and Horus; 8. Athor. Those of Thebes were— I. Amen-Ra; 2. Mentu; 3. Atum; 4. Shu and Tefnu; 5. Seb; 6. Osiris; 7. Set and Nephthys; 8. Horus and Athor. The gods of the second order were twelve in number, but the name of one only, an Egyptian Hercules, has been preserved. The third order is stated to have comprised Osiris, who, it will be seen, belonged to the first order."—*Guide to the First and Second Egyptian Rooms; Brit. Musæ.* S. BIRCH, 1874.

The Gods most commonly represented upon the monuments are Phthah, Kneph, Ra, Ammon-Ra, Khem, Osiris, Nefer Atum or Tum, Thoth, Seb', Set, Khons, Horus, Maut, Neith, Isis, Nut, Hathor, and Pasht or Bast. They are distinguished by the following attributes:—

Phtah, or *Ptah:*—In form a mummy, holding the emblem called by some the Nilometer, by others the emblem of Stability. Called "the Father of the Beginning, the Creator of the Egg of the Sun and Moon." Chief Deity of Memphis.

Kneph, Knoum, or *Knouphis:*—Ram-headed. Called the Maker of Gods and men ; the Soul of the Gods. Chief Deity of Elephantine and the Cataracts.

Ra:—Hawk-headed, and crowned with the sun-disk encircled by an asp. The divine disposer and organiser of the world. Adored throughout Egypt.

Amen-Ra:—Of human form, crowned with a flat-topped cap and two long straight plumes ; clothed in the schenti; his flesh sometimes painted blue. There are various forms of this god (see Footnote, p. 120 of this vol.), but he is most generally described as King of the Gods. Chief Deity of Thebes.

Khem:—Of human form mummified; wears head-dress of Amen Ra ; his right hand uplifted, holding the flail. The God of productiveness and generation. Chief Deity of Khemmis, or Ekhmeem.

Osiris:—Of human form, mummified, crowned with a mitre, and holding the flail and crook. Called the Good; the Lord above all; the One Lord. Was the God of the lower world; Judge of the dead; and representative of the Sun below the horizon. Adored throughout Egypt. Local Deity of Abydos.

Nefer Atum:—Human-headed, and crowned with the pschent. This God represented the nocturnal sun, or the sun lighting the lower world. Local Deity of Heliopolis.

Thoth:—In form a man, ibis-headed, generally depicted with the pen and palette of a scribe. Was the God of the moon, and of letters. Local Deity of Sesoon, or Hermopolis.

Seb:—The "Father of the Gods," and deity of terrestrial vegetation. In form a man with a goose upon his head.

Set:—Represented by a symbolic animal, with a muzzle and ears like a jackal, the body of an ass, and an upright tail, like the tail of a lion. Was originally a warlike God, and became in later times the symbol of evil and the enemy of Osiris.

Khons:—Hawk-headed, crowned with the sun-disk and horns.

Is sometimes represented as a youth with the side-lock, standing on a crocodile.

Horus:—Horus appears variously as Horus, Horus Aroëris, and Horus Harpakhrat (Harpocrates), or Horus the child. Is represented under the first two forms as a man, hawk-headed, wearing the double crown of Egypt; in the latter as a child with the side-lock. Local Deity of Edfoo (Apollinopolis Magna).

Maut:—A woman draped, and crowned with the pschent; generally with a cap below the pschent representing a vulture. Adored at Thebes.

Neith:—A woman draped, holding sometimes a bow and arrows, crowned with the crown of Lower Egypt. She presided over war, and the loom. Worshipped at Thebes.

Isis:—A woman crowned with the sun-disk surmounted by a throne, and sometimes enclosed between horns. Adored at Abydos. Her soul resided in Sothis, or the Dog-star.

Nut:—A woman curved so as to touch the ground with her fingers. She represents the vault of heaven, and is the mother of the Gods.

Hathor:—Cow-headed, and crowned with the disk and plumes. Deity of Amenti, or the Egyptian Hades. Worshipped at Denderah.

Pasht:—Pasht and Bast appear to be two forms of the same Goddess. As Bast she is represented as a woman, lion-headed, with the disk and urœus; as Pasht, she is cat-headed, and holds a sistrum. Adored at Bubastis.

APPENDIX III.

THE RELIGIOUS BELIEF OF THE EGYPTIANS.

Did the Egyptians believe in one Eternal God, whose attributes were merely symbolised by their numerous deities; or must the whole structure of their faith be resolved into a solar myth,. with its various and inevitable ramifications? This is the great problem of Egyptology, and it is a problem that has not yet been solved. Egyptologists differ so widely on the subject that it is impossible to reconcile their opinions. As not even the description of a temple is complete without some reference to this important question, and as the question itself underlies every notion we may form of ancient

Egypt and ancient Egyptians, I have thought it well to group here a few representative extracts from the works of three or four of the greatest authorities upon the subject.

"The religion of the Egyptians consisted of an extended poly-theism represented by a series of local groups. The idea of a single deity self-existing or produced was involved in the conception of some of the principal gods, who are said to have given birth to or produced gods, men, all beings and things. Other deities were considered to be self-produced. The Sun was the older object of worship, and in his various forms, as the rising, midday, and setting Sun, was adored under different names, and was often united, especially at Thebes, to the types of other deities, as Amen and Mentu. The oldest of all the local deities, Ptah, who was wor-shipped at Memphis, was a demiurgos or creator of heaven, earth, gods and men, and not identified with the Sun. Besides the wor-ship of the solar gods, that of Osiris extensively prevailed, and with it the antagonism of Set, the Egyptian devil, the metempsychosis or transmigration of the soul, the future judgment, the purgatory or Hades, the *Karneter*, the *Aahlu* or Elysium, and final union of the soul to the body after the lapse of several centuries. Besides the deities of Heaven, the light, and the lower world, others per-sonified the elements or presided over the operations of nature, the seasons, and events."—*Guide to the First and Second Egyptian Rooms: Brit. Mus.* S. BIRCH, 1874.

"This religion, obscured as it is by a complex mythology, has lent itself to many interpretations of a contradictory nature, none of which have been unanimously adopted. But that which is beyond doubt, and which shines forth from the texts for the whole world's acceptance, is the belief in one God. The polytheism of the monuments is but an outward show. The innumerable Gods of the Pantheon are but manifestations of the One Being in his various capacities. That taste for allegory which created the hiero-glyphic writing, found vent likewise in the expression of the reli-gious idea; that idea being, as it were, stifled in the later periods by a too-abundant symbolism."—P. PIERRET, *Dictionnaire d'Arch. Égyptienne*, 1875. Translated from article on "*Réligion.*"

"This God of the Egyptians was unique, perfect, endued with knowledge and intelligence, and so far incomprehensible that one can scarcely say in what respects he is incomprehensible. He is the one who exists by essence; the one sole life of all substance; the one single generator in heaven and earth who is not himself en-gendered; the father of fathers; the mother of mothers; always the

same; immutable in immutable perfection; existing equally in the
past, the present, and the future.   He fills the universe in such
wise that no earthly image can give the feeblest notion of his
immensity.   He is felt everywhere; he is tangible nowhere."—
G. MASPERO.   Translated from *Histoire Ancienne des Peuples de
l'Orient*.   Paris, 1876, Chap. I, p. 26.
	"Unfortunately, the more we study the religion of ancient
Egypt, the more our doubts accumulate with regard to the character which must finally be attributed to it.   The excavations
carried on of late at Denderah and Edfoo have opened up to us an
extraordinarily fertile source of material.   These Temples are
covered with texts, and present precisely the appearance of two
books which authoritatively treat not only of the Gods to which
these two Temples are dedicated, but of the religion under its more
general aspects.   But neither in these Temples, nor in those which
have been long known to us, appears the One God of Jamblichus.
If Ammon is 'The First of the First' at Thebes, if Phthah is at
Memphis 'The Father of all Beings, without Beginning or End,'
so also is every other Egyptian God separately endowed with these
attributes of the Divine Being.   In other words, we everywhere
find Gods who are uncreate and immortal; but nowhere that unique,
invisible Deity, without name and without form, who was supposed
to hover above the highest summit of the Egyptian pantheon.   The
Temple of Denderah, now explored to the end of its most hidden
inscriptions, of a certainty furnishes no trace of this Deity.   The
one result which, above all others, seems to be educed from the
study of this Temple, is that, according to the Egyptians, the
Universe was God himself, and that Pantheism formed the foundation of their religion."   A. MARIETTE BEY.   Translated from
Itinéraire de la Haute Egypte.   Alexandria, 1872, p. 54.
	"The Sun is the most ancient object of Egyptian worship found
upon the monuments.   His birth each day when he springs from
the bosom of the nocturnal heaven is the natural emblem of the
eternal generation of the divinity.   Hence the celestial space became identified with the divine mother.   It was particularly the
nocturnal heaven which was represented by this personage.   The
rays of the sun, as they awakened all nature, seemed to give life to
animated beings.   Hence that which doubtless was originally a
symbol, became the foundation of the religion.   It is the Sun himself whom we find habitually invoked as the supreme being.   The
addition of his Egyptian name, Ra, to the names of certain local
divinities, would seem to show that this identification constituted a

second epoch in the history of the religions of the Valley of the Nile."—VISCOUNT E. DE ROUGÉ. Translated from *Notice Sommaire des Monuments Egyptiens du Louvre.* Paris: 1873, p. 120.

That the religion, whether based on a solar myth or upon a genuine belief in a spiritual God, became grossly material in its later developments, is apparent to every student of the monuments. M. Maspero has the following remarks on the degeneration of the old faith.

"In the course of ages, the sense of the religion became obscured. In the texts of Greek and Roman date, that lofty conception of the divinity which had been cherished by the early theologians of Egypt still peeps out here and there. Fragmentary phrases and epithets yet prove that the fundamental principles of the religion are not quite forgotten. For the most part, however, we find that we no longer have to do with the infinite and intangible God of ancient days; but rather with a God of flesh and blood who lives upon earth, and has so abased himself as to be no more than a human king. It is no longer this God of whom no man knew either the form or the substance:—it is Kneph at Esneh; Hathor at Denderah; Horus, king of the divine dynasty, at Edfoo. This king has a court, ministers, an army, a fleet. His eldest son, Horhat, Prince of Cush and heir-presumptive to the throne, commands the troops. His first minister Thoth, the inventor of letters, has geography and rhetoric at his fingers' ends; is Historiographer-Royal; and is entrusted with the duty of recording the victories of the king and of celebrating them in high-sounding phraseology. When this God makes war upon his neighbour Typhon, he makes no use of the divine weapons of which we should take it for granted that he could dispose at will. He calls out his archers and his chariots; descends the Nile in his galley, as might the last new Pharaoh; directs marches and counter-marches; fights planned battles; carries cities by storm, and brings all Egypt in submission to his feet. We see here that the Egyptians of Ptolemaic times had substituted for the one God of their ancestors a line of God-Kings, and had embroidered these modern legends with a host of fantastic details."—G. MASPERO. Translated from *Histoire Ancienne des Peuples de l'Orient.* Paris: 1876, chap. 1. pp. 50-51.

APPENDIX IV.

EGYPTIAN CHRONOLOGY.

"The chronology of Egypt has been a disputed point for centuries. The Egyptians had no cycle, and only dated in the regnal years of their monarchs. The principal Greek sources have been the canon of Ptolemy, drawn up in the second century A.D., and the lists of the dynasties extracted from the historical work of Manetho, an Egyptian priest, who lived in the time of Ptolemy Philadelphus, B.C. 285-247. The discrepancies between these lists and the monuments have given rise to many schemes and rectifications of the chronology. The principal chronological points of information obtained from the monuments are the conquest of Egypt by Cambyses, B.C. 527, the commencement of the reign of Psammetichus I., B.C. 665, the reign of Tirhaka, about B.C. 693, and that of Bokchoris, about B.C. 720, the synchronism of the reign of Shishak I. with the capture of Jerusalem, about B.C. 970. The principal monuments throwing light on other parts of the chronology are the recorded heliacal risings of Sothis, or the Dog-star, in the reigns of Thothmes III. and Rameses II., III., VI., IX., the date of 400 years from the time of Rameses II. to the Shepherd kings, the dated sepulchral tablets of the bull Apis at the Serapeum, the lists of kings at Sakkarah, Thebes, and Abydos, the chronological canon of the Turin papyrus, and other incidental notices. But of the anterior dynasties no certain chronological dates are afforded by the monuments, those hitherto proposed not having stood the test of historical or philological criticism."—S. BIRCH, LL.D.: *Guide to the First and Second Egyptian Rooms at the Brit. Museum.* 1874, p. 10.

As some indication of the wide divergence of opinion upon this subject, it is enough to point out that the German Egyptologists alone differ as to the date of Menes or Mena (the first authentic king of the ancient empire), to the following extent:—

						B.C.
BOECKH places Mena in			.	.	.	5702
UNGER	,,	,,	.	.	.	5613
BRUGSCH	,,	,,	.	.	.	4455
LAUTH	,,	,,	.	.	.	4157
LEPSIUS	,,	,,	.	.	.	3892
BUNSEN	,,	,,	.	.	.	3623

M. Mariette, though recognising the need for extreme caution in the acceptance or rejection of any of these calculations, is inclined on the whole to abide for the present by the lists of Manetho; according to which the thirty-four recorded dynasties would stand as follows:—

ANCIENT EMPIRE.				NEW EMPIRE.		
DYNASTIES.	CAPITALS.		B.C.	DYNASTIES. CAPITALS.		B.C.
I. II. } This		. .	{5004 4751	XVIII. XIX. } Thebes XX.	. .	{1703 1462 1288
III. IV. } Memphis V.		. .	{4449 4235 3951	XXI. Tanis XXII. Bubastis	. . . .	1110 980
VI. Elephantine		. .	3703	XXIII. Tanis	. .	810
VII. VIII. } Memphis		. .	3500	XXIV. Saïs XXV. (Ethiopians)	. . . .	721 715
IX. X. } Heracleopolis		. .	{3358 3240	XXVI. Saïs XXVII. (Persians)	. . . .	665 527
MIDDLE EMPIRE.				XXVIII. Saïs XXIX. Mendes	. . . .	405 399
XI. XII. } Thebes XIII.		. .	{3064 ,, 2851	XXX. Sebennytis XXXI. (Persians)	. . . .	378 340
XIV. Xoïs		. .	2398	LOWER EMPIRE.		
XV. XVI. } Shepherd Kings XVII.		.	{ 2214	XXXII. Macedonians XXXIII. (Greeks) XXXIV. (Romans)	. . .	332 305 30

To this chronology may be opposed the brief table of dates compiled by M. Chabas. This table represents what may be called the medium school of Egyptian chronology, and is offered by M. Chabas, "not as an attempt to reconcile systems," but as an aid to the classification of certain broadly indicated epochs.

	B.C.
Mena and the commencement of the Ancient Empire . . .	4000
Construction of the great Pyramids	3300
VIth Dynasty	2800
XIIth Dynasty	{2400 2000
Shepherd Invasion	?
Expulsion of Shepherds, and commencement of the New Empire	1800
Thothmes III.	1700
Seti I. and Rameses II.	{1500 1400
Sheshonk (Shishak), the conqueror of Jerusalem	1000
Saïtic Dynasties	{700 600
Cambyses and the Persians	500
Second Persian conquest	400
Ptolemies	{300 200 100

It is, however, probable that M. Chabas will before long correct some of the earlier dates in this scheme, so as to bring them
into accordance with the date which he is of late reported to have
determined with respect to the pyramid of Menkara. The *Bulletin
Mensuel de l'Académie des Inscriptions* for the month of April 1876,
as published in the *Révue Archéologique* for the month of May following, announces this latest addition to M. Chabas's many learned
and important discoveries in the following terms:—

"M. de Saulcy annonce à l'Académie que M. Chabas est par-
venu à déterminer une nouvelle date dans l'histoire primitive de
l'Egypte, date extrêmement importante, puisqu'elle se rapporte au
règne de Menchérès. Cette date tombe dans l'intervalle qui sépare
l'an 3010 de l'an 3007 avant notre êre. M. de Saulcy a refait les
calculs de M. Chabas; il les trouve exacts. Ainsi serait définitive-
ment fixée l'époque de la construction des grandes pyramides, et
Ménès appartiendrait bien, comme d'autres calculs l'avaient fait
penser, au xxxxe siècle avant Jésus-Christ."—*Revue Arch.* No. V.
Mai, 1876.

Translation:—M. de Saulcy announces to the Academy that
M. Chabas has succeeded in determining a new date in the primitive history of Egypt—a date of extreme importance, since it refers
to the reign of Menkara. This date falls in the interval which lies
between the years 3010 and 3007 before our era. M. de Saulcy
has verified the calculations of M. Chabas, and finds them exact.
Hence we are enabled to attach a definite date to the epoch of the
construction of the great pyramids, and Mena will belong, as other
calculations have already led us to suppose, to the xxxxth century before Christ."

THE END.